Inside Tenement Time

Critical Caribbean Studies

Series Editors: Yolanda Martínez-San Miguel,
Carter Mathes, and Kathleen López

Editorial Board: Carlos U. Decena, Rutgers University; Alex Dupuy, Wesleyan University; Aisha Khan, New York University; April J. Mayes, Pomona College; Patricia Mohammed, University of the West Indies; Martin Munro, Florida State University; F. Nick Nesbitt, Princeton University; Michelle Stephens, Rutgers University; Deborah Thomas, University of Pennsylvania; and Lanny Thompson, University of Puerto Rico

Focused particularly in the twentieth and twenty-first centuries, although attentive to the context of earlier eras, this series encourages interdisciplinary approaches and methods and is open to scholarship in a variety of areas, including anthropology, cultural studies, diaspora and transnational studies, environmental studies, gender and sexuality studies, history, and sociology. The series pays particular attention to the four main research clusters of Critical Caribbean Studies at Rutgers University, where the coeditors serve as members of the executive board: Caribbean Critical Studies Theory and the Disciplines; Archipelagic Studies and Creolization; Caribbean Aesthetics, Poetics, and Politics; and Caribbean Colonialities.

For a complete list of titles in the series, please see the last page of the book.

Inside Tenement Time

Suss, Spirit, and Surveillance

KEZIA PAGE

Rutgers University Press
New Brunswick, Camden, and Newark, New Jersey
London and Oxford

Rutgers University Press is a department of Rutgers, The State University of New Jersey, one of the leading public research universities in the nation. By publishing worldwide, it furthers the University's mission of dedication to excellence in teaching, scholarship, research, and clinical care.

Library of Congress Cataloging-in-Publication Data

Names: Page, Kezia Ann, author.
Title: Inside tenement time : suss, spirit, and surveillance / Kezia Page.
Description: New Brunswick, New Jersey : Rutgers University Press, [2025] |
    Series: Critical Caribbean studies | Includes bibliographical references and index.
Identifiers: LCCN 2024003742 | ISBN 9781978837881 (paperback) |
    ISBN 9781978837898 (hardcover) | ISBN 9781978837904 (epub) |
    ISBN 9781978837911 (pdf)
Subjects: LCSH: Jamaican literature—History and criticism. | Surveillance in literature. |
    Reggae music—Jamaica—History and criticism. | Police patrol—Jamaica—Surveillance
    operations. | Jamaica—Social conditions.
Classification: LCC PR9265 .P34 2025 | DDC 820.9/3587291071—dc23/eng/20240709
LC record available at https://lccn.loc.gov/2024003742

A British Cataloging-in-Publication record for this book is available from the British Library.
Copyright © 2025 by Kezia Page

All rights reserved

No part of this book may be reproduced or utilized in any form or by any means, electronic or mechanical, or by any information storage and retrieval system, without written permission from the publisher. Please contact Rutgers University Press, 106 Somerset Street, New Brunswick, NJ 08901. The only exception to this prohibition is "fair use" as defined by U.S. copyright law.

References to internet websites (URLs) were accurate at the time of writing. Neither the author nor Rutgers University Press is responsible for URLs that may have expired or changed since the manuscript was prepared.

♾ The paper used in this publication meets the requirements of the American National Standard for Information Sciences—Permanence of Paper for Printed Library Materials, ANSI Z39.48-1992.

rutgersuniversitypress.org

In memory of my father, John Page
For my sons, Matthias and Jude

Contents

	Introduction: Flexible Hegemonies: The Tivoli Incursion and the History of Surveillance in Jamaica	1
1	In the Shadow of the Wall: Suss and Sussveillance in the Yard Fiction of H. G. de Lisser	26
2	"The Dungle Is an Obeah Man": Spiritveillance in *The Children of Sisyphus*	55
3	Smile Jamaica, for the Camera: Performance and Surveillance in 1970s Jamaica	84
4	Bongo Futures after Tivoli: The Reggae Revival and Its Genealogies	110
	Coda	131
	Acknowledgments	137
	Notes	141
	References	153
	Index	163

Inside Tenement Time

Introduction

• •

Flexible Hegemonies: The Tivoli Incursion and the History of Surveillance in Jamaica[1]

In May 2010 in Tivoli Gardens, West Kingston, Jamaica, security forces and West Kingston rebels fought over the fate of the area leader of Tivoli, Christopher "Dudus" Coke. Would he be extradited to the United States to face charges of drug trafficking, murder, and other crimes, or would he continue in his office as "president" ("Prezi") of West Kingston, overlord of the Shower Posse and the Presidential Click gang? Though easily the biggest and baddest shotta[2] versus security forces event of the twenty-first century in the Caribbean, what happened in Tivoli Gardens in May 2010 was not an aberration; it was, but for its scale, business as usual. That standoff-cum-siege-cum-incursion is the aporia that inspired this book project. From the drama that seized the Jamaican nation with the world looking on emerged a story with a long history, much longer than the story of Dudus or his father Jim Brown,[3] or the history of garrison communities like Tivoli, or the postindependence practice of what Jamaicans term *partisan politricks*,[4] which was felt by wide swaths of Jamaicans to be the behind-the-scenes driver of the incursion.

The plot twists, climaxes, and dénouements of the drama that unfolded were the spectacular quotidian or the quotidian spectacular of Caribbean life, spawned in the long shadow of the colonial plantation. The events inspired new music, literature, and visual art and new intensities of political and social commentary. Part of what stood out most clearly was that the security forces' incursion into Tivoli, as well as the incursion's prologue and aftermath, called for a renewed look at surveillance in Jamaica and the wider Caribbean. Both the events that took place between May 23 and 26, and in the months and weeks preceding these three days, exposed just how powerfully, intricately, and in some ways subterraneously the web of surveillance over and within the Caribbean works in local communities, across national spaces, and in geopolitical corridors.

I take the incursion as my point of departure for this discussion of surveillance in a Caribbean context because the event put on display many aspects of surveillance and its counter-systems in and beyond the nation in which it took place. Moreover, I begin here because the incursion was the contemporary moment that made surveillance visible as a fundamental dynamic of what David Scott (2004) calls the crisis of the (Caribbean) postcolonial state. The visibility was global, even if, ironically, surveillance as a primary issue did not play a major part in the masses of papers, reflections, commentaries, and publications that came in the aftermath of the incursion. Thinking about this issue led me back to an examination of literary and musical texts in which a critique of surveillance is central to both narrative and poetics. While the texts that made their way into this book address very particular moments (pre- and post-emancipation; the turn of the century; the Independence period; post-colony; now) and particular spaces (the enclaves of urban yards and their environs), collectively they track a long historical arc of the Caribbean's fight for sovereignty. The Caribbean situation reveals flexible hegemonies in sociopolitical arenas, so that even while the denudation of the people is effected through the state apparatus enabled by its surveillance technologies, countervailing factors are always *equally* at work. The frangible and unstable nature of state power, and the vernacular arts and sciences that ensure its instability are both on display. There is ultimately no triumphant panoptical agency available in the Caribbean context.

That this dynamic (flexible hegemonies) is rooted in performance is not an accident but the direct result of a history: we know the colonial territory was by definition a police/d enclave, in which control was intentionally displayed in visible acts such as the governors' inaugural "progresses" and the public staging of massacres and lynched bodies on plantations in response to uprisings.[5] We also know the practice of the enslaved and the colonized to use carnival, role-playing, and other cloaking devices to stage countersurveillance. Through the Tivoli moment and the texts and contextual histories I discuss in this book it is possible to see that this dynamic of flexible hegemonies is the tension that has made impossible the arrival of the postcolonial state. As I will discuss later in this introduction, one way I signal the specific historical grounds on which flexible hegemonies emerge in the Caribbean is through my use of terms such as sussveillance and spiritveillance, which run counter to the Foucauldian concept of the panopticon. In thinking with these terms, I bring a local specificity that also serves to add nuance to the application of generalized African diaspora and other current theories of counter and anti-surveillance.

My choice to close read fiction, a music concert, and a multi-art movement—the Reggae Revival—as opposed to cybersystems, CCTV trends, or other "hard" technologies that have no doubt played major roles in the surveillance of the Caribbean is undertaken in full disciplinary trust that the imagination is an unfettered gatherer of stories, social and historical truths and ways of knowing.

The literary texts I examine include two novels by H. G. de Lisser, *Jane's Career* (1913) and *Susan Proudleigh* (1915), *The Children of Sisyphus* (1964) by Orlando Patterson, and *A Brief History of Seven Killings* (2014) by Marlon James. Collectively they span the long arc of the history of the writing about surveillance in Jamaica from the beginning of the twentieth century to the contemporary moment. I read the 1976 Smile Jamaica concert headlined by Bob Marley (which Marlon James enters into conversation about in *A Brief History of Seven Killings*) as a real-life instance where the lead-up to the event and the event itself were deeply impacted by surveillance. My interest in the Reggae Revival, which I discuss in the final chapter, is motivated by the ways the influences and events discussed in the other chapters coalesce in this movement. The revival, which is in part a direct confrontation with the Tivoli incursion that frames the inquiries conducted in this book, draws on the legacies of music and other artistic and creative responses to surveillance from colonial times to the present.

Through the vantage point provided by these texts and contexts, we are able to see why certain concepts of surveillance apply or do not apply or undergo a sea change when mobilized within Caribbean space. My attention to vernacular or indigenous[6] forms of surveillance and countersurveillance underscores the prominence of these veillances[7] in Caribbean literature, culture, and everyday life. While the book focuses on Jamaica in particular, I place it against the backdrop that there are threads of connection that make the Jamaica case of regional concern, impactful beyond its borders or the source of inspiration. Such threads can be seen in Caribbean uprisings, political movements, and literary trends that cohere around time and motif. For instance, yard fictions from as early as the 1920s and up to the 1960s, exemplified by works such as C.L.R. James's *Minty Alley* (1936), Alfred Mendes's *Black Fauns* (1935), V. S. Naipaul's *Miguel Street* (1959),[8] Roger Mais's *Brother Man* (1954), and Alvin Bennett's *God the Stone Breaker* (1964), explore similar themes and spaces. James, Mendes, and Naipaul are focused on Trinidad while Mais and Bennett are writing about Jamaica, but collectively they allow for a broad picture of urban life over a twenty-year period in the Caribbean. They highlight the urban yard and its gendered equivalent, the street, as the vantage or lookout point from which inner-city dwellers deal with the experience of watching and being watched. We recall that the barrack yard (Trinidad) and tenement or government yard (Jamaica) emerged as twentieth-century repurposing of colonial space. Similarly, "independence fictions" such as Orlando Patterson's *The Children of*

Sisyphus (1964), V. S. Naipaul's *The Suffrage of Elvira* (1958), George Lamming's *Season of Adventure* (1960) and *Of Age and Innocence* (1958), and poetry collections such as Martin Carter's *Poems of Resistance from British Guiana* (1954) emerge contemporaneously in the decade of (failed) federation and (sometimes violently) emergent statehood for the larger Anglophone colonies such as Jamaica, Trinidad, Barbados, and Guyana. Carter, like Mais before him, experienced the full brunt of surveillance as he was arrested and put under observation more than once for participating in independence marches.[9] In that same moment, Lamming, phrasing the process of Caribbean intellectual freedom as a coming into sight, declares, "Prospero. . . . has been seen"—the tables have been turned, the surveilling power has become the object of the people's critical gaze (Lamming, 1992, 158). I am gesturing here toward patterns of regional flow and crosscurrents of influence.

Flexible Hegemonies and Surveillance in Tivoli Gardens and the Morant Bay Rebellion

The complexities that make the idea of a top-down surveillance questionable in the Caribbean context are apparent in the various layers of competing surveillances that emerge in the Tivoli affair. First is the relationship between the United States' "information gathering," the Jamaican government's obligated deference to U.S. power, and the government's simultaneous (at least initial) rejection of U.S. interference. The cross-national and inter/extra-national surveillance of Dudus produced damning evidence that some of his businesses and other activities were not legal, that he was indeed trafficking drugs and weapons, and that he was responsible for murders in the U.S. and Jamaica. Ironically (given the questionable nature of the Jamaican state's own surveillance methods), the ways in which U.S. surveillance agencies collected evidence proved to be an important point of argument in Prime Minister Bruce Golding's and the ruling Jamaica Labour Party's resistance to U.S. demands for Coke's extradition. The government was aware of the accuracy of the information, which had also been gathered by their own surveillance machinery.[10] This intersectionality and opposition is just one example of the relational nature of surveillance that begins to trouble hegemonic concepts.

Second, the Dudus-Tivoli story, though a Robin Hood story for sure, did not even pretend toward the easy pastoral associated with the folk hero. Dudus was able to maintain his narrative of a crime-free, carefully run Tivoli Gardens because of his singular power as don and area leader over the garrison and his own expertise as a surveillant. Dudus, head of the Presidential Click (clique), did not simply keep the police out of Tivoli, he also kept the utility companies from collecting payments for their services, thus diverting standard monthly expenses from the Jamaican state to the "state" of Tivoli.[11] As well, by capitalizing on the original infrastructure of the community, which facilitated self-containment, he created industry and enterprise and the context in which these could thrive. It is no surprise that a community unburdened from the costly inefficiencies of the state did not immediately see that in exchange they were living under the rules, laws, and rigorous surveilling oversight of Dudus and the Presidential Click. Residents of Tivoli Gardens and surrounding areas in West Kingston benefited from the Click's activities, and perhaps most especially from the version of law and order that the Click enforced. It was said that under Dudus there was no crime, no theft or rape. According to the report of the West Kingston Commission of Enquiry, "Former Commissioner of Police, Owen Ellington, described Tivoli Gardens under Coke's suzerainty as a 'state within the State'" (West Kingston Commission of Enquiry, 2016, 18).[12] Though the report distinguishes between the state and the State, there is no evidence that, in terms of its violence, the impact of Dudus and the Presidential Click's surveillance of the community under his rule was any different from the impact of surveillance by the Jamaican police, though certainly the context and the "rewards" were different.

The Tivoli people's pushback against the incursion further exemplifies how in the Caribbean, surveillance power is not a one-way street, but competing sets of spectacular performances. These allow for flexible hegemonies and reflexive aporias through which the surveilled, who in this case include both Dudus and the people of Tivoli, are not only surveilled, but also performers navigating power relations with skill and savvy. The people's pushback was powerful and immediate, a study in the counterstrategies of performative surveillance from the interior. When it became clear to people in West Kingston that their President Dudus had become a wanted man, many residents of Tivoli Gardens and neighboring Denham Town, as well as Dudus sympathizers and affiliates from other communities in Kingston and some from as far away as Clarendon, in the center of the island, attempted to stop Dudus's capture. A major part of this effort was the march of women on May 20. While the question of Dudus's physical protection from the Jamaica Constabulary Force (the police) and the Jamaica Defence Force (the army) was a multipronged operation that soon involved the people of Tivoli, Denham Town, Stadium Gardens, and allegedly shottas from Clarendon, the work of protecting Dudus and thwarting the efforts of the security forces by Tivoli residents was structured around gendered roles. Women and children were involved in choreographed performances of peace and wellness from the community—a public declaration that "not only are we not a public threat, but also, neither are we under any threat from Dudus." Importantly, these demonstrations used avenues that were generally considered decent and lawabiding even if the collective bodies read as not as decent (not respectable) and not as law-abiding as other women's and children's bodies (class, race/color, and place of domicile) might read.

The march of women and some children dressed in white and carrying signs pledging allegiance to Dudus and defying the power of the state by comparing Dudus to God and contradicting state authority, began early on the morning of

May 20, 2010. Some reports say that over 600 women participated in this march and that the number grew from where it began at the intersection of Spanish Town Road and Industrial Boulevard. The march proceeded through the commercial center of downtown toward North Street to the Gleaner Company, the headquarters of Jamaica's leading daily newspaper, and then toward Gordon House to the Parliament Building, where the marchers were eventually cut off and returned to Tivoli. The crowd got close enough to Parliament to rattle workers at the Parliament building and to draw ire and condemnation from political leaders on the public threat to the nation's democracy. This is because, though the march was peaceful in that the women were unarmed and there were no clashes with the police, the women themselves were not read as disarming. These were women already read in their bodies as inherently out of order and out of place once they were not quiet and subservient. Therefore, the fact that they were sent by Dudus, with a message of defiance, merely confirmed the general perception of them as dangerous and disruptive.

The choice of white clothing strategically aimed to signify peace and political neutrality and, in their numbers, even despite certain less than modest sartorial choices, the women looked like a religious order: a meeting of deaconesses, a Revival band, a stormy cloud of witnesses. It is not surprising, then, that many of their placards compared Dudus to God: "After God comes Dudus" and "Jesus died for us so we will die for Dudus." White clothing added another layer of protection and extended, for the rebel women of Tivoli, the possibility of *passing*: their white clothes were to signal that the Dudus issue was not about politics. Had it been about politics, they would have worn the green of the Jamaica Labour Party, the party that had given Dudus up for extradition. The women disavowed the pretense of political allegiance to protect their president.

This supremely choreographed, quasi-royal, quasi-religious progress of female bodies was intended to contradict, with over 600 as evidence moving through the streets of downtown Kingston, the news reports that, under Dudus, Tivoli residents were unable to leave and return to the community as they desired. In this way, the march explains the barricades erected earlier by men from Tivoli and neighboring Denham Town and proves that they were not erected to hinder Tivoli residents from leaving, but rather to hinder any unauthorized person from entering the community. The women brandished their cell phones, electronic testimonies and visible props showing not only their unfettered freedom but also that Dudus facilitated prosperity, contradicting news reports that the ruling gang had held law-abiding Tivoli residents hostage and confiscated their cell phones. And they spoke: "Anybody can come into Tivoli and see the situation. We can go and come as we want, we can walk peacefully and see mi phone here" and "Dudus tell we fi wear white today and not green because this is not about politics and the PNP dem a play politics and Dudus only want peace" ("Diehards Defend Dudus," 2010). The women were sent out or went out to perform for the keen eye of a tense nation as representatives of the community, and they did it with care and prepared style.

Part of what is interesting about this tactic is how oriented it is around perceptions of traditional (Western, white, uptown Jamaican middle-class) ideas of womanness. The women are meant to be symbols of peace, mediators between their men and the state. The organizers of the march expect that the state will be operating on this official social contract, that women and children will be afforded care, respect, and safety, especially in their numbers and even despite where they are from, whom they support, and what their bodies defy. But the reality of the march is that the bodies in white are more than delicate and peaceful, though both the marchers and police understand that they must be treated as such. The newspapers describe a certain kind of body, a certain kind of woman.[13] They are Black women. Working-class bodies. Strong and loud. They are historically poor, underrepresented, and though crucial (as voters and voices for the working poor) they are not often given a place in official and national issues. This is not a quiet march; rather, it is a boisterous throng. Many of the women are big-bodied, and some, expressly noted by the *Gleaner* reporter, are scantily clad.

While this body is a staple in Jamaican domestic affairs, it does not often weigh in on delicate international affairs. This is defiance of all kinds of codes of colonial decency and respectability, upstaging the government and underscoring the Tivoli women's version of the status quo: "No Dudus, No Jamaica" and "A Presi we seh, a no Bruce we seh"[14] ("Under Siege," 2010, A2, A4). In addition to the placards they carry, the women verbalize their message: they say why they are in white and why they have marched. The apparently intended message is: We are the innocents in support of the president, even if any reading by the listeners and onlookers found both the script and the fact of the march more double-edged (at the very least) than innocent. And indeed, the multiple axes of double-take in their costuming foregrounds their complex signification—the resemblance to a religious band such as Revival, even while the costume and posture also cross over into respectable Western and acceptable Jamaican womanhood. Revival as an Afro-Jamaican grassroots, "fringe" religion invested with woman power is regarded with both fear (of the prophecies of its warner women) and denigration (of its departure from mainstream religious expression).

The march of women in white tests the Jamaican imaginative capacity to read this kind of Black woman's body with the message they carry, as simultaneously inner-city and deserving of an audience for the issue. One *Gleaner* reporter calls the demonstrators "Diehards," and in another newspaper story that narrates the impact of the demonstration on Parliament, government workers complain that the demonstration made them feel intimidated. One worker called it a "scary experience." Then senior opposition parliamentarian, Dr. Peter Phillips, is quoted as saying this about the demonstration: "While the Constitution of Jamaica allows for peaceful protest, in the context where this protest is threatening

Parliament on behalf of someone for whom the courts of Jamaica have issued a warrant of arrest and in the context of the continuing parading of heavily armed men in the sections of West Kingston defying the security forces, such a demonstration raises the gravest implications for the country" ("Protestors Cause Panic at Parliament," 2010, A4). Phillips sees the women's march in tandem with the men erecting barricades as a threat not only to the law of the land but to the very existence of the sovereign state. His association of these white-clothed bodies with the heavily armed men of Tivoli is deeply influenced by partisan politics; if these had been supporters of his own party, it is unlikely that their exercise of the right to protest would have been interpreted in this way. Political affiliation adds another layer of necessity to the project of controlling and surveilling raced, classed, and gendered bodies. (It is worth noting that the demonstrators did not attempt to enter the building, though they "paraded" noisily in front of the building until they were dispersed.) In the Jamaican context, the gathering of these women from West Kingston in front of the capital "P" Parliament building is for some scary and for others threatening, precisely by suggesting that these bodies could influence or impact decisions or the course of justice or that their rebellious behavior might intimidate and thus force the arm of justice.

It is important that the march was staged among the other activities to prevent Dudus from being taken. The march may indeed be described as a front scene behind which other countersurveilling and guerrilla-war strategies, both offensive and defensive, were taking place. Media accounts first describe civilians barricading the entrances to Tivoli on Marcus Garvey Drive and Industrial Terrace with standard road-blocking paraphernalia: old appliances, shells of old cars, sandbags, garbage. As well, the security forces gave evidence that there was nonstandard paraphernalia that made some barricades explosive. This attempt to make Tivoli inaccessible to law enforcement deserves close analysis. Numerous anecdotal and official narratives circulate about how the Tivoli garrison was run. Many of these reports as well as research on gangs in the Caribbean by Anthony Harriot explain that Tivoli had not been penetrable by security forces for many decades. Residents in Tivoli are said to have paid their utility bills to the ruling Presidential Click, the more organized subgroup of the Shower Posse that Dudus ran, and that the relevant utility companies were unable to do anything about it. Similarly, the police in the area say that while they often knew what happened in Tivoli, they could not interfere or intervene. The barricading of Tivoli suggested that the residents were preparing to resist the state's intervention and defend Dudus, no matter what Bruce Golding or the U.S. government said. The nature of the barricades also sent a message to the security forces that Tivoli defenders were fully imbued with the tactical advancements and firepower appropriate to a small war.

As a vantage point from behind which the shottas could see without being seen, the barricade in combination with the hit-and-run ambushes inflicted on the police stations and other places of law, announces a countervailing maroon ethos and strategy to force concessions from the state and to provide a distracting front scene that would give Dudus time to escape. The shottas' Maroon War enacted to elicit various levels of shock and awe from various national audiences: the security forces, the government, the news media, the general public across class lines. This was equally a show of allegiance to the president of a state within the state. The fact that the terrain of Tivoli Gardens, especially with the barricades, was configured in such a way that the surveillance strategies of the security forces could not operate effectively within that space led to the unleashing of extraordinary powers by the state: mortar bombs, drones, and heavy artillery deployed with outsized sonic effect disoriented and crippled the resistance, exposed Tivoli residents to brutal surveillance strategies, and randomly treated men young and old as guilty. Stories of mass graves, missing relatives, destroyed homes and businesses marked the progress of the latest mass atrocity in West Kingston. In this show of power and fear of its own citizens, the extreme fragility of the Jamaican state becomes a national as well as an international spectacle.

Dudus's own (aborted) strategy of escape was an extension of the multifoliate performance strategy adopted by the women and the barricaders, an elaborate staging of the body as a pliable field of representation neither fixed nor transparent but deliberately aimed to present to the surveilling eye the impression of transparency. On June 22, 2010, at 5:56 P.M., the *Jamaica Gleaner* published an update to their online news platform that Christopher "Dudus" Coke, wanted for fleeing an extradition request signed by the Jamaican government, was caught and in the custody of the Jamaican security forces. Dudus had only become a wanted man in Jamaica on May 17, 2010, when, after a year of resisting U.S. pressure to extradite the area leader of Tivoli Gardens, Bruce Golding, then prime minister of Jamaica, recanted and yielded to the U.S. and signed the request for his extradition. Neither bloody nor fatal, Dudus's capture proved to be differently dramatic from the lead-up to the signing of the extradition papers. Dudus was captured at a police checkpoint on the Mandela Highway heading into Kingston. He was in a car driven by Reverend Al Miller, a well-known apostolic minister in Jamaica who was at the time head of the National Transformation Programme for the good of inner-city youth. Photos show that Dudus was wearing a half-hearted disguise of a short, curly woman's wig with a cap on top and a pair of glasses—no clip-on earrings, no skirt and blouse or dress, no church sister makeup to render the disguise more believable. There are reports that there was a second pink wig on the back seat of the car, but again, nothing to make this second possible disguise convincing. As a master tactician and president of a transnational criminal organization, Dudus must have given thought to this disguise. The obvious but intriguing question then is, why did he choose disguise, but choose it in such a way that the risk of getting caught was not much minimized?

Dudus was apprehended while traveling the safest, most direct route into Kingston—the Mandela Highway. He was caught in broad daylight traveling unconvincingly in the safest, most neutral body he could construct to face Babylon—a woman in the company of a man of God. Both Dudus and Al Miller claim that they were on their way to the U.S. embassy for Dudus to turn himself in. Indeed, Dudus, fearing his fate at the hands of the Jamaican police, was anxious to be safely with the American authorities rather than be held by the Jamaican police. His father, Lloyd Lester Coke, otherwise known as Jim Brown, the previous area leader of Tivoli Gardens, had died in a mysterious fire in a Jamaican jail cell while awaiting trial, and the fear of a repeat had dogged Dudus all his life. Was Dudus's disguise meant to make it past the Jamaican police or was it meant to impact how the police saw him and treated him should he and Miller be stopped? Are we to read Miller's body as part of Dudus's disguise even as he functions as a neutral mediator, or is Miller to function as a trusted witness to whatever the police do when they are apprehended? It seems that the costume was not the centerpiece of his disguise strategy but rather a deflection point that would earn him a certain delay; the moment of delay would in its turn inhibit any quick finger on the trigger of a soldier's gun. As the women's march had shown, the police were not as quick to shoot a perceived woman as they would have been to shoot a man, even if hers was a less than decent body. The presence of Miller had the potential not only to expand the moment of delay but almost certainly to open a space for dialogue, in which the outcome would not be the summary execution that Dudus feared. This exposure of Dudus's vulnerability has its own gendered complexities: the half-heartedness of the disguise might be a sign of haste, but it might equally be indicative of a conflict between his recognition of the power of performed femaleness on the one hand and the cultural association of female clothing with homosexuality, loss of masculinity, and the diminished authority of the male on the other. Dudus, then, inhabits a peculiar position within the flexible hegemonies spawned in the intersection between surveillance and the countervailing technologies by which it is opposed.

In sum, though, Dudus's and his supporters' performance strategies cannot simply be read as strategies that counter the effect of surveillance by the state. Rather, they emerge as overlooking technologies directed from the interior, that were in part enabled by the state machinery that sought to exercise control. To phrase this another way: the Tivoli incursion showed how overarching systems of surveillance generate various expressive relations that are not simply between the powerful and the powerless; instead, complex ways of seizing and deploying power emerge among the so-called powerless. These initiatives appear as a dynamic, contingent, and shifting yet systematically choreographed response to the stimulus from above. The response, which is both oppositional and symbiotic, is integral to the organizing dynamic of Caribbean culture from its inception.

Equally instructive is the way the geopolitics of Tivoli was perceived across the Caribbean region. While this was not the political tensions with Cuba from the Cold War to the present, or Grenada in 1983, or Haiti in 1915–1934, 1994, and 2004, Tivoli as a small-scale scenario played out of a particularly Caribbean moment in which were marshaled the kinds of activities and repercussions from the U.S. with which the region was familiar. In this light, it was both an example of the Caribbean quotidian spectacular and a tipping point that could wholesale reorder Caribbean-U.S. relations. The standoff between the Jamaica government and the U.S., a breath-holding affair, was at once a statement of Jamaican national self-determination and a statement of the true impossibility of political agency for a small state with any proximity to the Monroe Doctrine (1823)[15] in the current global order.[16] Across the Caribbean, the Jamaican government's refusal to sign Coke's extradition papers was met with fear and warnings. Caribbean newspapers noted this by commenting on the ongoing saga: what it meant for much-needed tourist dollars, what it meant to essential relations between the U.S. and the Caribbean, and whether the U.S. crackdown on a gradually more visible web of relations to Dudus Coke by confiscating visas and turning high-level travelers away at airports could have an impact beyond the *biggish* little island in the northern Caribbean.[17] Regional governments checked in with U.S. embassies and envoys to make sure Jamaica's recalcitrance would not be considered a strike against them. As the transgovernmental legal fracas became a full-on "gunfight" and the media amped up warnings to North American tourists traveling to Jamaica, reports of revenue loss because of violence flooded in. It is not unusual for Jamaica to be on the U.S. State Department's travel warning list at some level. However, 2010 was different because this was not just Jamaica versus itself, it was Jamaica versus the United States.

Critically, the Tivoli incursion exposed how surveillance works, not only as a technology to trace and track drug lords and underground criminal offenders but as a deeply embedded hegemony that has historically assigned some as the seers and others as the seen, some with extended power, others with only localized (strategically assigned or allowed) power, and still some with no power at all. The Morant Bay Rebellion of 1865 is a good place to begin tracing a genealogy, though of course, the history goes further back to the slave/colonial plantation itself. Morant Bay has been hailed by many as a post-emancipation tipping point in Jamaica—specifically, as the first significant attempt after emancipation itself to upset the status quo, which held Blacks, those formerly of the slave class, in the same if not worse position than during slavery.[18] Furthermore, the repercussions have been identified as going far beyond Jamaica and the Caribbean. Stephen Russell writes that the "Morant Bay rebellion has increasingly been recognized as a watershed moment in the history of Jamaica and the Transatlantic world. Coming on the heels of the American Civil War and some twenty-seven years after the end of the apprenticeship that followed slavery in Jamaica, it further crystalized Black identity in post-slavery society and helped pave the way for the pan-Africanism of the early twentieth century" (Russell, 2022a, 637–638). Though the root of the rebellion's organization was the Baptist church and not a transnational criminal organization/gang/clique, and though Tivoli and Morant Bay were over a century apart, the state's violent response to Black people mobilized in opposition to the state is strikingly similar. Equally, in both cases, those whom the state opposed also exposed the state. Morant Bay showed how the exposed (and believed to be attacked colonial state) responded out of fear with a repressive force not only for Deacon Paul Bogle, the ragged group of insurrectionists from Stony Gut, and the brown and Jewish supporters in Kingston such as George William Gordon and Sidney Levien, but for any rebellion *imagined in the future.* The overarching aim was to make surveillance and punishment a set of fixed, specific acts and activities that would endure in their power over time, transhistorically and even in perpetuity.

All of this, of course, may be questioned as purely symbolic associations. More compelling is the fact that the rebellion happened in the post-emancipation era, almost thirty years after "full free," in the open gateway of possibility for Jamaica becoming a postcolonial state. Morant Bay, therefore, can be understood as consequential for the state that Jamaica became. Indeed, because historians see it as an important turning point in the story of Jamaica, the rebellion is the most well-documented, the most public and publicly displayed, and the most artistically engaged event of that period. Still more crucial, though, is the part played by local policing at Morant Bay (1865) and Tivoli (2010). The most far-reaching aspect of the colonial government's attempt to cement power was the establishment of a very specific policing system that was to become the police force of independent Jamaica. According to the historical timeline on the Jamaica Constabulary Force's website, in 1716 informal policing began in Jamaica with "night watchman appointed to serve the cities of Port Royal, Kingston" (Jamaica Constabulary Force, 2019). Between 1832 and 1835 there were attempts to formalize policing in Jamaica, likely in preparation for emancipation, where the formerly enslaved would no longer be policed by slave masters and would have leeway to do as they pleased. But it was between 1865 and 1867—that is, in the aftermath of the rebellion—that the Jamaica Constabulary Force was formed. "The uprising demonstrated the vulnerability of peace and law in Jamaica and caused the establishment of an improved police force" (Jamaica Constabulary Force, 2019). Anthony Harriott put it succinctly in his article "Reforming the Jamaica Constabulary Force: From Political to Professional Policing?" when he says, "The JCF has operated on the colonial political model which is state protective rather than citizen protective and more concerned with public order than crime control" (Harriott, 1997, 1). The retired senior superintendent of police, Reneto Adams, in an interview with Eilat Maoz, describes the job description of both the post-Morant Bay Rebellion JCF and the contemporary JCF as a mandate "[t]o protect the rich against the poor" (Maoz, 2023, 13).

The rebellion in Morant Bay began with the peasant class in their determination not to starve as they were dried out by a multiyear drought, demanding that Governor Eyre see their condition. Governor Eyre's response, to seek and employ the power of the soldiers aboard a British military ship, with much more fighting power and weapons than the tired, hungry, drought-weary rebels on the ground, was to kill all Blacks on sight (all being guilty by virtue of their skin color), and to hang Bogle and his associates from the burnt remains of the Morant Bay courthouse as a lesson for all to see. Among those hanged was George William Gordon, a mixed-race anti-government agitator and supporter of the Black cause. Mimi Sheller, Stephen Russell, and others have found compelling evidence that many marginally white Jamaicans had rallied in support of Bogle, George William Gordon, and those in desperate poverty in St. Thomas in the east. Sheller's work highlights Jewish Jamaicans such as newspaperman Sidney Lindo Levien, who had been working against Governor Eyre's oppressive policies and was tried and arrested in the brutal anti-rebellion crackdown. Russell's work brings to attention Robert A. Johnson, who had served in the Jamaica legislature and was also a journalist before he emigrated to the United States and continued writing about events in Jamaica there (Russell, 2022b). Sheller uses the story of Levien and evidence from prior research to argue that Levien's case "opens new questions about the relation between Jews, Asians, Black, Colored, and varied white and 'marginally white' populations in Jamaica" (Sheller, 2019, 202). Sheller takes us "beyond the typical Black-vs-White framing of the Morant Bay Rebellion toward a more multi-sided emphasis on cross-racial and cross-class alliances, the politics of social justice, the social construction of race, and opposition within the imperial global economy" (Sheller, 2019, 202).

There is evidence enough that a Black-white framing does not attend to the complex pro- and anti-government racial politics that obtained in Jamaica in 1865—the maroons, after all, fought on the side of Eyre and killed many rebel Blacks. However, there is no evidence that marginal whites and Jews were cut down without trial or evidence, or that entire communities were murdered simply because they were marginally white or Jewish. In essence, their skin did not make them guilty; support of the cause of Black liberation and an anti-government stance did. These acts show how connected the need to control bodies is to the work of surveillance. The retinue of redcoats (British army men) unleashed to quash the uprising in Morant Bay, and their commitment to killing any Black person in sight, exposed the deep fear generated by organized and mobilized Black bodies. Equally evident was the way the body, once relegated to a certain category, was read as a transparent script. Its Blackness became the most consequential document by which the intention or animus of the body's inhabitant was assumed. Indeed, the Black body in and of itself became, was synonymous with, the intention. The British had failed in the eighteenth century in the first Maroon War[19] insofar as the result of this encounter was the forced compromise of a treaty, and the governor's fear was that they would fail again in 1865 unless the regime's tactics were more radically brutal. (It is instructive that even people in Britain were so shocked by the intensity of his reprisals that a royal commission was engaged, and Eyre was eventually sent home by the Colonial Office.)

One hundred forty-five years after Morant Bay, the Jamaican government's response to the rebels of Tivoli Gardens had a similar punch. As with Morant Bay in 1865, Tivoli in 2010 was not a clear-cut social-political situation. If in Morant Bay Blackness made one guilty without trial, the Tivoli rebels shot in cold blood were, in the main, Black, working-class, West Kingston dwellers. In both cases the perception of threat and the extreme violence of the response were similar. Class now crosses color in the postcolonial state. And in both cases, we see the necessity of a particular kind of police force and the redirection of the military, not for defense or offense against hostile nations, but against outsiders within the scope of the body politic.

The extremity of the violence meted out by the security forces in Tivoli Gardens is now legend. It did not take long for the public to know that the situation had far surpassed the last bloodbath of 2001, which had also taken place in Tivoli at the hands of the security forces. There were stories of men being rounded up, interrogated, and beaten, of others being shot, of mortar bombs dropped, the wrath of the Jamaica security forces unleashed and unfettered. Jamaica Constabulary Force (JCF) and Jamaica Defence Force (JDF) testimony before the Commission of Enquiry is corroborated by stories of Tivoli residents told to the media and in interviews with anthropologists.[20] According to these testimonies, after the security forces established dominance on the outside, they began a door-to-door sweep to find the gunmen and their arsenal that had assailed the lawmen by insurrectional acts such as ambush and burning of police stations following the announcement of the signing of Dudus's extradition papers. The most painful of the stories from the community are from the mothers, sisters, girlfriends, and wives who tell of their sons, brothers, partners, and husbands being shot in cold blood.

Chapter 10 of the report of the West Kingston Commission of Enquiry (2016) deals expressly with the conduct of the security forces under the Emergency Powers Act during a state of emergency. The chapter discusses how a state of public emergency curtails "some of the fundamental rights and freedoms guaranteed under Chapter III [of the Emergency Powers Act]" (17). The state of emergency (or period of public emergency) marks the fullest extent of the state's surveillance of its citizens. Periods of public emergency are significant because citizens are often temporarily stripped of their rights on the assumption that curtailing movement, privacy, and so on will ensure wider public safety. However, these actions often disproportionately impact those who are believed to be most in need of surveillance and bodily control—the Black, poor, and dispossessed. The Tivoli uprising and the government's response not only threw the continuity of policing from Morant Bay into stark relief, but also proved the limits of state surveillance, especially when faced with maroon/guerrilla warfare; that is to say, it became clear in Tivoli, as at Morant Bay, that the limits of state surveillance were most legible when facing maroon/guerrilla warfare. The extremity of the governor's response to peaceful protest, perceived as unorthodox warfare, was testimony to a sense of vulnerability that even pushed him beyond what Queen Victoria felt she could permit.

And as is the case with the Tivoli incursion, the close relation of the Morant Bay events to performance is apparent. In 1865, the rigid technologies of surveillance were paired with a radical return to the spectacular brutalities of slavery to quash the uprising. Here "spectacular" refers to the ritual staging of mutilated and hanged Black bodies, including those not involved in the uprising. This, then, was a dedicated focus on the lynched Black body as the visible proof and punishment, the material performance of colonial power. Not only were hundreds killed in and around Morant Bay, but, as previously noted, the body of Paul Bogle and the bodies of those closely associated with him as leaders of the uprising were hung from the Morant Bay courthouse as the most eloquent argument that this is the result of Black rebellion; our law and the institutions that house our law will make this the conclusion: broken necks, beaten bodies, dismembered parts, and the cause undone. The punishment of the rebels is performed to engender fear and to discourage more uprisings. Yet the staged bodies, like all performances, enact at least a double contradiction: not only is the depravity of the state equally on display, and not only is this preserved in memory and memorializing documents such as artistic renditions, but the bodies by virtue of the display express their own sentience, an inherent pushback that continued to play out in later uprisings, though in different contexts and in different ways. Beyond this inherent double pointing of the displayed body, we may think of the transhistorical reach of Morant Bay in word, poetic recitation, fiction, painting, and sculpture that made dynamic the pushback through material images and established Morant Bay as part of the Jamaican imaginary of resistance. These expressions include V. S. Reid's novels *New Day* and *Sixty-Five* as well the numerous poems about the uprising, some which are included in a choral speaking anthology for school children, as well as paintings by Barrington Watson, *The Morant Bay Rebellion* and *The Hanging of George William Gordon*, and Edna Manley's controversial sculpture *Bogle*.

In sum, I have given attention to the Tivoli incursion because of its profound significance in the contemporary Jamaican and Caribbean imaginary and because the events foreground three main tracks in the Caribbean experience of the relation of power that I refer to as flexible hegemonies within surveillance. I suggest the historical baseline of surveillance as an ongoing systemic machinery of the colonial and postcolonial state. Tivoli also provides a globally visible example of the relation between surveillance, performance, and flexible hegemonies within the Caribbean context. The specific forms taken by the people's resistance to the incursion opens a gateway to think about the relation of all these to conceptions of the body, and specifically the Black peasant or proletarian body. Tivoli as an emblematic field of narratives establishes the presence of a historical continuity that is sharply and variously focused on the literary works, documents, acts, and staged cultural performances from different historical eras with which this book is concerned.

My reading of how surveillance works in the Caribbean runs counter to some more traditional strands in surveillance studies but resonates with more recent approaches which emphasize context. Surveillance studies are often concerned with two key issues: visibility and power. Both have their roots in Michel Foucault's study of Jeremy Bentham's "panopticon," which has been called the leading scholarly metaphor for analyzing surveillance. Through Foucault's study of the panopticon, we get some insight into the relationship between visibility and power in the twentieth century, and, through analysis of the designs responsible for the few watching the many, we see power relations grounded in those who have the power to surveil. However, if Zygmunt Bauman is right to consider "surveillance [as] a central theme of modernity" (Lyon, 2010, 326) and Haggerty and Ericson are correct in positing that "society is organized through surveillance systems, technologies, and practices" (Haggerty and Ericson, 2006), it is obvious that different societal orders and their necessities produce different relations between visibility and power. Thomas Mathieson's work on synopticism, "the ability of the many to watch the few," comments on the role of "mass media in fostering a culture of celebrity where fame, or even notoriety, have become valuable" (Haggerty and Ericson, 2006, 5). Though Bauman does not use the phrase "liquid surveillance," Lyon argues that the term captures Bauman's contribution to surveillance studies. Liquid surveillance describes "today's surveillance [that] does not keep its shape; it morphs and mutates. Surveillance not only creeps and seeps, it also flows. It is on the move, globally and locally" (Lyon, 2010, 330). Lyon asserts that Bauman's concept "speaks to the looseness and frailty of social bonds" (Lyon, 2010, 331), seen in surveillance terms as the transformation of ordinary citizens into suspects and their relegation to consumer status across a range of life spheres. The banopticon, conceived of by Didier Bigo, considers people who are banned or excluded from society and surveilled not as part of the populace but as exceptions. He gives as examples refugee camps and offshore prison camps like Guantánamo Bay. Stephen Mann and colleagues have coined the word *sousveillance*, which means watching from below. According to Mann and colleagues, sousveillance "from the French words for 'sous' (below) and 'veiller' to watch" is an example of "inverse panopticon" (Mann, Nolan, and Wellman, 2002, 332). Sousveillance considers how an ordinary device like a cell phone can capture big events, reordering the location of power.

Simone's Browne's *Dark Matters: On the Surveillance of Blackness* suggests that race plays a central part in surveillance, as evidenced in the organization and monitoring of Black bodies on slave ships and in more contemporary times what she calls the "white eye." The "white eye" from the earliest encounter of Africans with whites is understood to be a labyrinth of power—economic, political, and social—deployed for the purpose of disciplining Black subjects in whichever way was appropriate to the particular brand of whiteness doing the work. Browne contends that race is undertheorized in surveillance studies and extends Mann's concept of sousveillance with the term "dark sousveillance" "as a way to situate the tactics employed to render oneself out of sight, and strategies used in the flight to freedom from slavery as necessarily ones of undersight" (Browne, 2015, 21). Browne's description of dark sousveillance operates three-dimensionally. Browne says:

> I plot dark sousveillance as an imaginative place from which to mobilize a critique of racializing surveillance, a critique that takes form in antisurveillance, countersurveillance, and other freedom practices. Dark sousveillance, then, plots imaginaries that are oppositional and that are hopeful for another way of being.
>
> Dark sousveillance is a site of critique, as it speaks to black epistemologies of contending with antiblack surveillance, where the tools of social control in plantation surveillance or lantern laws in city spaces and beyond were appropriated, co-opted, repurposed, and challenged in order to facilitate survival and escape.
>
> Dark sousveillance charts possibilities and coordinates modes of responding to, challenging, and confronting a surveillance that was almost all-encompassing. . . . As a way of knowing, dark sousveillance speaks not only to observing those in authority (the slave patroller or the plantation overseer, for instance) but also to the use of a keen and experiential insight of plantation surveillance in order to resist it. . . . Dark sousveillance is also a reading praxis for examining surveillance that allows for a questioning of how certain surveillance technologies installed during slavery to monitor and track blackness as property. (Browne, 2015, 21–24)

Given the Caribbean's unique experience as the earliest crucible of modernity, and Blackness as modernity's most consequential invention,[21] it becomes easy to locate the Caribbean within Baumann and Browne's theorizations on surveillance, modernity, and Blackness. In particular, the practices of veillance in the Caribbean fall broadly under what Browne defines as dark sousveillance. However, there are peculiarities of Caribbean space that impact how countersurveillance and anti-surveillance happen, and the reading practices that track Blackness have differently malleable and interpretive ways of understanding that are specific to the Caribbean.

I identify four qualities or characteristics of the region that impact how veillance happens: the size of the Caribbean's predominantly island nations and other geographical spaces; its demographic makeup; how race, skin shade, and class signify and command power differently, shifting the meaning and interpretation of words like "dark" ever so slightly, often contingently and yet crucially; and finally, the intermingled worlds of the spirit and the physical.

The Brathwaitian metaphor "[t]he stone . . . skidded arc'd and bloomed into islands" (Brathwaite, 1988, 48), of stone skipping and the splash forming an arc of islands (the arc referencing the geographical classification, archipelago), states a basic fact of scale. Whether the small islands are the ones in the arc surrounded by water or the forest-bordered bigger "islands" of the Guianas that, located on the South American mainland, are the archipelago's southernmost base, small spaces in the Caribbean have influenced how we see each other. On large plantations enslaved people were housed in small huts, and in urban spaces they were housed in yards for the purpose of being watched and controlled. The veillances that come out of these contexts are of a particular size-inflected vernacular. And they respond not only to the size of the islands, but to the space and scapes they make. St. Marten/New Jersey artist Deborah Jack comments on this in a talk on her installation, "Saltwater Resistance: Visualizing the (un) Geographic and Resonance of Archipelagic Memory in the Caribbean." Jack posits, "if you live on a small island you are always aware of the edges of the land" (Deborah Jack, "Saltwater Resistance," public lecture, Colgate University, March 22, 2023). I am intrigued by what this must have meant for the surveilling class and what it must have meant for freedom seekers. In island spaces, where there was no North to run to and conversely no North with miles and miles of freedom to fear, being aware of the edges of the land meant different visions for freedom, resistance, and anti- and countersurveillance. And while the chapters in this project do not go back to the days of slavery, the physical landscape of the Caribbean remains a starting point, an imaginative source in the reading and understanding of Caribbean vernacular veillance. Another key element in reading veillance in the Caribbean is bound up in Browne's signifier "dark." As Browne argues, "the historical formation of surveillance is not outside of the historical formation of slavery" (Browne, 2015, 50); thus, any place touched by the slave trade has surveillance and countersurveillance practices impacted by race. It makes full sense to adopt a color/shade marker and not a racial category to describe acts of veillance in the Caribbean context as the categories Black and white do not hold the same anxious definitive power as they do in the United States, for instance. In the Caribbean, race is important and defining, and yet it is a malleable category. Arguably, dark or Black in the Caribbean has always meant the intersection of two factors: being of the surveilled class—the enslaved, laborers, working people—and dominant African heritage.

Finally, veillances in the Caribbean often emerge from the close association of the spiritual with the physical and the spiritual with the revolutionary. Indigenous and African spiritualism driven underground by surveilling colonial power evolved with countersurveillance and anti-surveillance in their liturgies. The famed Bois Caïman ceremony, a gathering led by the Voudun priest and revolutionary Dutty Boukman, is often understood to be the beginning of the Haitian Revolution. The illegal gathering of the enslaved in many colonial territories was not only a chance to practice their forbidden religions, but also to share news and plans for the many revolts. It is also no surprise that the syncretic forms that emerged not only resisted surveillance but performed surveillance.

While the physical design of the plantation panopticon has been largely dismantled, the colonial cog that relied on plantation discipline has reproduced itself in top-down hierarchical systems, and more insidiously within the minds of the historically surveilled.[22] Yet, in the Caribbean, top-down surveillance succeeded and failed in further interesting ways. The best evidence of this is not in discipline but in indiscipline. If discipline is "a type of power, a modality for its exercise, comprising a whole set of instruments, techniques, procedures and levels of application; targets" (Foucault, 1995, 215), indiscipline is another type of (brooding/rising) power that resists the techniques and procedures of discipline, in this case colonial ideas of law and order, colonial ideas of decency and respectability, and, of course, the wielding of power through surveillance and surveillance systems. Indiscipline is not just stepping out of the evenly spaced, single-file queue or line; it is the regularizing ([counter]institutionalizing) produced by the "bungle": the willful congestion, en-massing, and pushing out of the contours of the line to produce a different, anti-order choreography of movement in space. Inherent in the "bungle" or "bungling up" are the prohibited intimacies that are antithetical to rules of public order.

In other words, I am not just referring to the disruption of rules and laws in the traditional sense, but to a more general response to the idea of order. An obvious place to go here is Carnival. Calypso and soca in Trinidad—music expressing the jamette sensibility (the sensibility of people coming from the diameter, the margin dividing proper and improper society)—often is spoken as a rallying call, a call to dance and move vigorously, to "get on bad" and misbehave, a call to total disorder, with the frequent declaration, "we nuh have no behavior."[23] In the historical sense we know that this call was made precisely because the Black population and previously enslaved were always being watched by the surveilling powers, and so under the guise of play and bacchanal they could perform disobedience, rebellion, and threat. Sussveillance, spiritveillance, and modern-day variations on watching the watcher belong to this same indiscipline, that is, local versions of power grown out of emerging antipower structures in the jamette hemisphere.

If the jamette hemisphere signifies deep contentions over space and definitions of space, it also signifies deep chasms among the ways different communities encounter time. *Inside Tenement Time* engages spaces that are highly surveilled—from within (the yard and the tenement) and from outside in geopolitical corridors (the young nation). In such spaces, terms used to mark time—past, present, future—lose their efficacy as stable sets of referents to codify experience, even where no teleology of history is intended. Time in the experience of the surveilled is often an experience of (both inner and outer) crisis. Time in such contexts becomes deeply compressed and expanded—that is, flexible outside of usual understandings. Of course, it is a given that time is always marked in terms of place: in 1492 (the time/date), Columbus "discovered" Jamaica (the place), and so the perception and the narrative experience of Jamaica is colored and even directed by this marker of 1492. However, the inner psychic and emotional experience of the Taino who encountered Columbus in those days of the 1492 incursion calibrates the time in a different way, and to a different rhythm than either Columbus's or his mariners' or the historical reader's. Beyond the literary and historical readings it undertakes, this book seeks to bring into our line of vision a timescape that exhausts the discourse of history or of time passing. My point of departure is Tivoli Gardens, West Kingston, Jamaica, in the week of May 24–27, 2010. The narrative I excavate is how the event put on display the practice of surveillance and its counter-systems in, of, and beyond Jamaica, the nation in which it took place. Moreover, I begin here because the incursion made visible contemporary iterations of the long historical arc of surveillance that has made crisis and global visibilities of shame fundamental dynamics of the postcolonial Caribbean state. The texts and contexts I examine are markers of specific moments of crisis within tenement time. More than this, Tivoli, the night of the Smile Jamaica concert, the imagined inner lives of the characters of James's, Patterson's, and de Lisser's novels, and the personal narratives of members of the Reggae Revival group, point explicitly or implicitly to the inner timescape—the space of compressed and expanded psychic time— within which life is encountered in spaces marked, marked off, or "cordoned" off as zones of exception. Tenement time is both how the space is marked by time in outside perceptions, and how time is encountered in the innerscape, and, further, the intersection and conflict between the two.

In chapter 1 I highlight the long historical arc of surveillance in Jamaica and the Caribbean by examining H. G. de Lisser's early fictional work, which may be read as a close observation of surveillance contexts in Kingston yards in the first two decades of the twentieth century. The chapter takes as its focus de Lisser's representation of suss/gossip/talk/women's talk, sources that are often silenced and discredited, about topics that are similarly dismissed, to tell ear-to-the-ground stories about young, Black Jamaican women who climb the rough ladder of social mobility in Kingston and Colón, Panama, at the beginning of the twentieth century. The period is significant as the moment of a nascent Jamaican national identity in the making, an identity already being imagined in terms of a distinctive literary and more largely cultural character of its own. The role of Panama in reconfiguring class, economics, and gender ratios in the urban workspace during this period is also significant. Before the passing of the Emigrant Labour Law in 1893, sources say 15,000 Jamaicans were recruited to work in the Canal Zone each year. This number lessened after the passing of the law and became difficult to track because of the number of illegal migrants to the Canal Zone. Barbados sent large cohorts of working men to the canal building project—10 percent of the adult population and nearly 40 percent of the island's adult men. George Lamming in *In the Castle of My Skin* attributes the relative absence of fathers and the overarching presence of mothers in 1930s Barbados to this phenomenon of men leaving. The claiming or shaping of a literary character for Jamaica was already arguably evident in the early work of Claude McKay and Tom Redcam. De Lisser's acute awareness of the *presence* of urban working-class women, an awareness fueled by their perceived threat to the class system within which his privilege was entrenched, has been extensively discussed, with an emphasis on these gender and class dynamics. What strikes me most in this analysis is de Lisser's equally strong awareness of the surveillance machineries that operated at the micro level, in intimate domestic and urban yard spaces, and the ways that in his work the technology of "suss" becomes a countervailing, often productively contradictory force within and against such machineries. De Lisser recognizes and appropriates the power of suss as both narrative form and authorial vantage point. His self-positioning as a master "sussveiller" from outside who writes the story by participant observation from within implicates the questions of cultural nationalism, and literary and ethnographic authority, in very interesting ways.

Orlando Patterson's 1964 novel *The Children of Sisyphus*, discussed in chapter 2, takes us to the moment of Jamaica's independence from British rule, highlighting the questions with which the new nation struggled in the public sphere as it sought to establish for itself a distinctive identity set apart from its former masters, yet fully conscious of England's eye on its endeavors. On the one hand, there were those who thought it important to match the British "civilization," to prove to the presumed watching eye from outside how well Jamaica could handle the demands of Western-style nationhood; on the other hand, there were those who felt that only a radical resetting, a revolutionary turn to the postcolony's own indigenous cultural and ideological products and/or ancestral Africa, would suffice. Such a turn would be ontological in its consequences; that is, it would reset the parameters of what it meant to be human, a counterclockwise turn away from the "epochal break"[24] initiated by chattel slavery. Between these two extremes, of course, were those who embraced the sociopolitical equivalents of what Sylvia Wynter (1971) described as "creole criticism" in Caribbean discourse, a form of compromise between the British antecedents and independent self-fashioning. Patterson's novel brings into unprecedented literary focus two crucially related poles of the governing establishment's practical attempts to create the new nation: one, the configuration of the capital city, Kingston, as the shining emblem of national identity, and in light of this, two, what do with the urban poor, which included an ever-swelling mass of refugees from the countryside looking for work and a place in the city. Within the performance of nation-building through the erection of new buildings and the establishment of new residential and industrial enclaves, in their visible bodies these rural-to-urban masses were a singular eyesore.

The Children of Sisyphus, set just before Jamaica's independence in 1962 and published in 1964, shifts radically from the focus we see in de Lisser on the lower classes struggling to get into the class above—arguably, the class of poor that his middle-class readership could imagine or render acceptable as part of the national body politic. Patterson's concern, in contrast, is with the nation's *Homo sacer*[25]—those whose lives and perceived habits often tested the imagination of onlookers: "is it possible to be *this* and still human?" With sociologically accurate commentary on the formation of the new nation, Patterson focuses on the great slums of West Kingston and its denizens—the parts and people of Kingston put aside on the periphery from the city's foundations and often the builders and maintainers of those very foundations. In these depressed corridors of West Kingston, called "the Dungle," state surveillance is always at work, never seeing the community as a collection of individuals, but as flattened types. What I term spiritveillance, the slum-dwellers' form of both pushback and self-fashioning, however, is arguably a more potent (and permeating) form (of seeing and) of disciplining power in the slums. Because of the Dungle's and surrounding areas' myriad commitments to spirit work, this form of political and, ultimately, metaphysical counter/action has an abiding presence in multiple forms via African-Caribbean religious practice, and most powerfully via a commitment to and belief in individuals as active agents, visionaries, and enlightened followers. Obeah, Rastafari, and revivalism have their provenance and supporting numbers in the slums. *Sisyphus*, then, is grounded in how these tentacles of power work in the spiritual and physical realms. The novel both reveals the fissures in the public performance of nation enacted through the construction of literal façades and offers the naked semiotic of the Dungle as an alter/native[26] way of reading Jamaica in its postcolonial beginning. Of major importance in my discussion in these two chapters is the geographical setting and built enclosures within which the stories take place. In chapter 1 I give analytical focus to de Lisser's setting of the urban yard and the spaces to which it is contiguous. In chapter 2, the setting of the Dungle, an outre-sphere that is outside the "walled" city, including its contiguous yards, is central to Patterson's critique of the new nation and city. The cultural, social, and physical topographies of the two spaces are integral to our understanding of how suss and obeah as spiritveillance operate in relation to surveillance.

If there was a decade in Jamaica's history when anxieties about surveillance gripped the nation, it was the 1970s. Prime Minister Michael Manley's left-leaning and association with the likes of Fidel Castro upset U.S. doctrine enough for the United States to send out undercover missions to check up on backsliders. This larger backdrop is one of many scenarios implicated in chapter 3. In this chapter, I use as my main text a key performance in the complex political story of 1970s Jamaica: The Smile Jamaica concert headlining reggae superstar Bob Marley. Smile Jamaica brings performance and surveillance into relief, as only two days before the concert there was an attempt on Marley's life, presumably with the intention of preventing his performance and canceling the concert. Documents from the period reveal how closely Marley was watched from multiple platforms, including the U.S. surveillance system, in the backdrop of events leading up to this moment. The entire performance, from Marley's choice of music to the vocal and instrumental accompaniments, from the MC to the crowd on stage, to the *bruggudup*[27] of reggae music, and finally to the audience that showed up in record numbers to witness Marley's performance in defiance of the attempt on his life, was clearly a response to the powers of surveillance. The attempt on Marley's life has been extensively glossed as the result of partisan politics. Paying attention to registers such as Marley's body "politics," the sequence of events, and particularly the performance itself as the playing out of a multipronged contest among surveillance powers, allows us to see continuities in the larger picture of how hegemonies are sustained in the Jamaican/Caribbean quotidian, how power becomes flexible depending on who has the "bigger eye" in a given moment. The concert takes us from both yard and Dungle to the designated inclusive community setting of the National Heroes Park near Crossroads, where uptown, downtown, yard, and all of Kingston and Jamaica supposedly meet without restriction to access. The park's connections with meetings across class lines and the imagination of a new nation are amplified by Marley's and reggae's own originations in the urban yard of Trench Town. The uptown yard of 56 Hope Road, Marley's residence, is also an important locale in thinking about the geopolitics of surveillance.

The final chapter takes us back to where we began: it looks at artistic production after and in response to the heightened surveillance state that emerged from the standoff between Dudus's Tivoli Gardens and the Jamaican and U.S. governments. The Reggae Revival was a youth-inspired response, not expressly to the political climate of the day in which Jamaica had become openly subject to U.S. dictates, but rather to how politics and the system had impacted the music, music culture, and visual art. Reggae revivalists saw the art culture as having prostituted itself to the tastes of gangsters and power grabbers and having flattened the culture of "we" (we are all together in the struggle, one family, working for the same goals, the word is love) into the ways and the wiles of "dem"—the enemy, the competition, the people working for their own gain). The chapter argues that the young people of the Reggae Revival were able to emerge under the proverbial radar precisely because their art had not yet made a name for itself or been established. They were too green, too "new" and "clean" to be on Dudus's or the government's payroll. Besides, they sought among themselves an artistic community that engaged the spirit of "we-ness," a creative community that they saw as having existed in the first days of reggae and which they thought was in danger of being erased or had been completely expunged from the art scene, through the affiliation of well-known artistes, either with government and other establishment or with anti-establishment authorities. Among the latter was Dudus's Presidential Click, whose support had helped artistes from the inner city to flourish through installations such as Passa Passa, the popular downtown dance party. The rejection of establishment patronage by these revivalists is, then, by extension, at least in theory, a rejection of the patronage of the surveillance state and state.

The revival flourished in its time because of a set of ironic confluences. As a perceived antithesis to the long arc of Tivoli, it became noticed as a breath of fresh air, so to speak. It became visible *and* viable also because, first, the moment of the incursion, which is also the moment of the revival's emergence, preoccupied the attention of the establishments, and second, even if the Tivoli crisis had not consumed the establishment's attention, the group was as yet too new and negligible to be considered worth the expenditure of courting or corralling their affiliation. In other words, then, the Reggae Revival emerged through the fissures of surveillance in a particular moment. It is worth noting that the revivalists presented themselves not as individual artists but as a single body, a composite "we" invested/sutured with "true rebellion" and the accoutrements, including sound (musical instruments) of "true" art. A comparison may be drawn with the Caribbean Artists Movement of 1966–1972, also an eclectic artistic movement but a cross-Caribbean community with a strong Caribbean nationalistic ethos.

The chapter examines, as well, the implications of the fact that these were largely middle-class bodies, antithetical to the inner-city bodies associated with the emergence of roots reggae for which they spoke even while articulating a different positionality and aesthetic. These intersectional asymmetries are aligned as well to the acute paradoxes inherent in the revivalists' careful staging and monitoring of their own identity-performance as a counter to state and don-man-sanctioned creative production and as a rejection of the blatant ethos of music or art for money. The question of their ability to survive arises in this context as well—could their subaltern economic strategy function outside of negotiation with the surveillance systems associated with big business conglomerates that often circumscribe even local music production outfits?

By identifying surveillance as a critical force in power relations in the Caribbean, this book offers a different take on the historical, political, and geopolitical issues that have plagued the modern region since its inception. The case study of one island nation over the arc of a long century-plus—from the first decades of the twentieth century to the first decade of the twenty-first—allows for a granular focus on specificities that are erased in a diasporan approach and yet bear broad applicability within the region. As a methodology, the approach of this book invites fresh conversations about the inter- and intra-Caribbean and about the nuances that allow us to speak of national arts within larger regional and diasporan frames.

Inside Tenement Time explores how power operates at different scales and across different sites in macro and micro forms through the spirit, through suss, and via the surveillance machinery of the state. But surveillance also operates as a method of reading that teaches us to look at its multifarious axes by drawing attention to the margins, by which I mean the Black subjects of Kingston—in particular, East and West Kingston on the edges of the city. Reading for surveillance then centers the margins and articulates why stories from the margins are critical to the story of the nation at all its key moments. Such an approach underscores how these lives have mattered to the idea and the frame of the nation. Reading for surveillance also looks to the extranational. It acknowledges the very early presence of elsewhere in Jamaica: Panama, Ethiopia, England, the United States, not simply as places to emigrate and repatriate to, but also as places that directly impact domestic relations in Jamaica. Finally, surveillance is identified as a source of anxiety that unleashes multiple outgrowths of creativity.

1

In the Shadow of the Wall

• •

Suss and Sussveillance in the Yard Fiction of H. G. de Lisser

> She strolled toward the eastern section of the city, and in half an hour had arrived at one of the innumerable yards in one of the numerous lanes of Kingston. She pushed the gate and went boldly in, and entered the third of a long low range of tenement rooms which formed the habitations of a good many families.
>
> (de Lisser, 1972, 95)

The conspiratorial tone that de Lisser's narrator (*Jane's Career: A Story of Jamaica*, 1913) uses to tell the story of Jane Burrell's emancipation from her domestic apprenticeship under the class- and color-anxious curmudgeon, Mrs. Mason, presents the tenements of East Kingston as a plain yet categorical promised land. Running away from Mrs. Mason's single-family home on Heywood Street, where Jane is cowed and beaten, to the tenements in East Kingston is not the beginning of her poverty and destitution but rather the first steps toward Jane's emancipation and her career as an independent woman in Kingston. The space of the tenement itself, even with its emergent challenges, is radically empowering for Jane. When she first arrives in the yard her co-conspirator underscores that Jane should no longer fear her employer: "y'u not a slave—slavery done away with long time ago" (de Lisser, 1972, 96). She outlines a different economy in which Jane is quickly a contributor, and in addition to finding Jane a job she tells her of a social order that obtains whereby young women openly seek "meal tickets" or "friends" in eligible young men to help them along. It is in other urban yards that Jane and her peers find entertainment and social engagement, and it is in the yards that a labor movement foments. Finally, it is in the yards that alternative forms of power: word of mouth, suss, and "watchie-watchie" are performed—very different from the top-down surveillance tactics of Mrs. Mason.

As Obika Gray argues, "the social power of the urban poor expressed itself through autonomous, small, persistent, and cumulative acts of individual and group empowerment inside and outside of state apparatuses. These small acts of empowerment, and the compulsion they exert on the society and on power holders, are referred to here as the social power of the urban poor" (Gray, 2004, 12). The novel's focus on the personality and complexity of the yard and its dwellers as navigators and movers and shakers of difficult social and financial situations and as challengers of a daunting, persistent history is instructive. De Lisser performs more than an intense scrutiny of yard power. Rather, the novel is crafted around what we might call a poetics of suss—an ironic appropriation of the technologies of yard power through which de Lisser creates a literary persona for himself. This aspect of the novel's intention is made legible in the context of an emergent idea of Jamaican literature and authorship at the turn of the century.

In de Lisser's yards, as in Tivoli Gardens in 2010 (before and during the incursion, that is, from colonial times to deep in the postcolonial state), "the social power of the urban poor" constantly exposes the fissures in the top-down surveillance machineries. To call Tivoli Gardens a yard is to acknowledge an unsettling thing. Before Tivoli was Tivoli it was Back O' Wall. Back O' Wall, one of the great slums of Jamaica, was demolished in an effort to remove the scourge of extreme poverty and to contain the terror of West Kingston before it spread across the city of Kingston, already for some "a negro slum" in the main (Franck, 1920, 404).[1] The demolition of Back O' Wall and the erection of Tivoli was supposed to fix the blight of the slum with government-approved walk-up apartments, open public spaces, and working infrastructure.[2] It was also an attempt to correct the threat of an emerging Black power made audible in the chantings of anti-nation, back-to-Africa "cultists." Though different in design from the yard described in the epigraph, the Tivoli yard shares similarities with this and other Kingston spaces referred to as yards. One primary similarity that emerges from the history of Tivoli outlined above is that Tivoli, like all urban yards, was and is an enclosure. Indeed, this is a basic principle of yard space. The terms by which Tivoli substituted for Back O' Wall make it clear that enclosure was not accidental but rather a fundamental intention of the state. This is to say that the design of Tivoli and other government-built tenements was never aimed at integration with mainstream society except for the purpose of service.

In fact, the invisible wall around Tivoli dwellers and others from slums, tenements, and urban yards in general was the purposeful maintenance of a society keenly sensitive to caste and class distinctions. The irony is that Back O' Wall was demolished in an attempt to contain the slum yard and yet in its reincarnation as Tivoli Gardens the principle of the yard is propagated. Back O' Wall was regarded as potentially dangerous and to be watched; Tivoli, the corrected version of the slum, is regarded as potentially dangerous and to be watched.

This chapter is concerned with how the social power of the urban poor is manifested in the technology I refer to as sussveillance: for the surveilling establishment, a crucial aspect of the perceived danger of urban yard space. I explore this relation through the early work of H. G. de Lisser, placing his two yard novels, *Jane's Career* (1913) and *Susan Proudleigh* (1915), in conversation with his journalistic writings and his editorial work. I read these texts as surveillance/sussveillance documents: not only does de Lisser's approach as literary ethnographer depend on these technologies, but his acute observational strategies reveal sussveillance and surveillance as dynamic sites of power within the intimate spaces and relationships of the yard. I argue that de Lisser manipulates sussveillance in his voyeuristic project among Black working classes, women, and aspiring (not well-enough colored) middle class. As writer and would-be man of letters, de Lisser is, in essence, a political operator (double agent) mining both surveillance and sussveillance strategies as a way of harnessing for himself literary capital, writerly authority, and the kudos of authenticity. I contend that these were crucial for de Lisser at a time when the issue of how to represent the people of the colonies was an emergent strand in the discourse of freedom, both (pre)national and literary. The chapter then highlights the fundamental role of the yard and the lives of the poor in the image of the literary/cultural nation. Ultimately, the spotlight on sussveillance is an aperture through which to read the pre-independence moment in colonial Jamaica.

Part of what appears from de Lisser's granular, up-close representations is that in the enclosure of yards, relationships are built across domestic space. From one doorway to another, at standpipes, on shared clotheslines, the reverberations of living everyday life in close proximity to others and in shared circumstances of economic need underscore the existence of a competitive, supportive human community. But also, crucially, these representations underscore the poor Black community dwelling together against the force of the modern city and creating spaces for fomenting resistance, articulating difference, and constructing decolonial, independent selves. These valences of the yard were played out in the Tivoli incursion, though in that scenario the focus on Tivoli as a systematized quasi-state could easily obscure the reality of Tivoli as yard—or more accurately as yard system. In that setting it was the public face of yard revolt that was made apparent. De Lisser's microcosmic portrayal of individual yards allows us to see how various facets of the yard "grow" to become dangerous from an establishment viewpoint, and how the "domestic sphere" comes to be involved with the public sphere.

We see such facets of the yard in the diction of the epigraph. De Lisser's emphasis on Jane's movement shows a narrative persona who is closely watching and registering potential threat: in Jane's passage from the enclave of aspiring middle-class Kingston to the tenement yards of the city. Jane "strolls" toward the yards—hers is a movement of leisurely ownership in the geographical space, such as one associates with the movement of the moneyed classes on a fictional summer evening. Strolling, she nevertheless arrives at the third house in the slum yard in a very short time, a mere half an hour. With Jane we stroll into her new life finally unhurried by Mrs. Mason's shrieks and orders. What the reader had always guessed about the proximity of Mrs. Mason's household and the working-class way of life is confirmed. The yards' unnerving proximity to the more respectable part of Kingston is signaled and then amplified in the sense of their movable proliferation: they appear as "innumerable" enclaves on "numerous" lanes—a growing encroachment of paths that chart the uncontainable geography of the city within the city. Jane's progress toward "housing" or "homing," we recall, had begun in her move from her rural village to Kingston and Mrs. Mason's home. There had as yet been no ease; it had all been part of the furtive desperation to leave the dead ends of the fields and the poverty of rural Jamaica. In the language of the epigraph, however, is the image of a woman in possession of space. She strolls toward her new life, and in her journey by foot shrinks the space between the middle-class home and the tenements, stepping us through the cartography of the city as though there had been neither border nor enclosure. Yet this does not signal an arrival but a new sphere of confrontation with the powers of surveillance. Equally, it signals Jane's introduction to the vernacular powers constructed within the space of the yard, among them the counter-operative arts (arguably sciences) derived from suss.[3]

Sussveillance may be defined as the surveillance strategy often (but not exclusively) practiced by the underclass, in which the power of rumor, of talk, of suggestion and suspicion are employed to wrest control or manipulate circumstances or opponents. It operates in the space created by the yard and the surrounding wall, that is, between confinement and the enforced intimacy that such confinement produces. Sussveillance is both organic, in that it emerges as a spontaneous, creative response to coercive power, and forced, in that coercive power from above establishes the conditions for it to flourish. At the same time, the recuperative power of sussveillance is not only its ability to "stare down" coercive authority, but also its capacity as an independent locus of power creatively sourced by those considered powerless, for their own self-reflexive ends.

I coin the neologism as a way of more accurately describing the Caribbean's experience of surveillance than Bentham's panopticon and Foucault's panopticism can accommodate. Related to this is Simone Brown's observation that race has always played an important part in surveillance.[4] I refer here to Mann and Ferenbok's concept of sousveillance. Sousveillance, according to Mann, means "'watching from below,' and its etymology derives from replacing 'sur' (over) with 'sous,' which means 'under' or 'below' or 'from below' (as in words like 'sous-chef')" (Mann and Ferenbok, 2013, 19). Mann's work on sousveillance considers how power is wielded and inverted more particularly through "social innovations being catalyzed by networked mobile, portable, and wearable computing" (Mann and Ferenbok, 2013, 19). The work of the network happens intuitively and organically at the turn of the twentieth century as a harbinger of sousveillance, as it arrests power from the usual suspects even without the computing of the late twentieth and twenty-first centuries. Mann's creative acknowledgment of different kinds of surveillance resonates in the Caribbean cultural context. It provides a helpful framework to acknowledge different levels and layers of surveillance power. Sousveillance, then, allows the questions: How do you talk about surveillance from below without the gadgetry that Mann describes? What are the technologies of sousveillance before there is wearable computing?

Inspired by Mann's term, I draw on the Caribbean word "suss" to offer the concept of "sussveillance" as applicable to the Jamaican and the larger Caribbean context.[5] Sussveillance comes out of close community interactions, usually of people and spaces that are already highly surveilled. That is, the purposeful arrangement of Black bodies in small closely monitored spaces produces the infrastructure of sussveillance. Early twentieth-century yard fiction provides literary context to see sussveillance at work. Sussveillance uses the prefix "suss," which, according to the *Jamaican Patois and Slang Dictionary* online, is a noun that means "rumor" or "scandal"—"Yuh hear di suss bout seh Stacey deh gi har man bun." Suss is also a verb, "to talk behind someone's back"—"me hear seh yu did a suss bout me." Cassidy and Le Page do not have suss listed in the *Dictionary of Jamaican English*. The word susu, a verb, from the Twi word "susu ka" is there, however. It means "to utter a suspicion.... To whisper (behind one's back); to gossip; to speak ill" (Cassidy and Le Page, 2002, 430). Allsopp's *Dictionary of Caribbean English Usage* adds a subtle layer to the meaning of susu: "[a] confidential whispering," which suggests both conspiracy and rumor as a continuous verb tense (Allsopp, 2003, 540). Paired with the suffix "veillance," the idea of "talking what you see" or watching (performing "watchie-watchie") so that you can carry news is born. Based on my discussion of Alexander Bedward's case below, we see that "suss" conveys various other ideas: the idea of "sniffing out" the truth and the idea of putting into circulation a rumor, based on fact or not, in order to achieve a particular effect or result. Suss can also be characterized as the proverbial grapevine. "Suss," then, as a complex of meanings or even a particular meaning at any one time has an alchemical or organic effect of changing situations, relationships, discourses, and power relations in ways that may be controlling but also unpredictable.

Sussveillance, then, suggests a developed technology of watching with the intention to speak or to tell. In the same way that suss can be based on untruths or falsehoods, sussveillance has the potential to create a way of seeing that is also based in falsehoods. Sussveillance, like its parent activity, suss, is generative; it has the ability to grow, to be more than what precisely is seen, so we could say it has creative potential. That is, it does not simply watch from above or below to monitor to maintain order or to contradict some official version of order or narrative; it is a more organic, phenomenological outgrowth that flourishes particularly in close spaces with many people and scarce resources. Its paradox, of course, lies in its generative capacity; so, while "suss" and "sussveillance" are major sources of power and power-brokering among neighbors in spaces such as the urban yard, they are also collusive as they can be adapted into any form of surveillance in any context.

I contextualize the examination of de Lisser's surveilling/sussveilling work with a brief history of the urban yard as an important locus of culture and community in colonial Jamaica. Out of the close quarters of the Black working poor in the yards of Kingston, the emblematic post/colonial city emerges anti-colonial radicalism and pro-Black sentiment. In these spaces, African Jamaican religious practice is born—Bedwardism, Revival, Kumina, and Rastafari; also in these spaces, anger over generational poverty and limited opportunity fans the flames of labor unrest. Kingston yards are also creative hotbeds. In the 1970s, at the height of nationalist contestations in Jamaica, the lyrics of reggae poetry and music repeatedly return to the conditions of these close quarters: the aggrieved persona of Mikey Smith's famous dub poem, "Mi Cyaan Believe It" (released 1982) describes the realities of moving into a tenement yard: "room dem a rent / mi apply widin / but as me go een / cockroach, rat an scorpian also come een / . . . but me naw siddung pon high wall / like Humpty Dumpty / me a face me reality." In Mutabaruka's "Siddung pon di Wall" (2005),[6] the speaker has a confrontation with another resident: "long time mi siddung pon di wall / a watch him a watch me" (Mutabaruka, 2005, 33). Similarly, Jacob Miller protests "dreadlocks can't live inna tenement yard / too much watchie watchie / too much susu susu susu" (Miller, 1975),[7] and Bob Marley's "No Woman No Cry" (1974) recalls "when we used to sit / in a government yard in Trench Town / Oba-observing the hypocrites / mingle with the good people that we meet" (Bob Marley and The Wailers, 1975). Taken together, the poems and lyrics convey a sense of the yard as a constricted space—whether because of the presence of literal walls, as in Smith and Mutabaruka, or as a space deeply stressed by the seeming inability to escape exposure: whether to rat, cockroach, suss, scorpion, or the surveilling eye. At the same time, we recognize a doubleness that refuses the "single story" of oppression: Smith and Mutabaruka invoke walls not only as a defining but as a contemplative place for tenement dwellers, and Marley's lyrics come in the context of a nostalgic longing for the Trench Town yard as home, community, and generative space. The deeper paradox of the yard is that it is a space where creativity thrives.

Many would argue that reggae music was birthed out of the yards where sounds, images, and experiences collided and transformed the city. Part of what is responsible for this creative bounty is that the yard functions as both stage and audience and, of course, the dastardly conditions of the yard provided steady inspiration to find a way out. Surveillance and its yard partner—sussveillance—are crucial to this emergence of African indigenous Jamaican art, culture, religion, and politics. And de Lisser's sussveillance/surveillance texts set in Kingston yards suggest that beyond its fueling of artistic bounty, yard culture, specifically the clash between surveillance and sussveillance, played a role in the labor movements and the evolution of a Black middle class.[8]

Contextualizing Sussveillance: A Brief History of Kingston's Yards

From as early as 1770, the cartography of colonial Kingston established the gathering of Black people, free and enslaved, as an occasion for surveillance. Seven-foot walls legislated around the dwellings of Blacks marked the subaltern who was not allowed to speak, and constructed race as a visible sign, the fence between human and its other. The space of the yard then begins in these enclosures, not exposed to panoptic surveillance like that of the plantation, but shut in and monitored by "fences of bricks and stones" ("The Laws of Jamaica," 1770) and by the assumptions that these high walls would confirm that those within them needed to be surveilled and monitored. But how does the wall come to be a prominent place for surveillance in its different permutations?

Arguably the inception of the tenement yard or the earliest form of the urban yard in Kingston grew up inside mandated walls. The law ratified in 1770 and referenced in both Erna Brodber's *A Study of Yards in Kingston, Jamaica* (1975) and Wilma Bailey's "Kingston, 1692–1843: A Colonial City" (1974) is the earliest mention of a surrounding structure (wall or fence) to encompass or yardify Negro dwellings. The law was specifically intended for "all and every Owner or Owners of Lots of Land in and about the said Towns of Saint Jago de la Vega, Port-Royal and Kingston, whereon now is built, or on which any Owner or Owners hereafter may build . . . any Hut or Huts, House or Houses, for the habitation of any Negro or other slaves, being separate and apart from the Dwelling house of such Owner or Owners" ("The Laws of Jamaica," 1770).

The clause concerning the residence of urban slaves in huts or houses apart from their owners underscores the extremism of slavery and the deeply held belief that enslaved men and women who did not live in close proximity to their masters needed some alternative physical structure to contain and remind them of the all-seeing eye of the master class. The law delineates further that "every hut or house, so built or to be built (not exceeding the number of four) shall have but one door of entry, but where there shall be four or more huts, or houses, belonging to the same owner or owners, then each hut or house shall be enclosed or compassed round with a fence of bricks, stone, boards, or palisades, of the height of seven feet, which shall be kept in good and sufficient repair . . . each of which enclosures shall have but one door of entry" ("The Laws of Jamaica," 1770).

In other words, the mandatory erection of seven-foot walls and the allowance of only one entrance/exit to any compound with Black dwellers was a cornerstone of surveillance in colonial cities in Jamaica and the wider Caribbean. For Blacks to be kept in order they had to be seen, surveyed, and monitored from up high/above (all of seven feet)—much in the way described by Foucault's panopticism. But further still, the single narrow entrance that characterized the yard dwellings was not only to confine and corral to minimize the possibility of escape or gatherings for the purpose of insurrection. It was also to reduce, singularize, and isolate from community. This constituted an assault on any sense of themselves as human; it served as an architectural reminder of this flattening out of identity.

The walls and fences of the colonial Kingston city yard carry on through independence as relics of the slave code. These walls are meant to race and segregate, and like the slave ship and slave quarters enclose large numbers of poor Black Jamaicans in small spaces—government (public) and tenant (private) yards of Kingston. These communities were established as urban dwellings from slavery days until the present day; the residents have limited control over the spaces they occupy, and this becomes the occasion not only for resistance but the spawning of radical forces that arguably become uncontainable. Erna Brodber's and Wilma Bailey's works provide sociological and historical detail, where writers before independence such as H. G. de Lisser and Roger Mais, and literary artists and filmmakers after independence such as Orlando Patterson, Mikey Smith, Storm Saulter, playwright Trevor Rhone working with filmmaker Perry Henzell, novelist Michael Thelwell working after Rhone and Henzell imagine and recount the lives of rural folk come to town. Brodber and Bailey examine themes of urban poverty and political partisanship, of violence, of space and agency in the Kingston yard. This continued preoccupation with the spaces the urban poor occupy is one way artists and academics have continued to reckon with class and color inequities on which Jamaican society is built.

Brodber's historical perspective on the yard is a useful place to begin. Brodber cites Bailey's work, where Bailey points out that "the Negro Yard during the period 1745–1826 was a conspicuous feature of the Kingston tax rolls" and that "large slave proprietors must have housed their slaves in these yards" (Brodber, 1975, 5). This fact is helpful as we come to understand how the concept of the yard is variable for different Kingston residents. Brodber indicates, then, that the term "yard" "must have become for black and white Jamaicans, a place in which non-white enslaved people live. The affective connotation would have been different however. For the one with a cultural experience of *yard* 'as an enclosure in which cabs, trains etc. are kept when not in use' (1827), the Negro Yard would have meant storage for property or residences for non-human beings; for the enslaved Jamaican, it would have meant 'where our kind find a respite from enforced labour and are exclusively exposed to each other's company'" (Brodber, 1975, 5). Brodber's comment here highlights a crucial source of the radical possibility that the yard became for Black Kingstonians a respite from enforced labor and a place of exposure to each other's company—it was essentially home.

After slavery and well into the nineteenth century, Kingston yards continued to house large numbers of African Jamaicans—now including migrants from rural Jamaica.[9] This population also grew to include Chinese and Indian immigrants. Low-income housing in Kingston began on the premise that slaves' bodies were for labor and profit exclusively and that they could be kept alongside tools and machines used for the same purpose. After emancipation, the push for cheap housing for as many as could be held continued, with both the government and private landlords building projects or converting single-family homes into government yards and tenant (or tenement) yards, respectively. This housing was needed to accommodate the steady stream of rural migrants leaving the poverty of the post-plantation where conditions remained desperately close to those under slavery. The fact that there was inadequate housing in Kingston, that unsanitary and dangerous situations awaited, did not make Kingston less attractive to rural migrants. There is plenty of evidence that the conditions in these dwellings were uniformly poor, though tenant yards were almost always thought to be worse situations and more expensive than government housing and government yards (Brodber, 1975, 10–24).

For many seeking housing, Kingston's yards were not often considered to be permanent dwellings, just stops on the way from the rural, post-plantation situation before finding the means to settle properly in town, and sometimes a necessity on the way out of a bad situation. Bailey identifies the yard as the place to adjust to city life; Kaneesha Parsard describes the barrack yard as the answer to "the need for housing in the late nineteenth and early twentieth century in the British West Indies" (Parsard, 2018, 21). Yards were for many, as they are for de Lisser's Jane, a transient place but with a consistent culture of African (creole) Jamaican abundance, certainly the space where one would find, as de Lisser claims for his novel, "a story of Jamaica."

In "What the Yard Is Said to Be" Bailey analyzes what these dwellings would have looked like in the geography of Kingston as raced spaces in a city where race and skin shade mattered:

> The black population of Kingston menaced the urban society and from
> the late 18th century their control became an obsession with the Kingston
> Vestrymen. The closeness of the group in an urban setting made the merchant

community more vulnerable than the rural plantations. Further, the association of enslaved and free, of domestic tied to the home and independent jobber, must have disturbed the ordinary relationship between master and slave. The Yards, their own communities, may have been the focal points of their very real and positive efforts to subvert a society in which they had no stake. (Bailey, 1976, 172)

Bailey suggests that yard spaces were not simply perceived differently, but that the collective living of Kingston's poor, initially meant for control, created situations that *needed to be controlled*. Bailey also suggests that different kinds of power and agency emerge from the urban yard. The power is in the association across status and role, but especially in the space walled off from polite white society. Bailey's emphasis on yards as Black people's "own communities" suggests that despite poor conditions residents found power and creativity possible in the yard. Sussveillance emerges as part of that power and creativity.

The structure of the yard, its positioning as the object of surveillance, and the identity of its denizens allow for the emergence of sussveillance as a self-reflexive practice that also counters and colludes with surveillance to achieve contradictory ends. (By self-reflexive, I seek to underline that the yard dweller had an existence in their own right, exceeding and preceding the necessity of "answering back to" or countering the surveillance by the state, and so the emergence of sussveillance as a creative strategy of survival and agency is also taken into account.)

Given the history of walls as a form of apartheid and ghettoization in Kingston and its environs, it is not surprising that several decades after emancipation in Jamaica, in the early twentieth century, Alexander Bedward, prophet, levitator, and minister of the Jamaica Native Baptist Free Church, uses the metaphor of the wall to describe the power-brokering whites used over Blacks in colonial Jamaica. In one of his famous sermons, Bedward intones: "There is a white wall and a black wall, and the white wall is closing around the black wall; but the black wall is bigger than the white wall and they must knock the white wall down. The white wall has opposed us for years. Now we must oppress the white wall. The governor passes laws to oppress the black people. They take their money out of their pockets. They rob them of their bread and they do nothing for it. Let them remember the Morant Bay Rebellion. I tell you the government are thieves and liars and the head of the government and the governor is a scoundrel and a robber" (quoted in Satchell, 2004, 37). Bedward gave this sermon knowing his activities were highly surveilled. The sermon begins with loosely coded language about race relations in Jamaica, but the metaphor of the wall soon gives way to a direct reference to the government. The sermon does not simply describe white oppression of Black Jamaica; it animates the wall and suggests a Black response to white confrontation; his call to remember the Morant Bay Rebellion of 1865 is both a threat and a rallying cry. And it acknowledges the radical Black perspective on the island still grounded in religious practice.

Bedward's employment of the wall metaphor to express Black Jamaica's refusal to be oppressed is noteworthy. He very likely used the metaphor without knowledge of the 1770 statute, but with firsthand and lived experience of white wall opposition, white wall oppression, thievery, and lies. Bedward's Native Free Church in August Town, a working-class, near-urban community located among yards and spun off from the Mona Plantation, was the space out of which these ideas emanated. The church, like other revival structures, was likely closely adjoined to yards. The sermon illustrates Bedward's deep understanding of yard culture; he is attuned to the fact that the walls and fences were erected to surveil the actions and words of dwellers, so he speaks to his congregants, and he speaks to the ears beyond the wall that he knows are listening. Bedward knows that his sermon is fodder for carry go bring come[10] suss and gossip, and he seems to invite and bait the audience beyond the audience by speaking to them. In this way, he understands Kingston, the governor and his lot included, as operating within this culture.

Bedward's power is like surveilling power. In his sermon about walls, he climbs atop "the wall" to watch them watch him. If it is true that he was mad, his refusal to acknowledge the combined powers of the white, English governor against (even) his spiritual insight and power of flight is evidence. Albeit at a different level, some of Bedward's sermons were published in the newspapers and were codified to build a case against him and his followers. At the national level, if we call the case against Bedward national suss, we can begin to see the dangerous intersection of surveillance—the governor monitoring Bedward and his influence—and suss, the alchemization of facts or intimated facts through the filters of rumor and suspicion that the press used to construct a narrative about Bedward, to lock the prophet away.

Rumor, a form of suss that mushroomed around his sermons, was circulated through the press and orchestrated by the authorities and was the basis of his "indictment."[11] In other words, the government harnessed sussveillance as the major part of its surveillance of Bedward. It is instructive that he was not arrested as a criminal but institutionalized as a madman, based not so much on Bedward's own utterances, but rather on the fields of distortion and innuendo that they enabled. While it seems clear that Bedward fully expected that word would travel, and he certainly wanted his anti-colonial rhetoric to reach the people's ears and the governor's conscience, it is not as clear whether he anticipated the exact way in which state power would spin his truth against him. It is possible that Bedward expected some official arraignment based on strict legal codes and was likely caught off guard by this use of suss against him. The unexpected use of sussveillance, the resistance technology of the yard, against the prophet of the yard is a powerful indication of the stakes the people were up against in the imperium of the colonial government.

H. G. de Lisser's "Story of Jamaica"

The work of H. G. de Lisser shows a growing interest in the urban poor and tells us that the lives of these Jamaicans, previously ignored and undervalued, were at the beginning of the twentieth century understood to be critical to the story of Jamaica. De Lisser's work exhibited a kind of watching that could be described as surveillance of the poor, presented as ethnography.[12] De Lisser's show of ethnographic expertise is not based on academic study, but rather on the fact that he was brown (not Black, and in his career progression, gradually white), interested, and perhaps objective. This watching was for the purpose of learning and writing. Using his initials HGD, he wrote a series of articles for the *Jamaica Times* in August and December 1899 and from January to February 1900 (Moore and Johnson, 2000, 7). In one of his early articles, collected and published as chapter 3 of Moore and Johnson's book *"Squalid Kingston" 1890–1920*, he introduces his jaunts around Kingston in this way: "Now you and I are going for a walk round and about Kingston for the object of learning something of how the people of Kingston and those whose business fetches them here week by week, live and work. We will confine ourselves chiefly to the poorer classes. We will watch them at their occupations, and, perhaps, we may be able to learn something more about them than we know at present" (Moore and Johnson, 2000, 51). De Lisser's work as a staff writer at the *Jamaica Times* marked the beginning of his journalistic career. The language in this early piece, "Now you and I are going for a walk round and about Kingston for the object of learning . . . how the people . . . live," is the casual language of walk and talk, and it signals, in tone at least, an earnest ethnographic- journalistic interest in the lives of the poorer urban classes. Here at the beginning of his career, de Lisser takes the posture of learner, not authority; of sussveiller, not surveiller; as brown man, not white; as aspirational, not established writer. "Walk and talk" suggests a shared friendliness of conversation among putative equals; "for the object of learning . . . how the people live" suggests a willingness to accept talk, the slipperiness of the oral, including, implicitly, "suss" as a form of authentic representation of "the people's" culture. But of course, his brown outside-observer status and aspirational careerism already rephrase walk and talk as quite firmly sussveillance in the service of a larger, authorizing power system.

The arc of de Lisser's career explains the evolutionary magic of his transformation, which he accomplished via a consolidation of power and influence in his work at the *Jamaica Times*, his editing of the *Daily Gleaner*, and his prolific influence as a writer of fiction and nonfiction. One side effect of de Lisser's advancement as a man of letters was his radical change of perspective—gradually becoming more conservative as he became more white. In de Lisser's yard fiction and its fascination with suss, we begin to see some of the strategies he used for his progress. I am interested in how de Lisser manipulates the interplay between suss, sussveillance, and surveillance to lay claim to the nationalist moment as a form of literary

38 • Inside Tenement Time

and economic capital. Certainly, his fascination with suss and surveillance in *Jane's Career* and *Susan Proudleigh* reveals his close observation and celebration of the Black working class as foundational to his success. As journalist-author-ethnographer, he goes into the villages, yards, rooms, and huts to write what he sees and hears. His particular fascination with the lives of young women, their aspirations and romances, is itself fascinating. And his ambitions are plain to see in the full-page advertisement in the January 8, 1914, edition of *The Gleaner*.

At the center of the page above and below the image of the cover of the novel are the words "A Book You Will Like" and "Buy A Copy To-Day." On either side of the centered image are descriptors of *Jane*, five on each side, all ending with the words, "THAT'S *'JANE.'*" One descriptor asserts: "A BOOK [*sic*] of Jamaican Life, written by a skillful native writer, perfectly acquainted with every detail of Jamaican character and the habits of Jamaican people, and with an intimate knowledge of all parts of the Island . . . THAT'S *'JANE.'*" Another reads, "A BOOK which every Jamaican should be proud of, and which all in Jamaica should buy and read. THAT'S *'JANE.'*" Of course, the cost of *Jane* is listed (1s 3d), as are the cost of post, locations where it can be purchased, and the call for country agents to sell the book in rural areas ("A Book You Will Like," 1914, 11). De Lisser using the *Gleaner* as his market is not particularly noteworthy. It might have been a completely standard way to sell a book. What is arresting is to read how de Lisser's "journalistic" interest in the working class becomes fiction and how this fiction is then marketed.

De Lisser's interest in the lives of country girls taken to town as white or brown lady's servants animates his simple ethnography enough for him to be inspired to write a novel about the subject. His findings are clearly the source not only for the *Times* articles but also the novel *Jane's Career* and the serially published story, "Susan: Mr. Proudleigh's Daughter," later published as a novel organized in three books, *Susan Proudleigh*. In his nonfiction work *Twentieth Century Jamaica*, published in 1913, before *Jane's Career*, de Lisser identifies the source of Jane's story, a story he believes was repeated many times over in Jamaica at the time. A rural woman brings produce to a town market and knowing that there is a woman from Kingston of a certain class location, she brings with her a girl, her daughter, whom she will hopefully find shelter and food for in exchange for the girl's "simple services" (de Lisser, 1913, 99).

> This person may be a stranger in the town, maybe a visitor from Kingston, that far off city, where (as the story runs in country districts) cars run about without the aid of mules and carriages without the help of horses; where wealth is abundant and life a long series of intoxicating enjoyments. News of the stranger's arrival somehow reaches the old woman's ears; an interview is solicited; does the mistress want a school girl? Probably the mistress does, but is she a good girl? Oh, yes; the parson is prepared to give her a good character and protest to the excellence of her Christian upbringing; her mother has also taught her how to

In the Shadow of the Wall • 39

FIGURE 1. "That's Jane": H. G. de Lisser advertises his novel *Jane's Career* in *The Gleaner*, January 8, 1914. © The Gleaner Company (Media) Ltd.

work, and now suggests an unfailing remedy for all indications of insubordination or laziness on her part: "Flog her well, missis, if she don't wants to h'obey yu; flog her well, ma'am, if she take up with bad company." . . . Thus the bargain is struck. The girl is handed over to her first mistress to be taken away and trained in the way she will go in the future. The mistress may be a "white" or "colored" lady or a "brown female." (de Lisser, 1913, 99–100)

40 • Inside Tenement Time

Both *Twentieth Century Jamaica* and *Jane's Career* are dedicated to Sir Sydney Oliver, governor of Jamaica, who served thrice as an interim governor and then from 1907–1913 as governor of Jamaica. Scholarship on de Lisser generally agrees that his interest in the working poor was influenced by the patronage of Sir Oliver, who was a Fabian socialist. Historian Matthew Smith tells us that de Lisser began his writing career "motivated by a desire to contest the interpretations of the Caribbean by non-Caribbean writers" (Smith, 2010, 185).[13]

Smith's discussion of de Lisser's work on Haiti, and Rhonda Cobham-Sander's work on the arc of de Lisser's life and work, suggest that while de Lisser may have had moments of patron-inspired sympathy for working Jamaicans (and for Jamaica's neighbors), he was certainly at the beginning and end of his career ambivalent about them at best. Cobham-Sander argues that he rather had a firm belief in the "goodness of patrons" and was mostly inspired by the (ideological) encouragement of Oliver's patronage (Cobham-Sander, 1987, 31). Leah Rosenberg is much less generous in *Nationalism and the Formation of Caribbean Literature* (2007), where she suggests that even when de Lisser is in line with Oliver's positioning, his work betrays the truth of his conservative leanings.

De Lisser's indulging the fascinations of his patron is not the only result of his study of poor Black Jamaicans. De Lisser's work is not simply outsider fascination, but serious observation that occasioned enough close-up intimacy to make his work valuable as ethnographic history of the period.[14] What is also noticeable is de Lisser's lubricious enjoyment of what he sees. He comes to us as someone who is speaking from the vantage point of suss as gossip, suss also as *labrishing* your tongue, that is, expansively telling what you have seen—the essence of carry go bring come, spreading the news.

De Lisser is critical of the brown middle class in *Jane's Career*.[15] He paints Mrs. Mason, the brown woman who hires Jane into her service in Kingston, and her nieces and nephew as exploitative and corrupt, and by the end of the novel, Jane's success is even more victorious because Mrs. Mason and company will witness it without the power they originally have over Jane. In fact, by the end of the novel, Jane chooses to stage her success—that is, her wedding in a church near the Masons' side of town—precisely for the hungry eyes of the Mason clan. So much so that there is little evidence that the joy Jane feels at her nuptials has anything to do with the formalized relationship itself. The novel ends with Mrs. Mason's nieces congratulating Jane, "and Jane's cup of joy was full" (de Lisser, 1972, 207). Here, as elsewhere in moments of political awareness, de Lisser's sympathy with Jane morphs into an interesting reduction: the overlooking presence of those of a "better" class a stone's throw beyond the tenements plays such a circumscribing role in Jane's consciousness that it dictates even so serious an undertaking as marriage. The desire to send news of her arrival in respectability to the *badminded*[16] watchers functions as a statement of being, codified in the religious paraphrase her "cup of joy (runneth over)." As an expression of selfhood at the novel's climax, Jane's marriage is no more than a performance, spectacular. That de Lisser's working class construct cannot see any aspect of self outside of class surveillance in this moment speaks to his ultimate sense of class power as unbreachable by those from below. He has sussed out the working-class woman and found her limited.

The clash between this sense of white and brown class power and de Lisser's acute sensitivity to the powers of sussveilling counterculture is a large part of the novel's field of play. *Jane's Career* is the story of a rural girl conscripted to work as a schoolgirl (assistant and apprentice to the maid) in the house of a Kingston mulatto woman, Mrs. Mason. Jane joins an army of Black women who transgress the spatial and racial boundaries of this Jamaica and find themselves proximate to the brown to white middle to upper classes as paradoxically free agents. Jane's story and the stories of Sarah, Amanda, and Sathyra, Black working women in Kingston, answer the questions of who the women are who are inside the houses of the "upper classes" and what they see. The story, told by an omniscient narrator, juxtaposes Jane's expectations of liberty in the great city of Kingston, with Mrs. Mason's constant, oppressive, yet selective surveillance of her employees and her household. In this novel and in *Susan Proudleigh*, the theme of full freedom and realizing personal agency (among the limited options for Black women) are set against and within societal and familial restrictions. These restrictions and codes are most often exercised through surveillance and the equally powerful control of sussveillance.

In the opening chapters of the novel, set in a small dying village in rural Jamaica, Jane's family and friends live a life of Sisyphean struggle and monotony. Her brother hails her going away to Kingston with jealous hope, saying "there is not much for a man to do here" and calling the field where he plants yams "stuppidness [*sic*] for man like me" (de Lisser, 1972, 14). De Lisser's commentary on gendered forms of mobility is enormously important because we at once understand the full gravity of Jane's opportunity through the perspective of her brother, who sees none for "a man like [him]" on the island; for women of their class, opportunity comes through subservience; for a man the imperatives of masculinity rule out this option. In a more direct assessment of the trouble in Jamaica, Jane explains to her mother that she is glad to be going to Kingston because there "is plenty of money dere," though her mother contradicts her, saying "it belong to white people" (de Lisser, 1972, 15). Jane's retort, "Everyt'ing belong to white people ... and brown people.... We only have the leavings" (de Lisser, 1972, 15), is a view generally accepted by poor Black Jamaicans. But what is clear as Jane moves around her village in the days before her departure is that except for the warnings to be a good girl and not allow a young man to "tek liberty" with her, Jane has full liberty in her movements outside of her familial responsibilities. She moves around the village freely and without thought of being watched, but Kingston, even with all its opportunities, is for Jane a place of surveillance and direct control by her employer and the closer and even more potent sussveillance of fellow denizens of the tenement yard. De Lisser's observation of the differences between town and country, and more so, implicitly, between rural and urban yards, and the possibilities of movement within each, is evidence of his careful ethnographic eye.

In Kingston as a single woman, Jane is attractive and vulnerable. Before she understands what the possibilities are for her mobility, she is appraised by all who have contact with her, and all except for Jane herself find her womanly potential intriguing or threatening. Her sexual potential and her industriousness themselves question the stability of a social order that is changing, but along the same color and power lines established during slavery. If Kingston is where the possibility of wealth and social mobility are located, they are guarded very carefully—so much so that there is much anxiety over access to opportunity and respectability—not just her own but for the Mason family as well. Mrs. Mason, then, is just as committed to guarding the reputation of her name against the actions of wayward schoolgirls, so that even those who are considered to be the human "detritus washed down from the mountains" have to be studiously and systematically watched (de Lisser, 1972, 26). In post-emancipation, colonial Jamaica, surveillance is a particular necessity in Kingston, the emblematic city of progress where scarce resources must be guarded from the ascending horde, as compared to rural areas where such technologies are not required. The constrictions of agrarian life signaled in Jane's brother's comment are already inherently a way of keeping the Black masses who remain there under control.

De Lisser's presentation of Mrs. Mason, Jane's employer and moral caretaker, underscores the power bound up in surveillance. Mrs. Mason is clearly only marginally brown and marginally privileged, perhaps an explanation for the anxious power she wields over her maids and schoolgirls. Indeed, her maid and schoolgirl are the only people over whom she has power. As a result, she is portrayed not only as a curmudgeon but as a master surveillant. Sarah, the maid who is in Mrs. Mason's service when Jane first arrives in Kingston, is "startlingly frank" when Jane asks her opinion of Mrs. Mason (de Lisser, 1972, 33). "A real wretch! . . . I just stayin' here tell I can get anoder jobs. She quarrel about everyt'ing, and she so mean dat if y'u teck a piece of stale bread dat she don't want, she will miss it and ask y'u 'bout it" (de Lisser, 1972, 33). Sarah's description of Mrs. Mason's meanness seems so stark it could be read as hyperbole. Sarah's contention is not simply that the Masons (Mrs. Mason and her nieces) are mean, but that they would miss and quarrel over a slice of stale bread taken without permission. This proves her bigger point to Jane: the Masons don't quite belong to the middle class. Because of this, Mrs. Mason uses surveillance to assert her fragile power, an act that signals the Masons' economic insecurity. Of the nieces, Sarah says, "Dem t'ink dem is young lady because dem can dress up, but I doan't t'ink noten of dem, for if dem was young lady dem would a live in a better 'ouse dan dis, an' would keep more dan one sarvant an' a schoolgirl" (de Lisser, 1972, 33). Sarah's suss about the Masons does not have the same power as Mrs. Mason's surveillance of Jane, but it is enough to destabilize the Masons' power in the small space that she and Jane occupy, and Sarah tells Jane that she, Sarah, will quarrel with Mrs. Mason before long, proving that her respect for her employer is grudging at best, and that her employer's power is precarious. De Lisser's decision to give Sarah the first word on the Masons and on life in Kingston, and not the other way around, significantly subverts the order of surveillance. By the time Mrs. Mason has her first formal conversation with Jane to warn her of the pitfalls of following Sarah, both Jane and the reader have already heard (and believed) Sarah's sussveilling version.

In addition to the multiple ways Mrs. Mason surveils all the young women who pass through her yard with her own eyes, she initiates Jane into her network of control, as we imagine she has attempted with Sarah. This plantation overseer strategy, to pit one against the other, is part of a carefully plotted modus operandi. Mrs. Mason encourages the two women to carry news on each other, in effect plaiting surveillance and sussveillance together in a complex web of intrigue. She promises Jane a promotion to Sarah's position "the moment she becomes efficient enough to justify Mrs. Mason's bundling Sarah 'neck and crop' out of the house. . . . Later on in the day she tells Sarah that she must keep a sharp eye upon Jane and report to her any laxity on the girl's part" (de Lisser, 1972, 35).

Mrs. Mason's surveillance of Sarah and Jane extends beyond her concern with the quality of work they do for her and beyond what her eyes can see. Her surveillance, particularly of Jane, is patronizing and somewhat brutal, exposing the full nature of their relationship and the full extent of her tenuous respectability. As a brown woman with marginal status, Mrs. Mason has full power over Jane, especially when she can see or hear her or when she is within the walls of her yard. It becomes clear that the unwritten contract of their relationship is that as a schoolgirl, Jane has surrendered her voice and agency to Mrs. Mason. Under this contract, Jane's future advancement is limited to domestic work—from schoolgirl to maid—and her body is subject to Mrs. Mason's authority. This dynamic is best seen when Mrs. Mason believes she hears Sarah and Jane entertaining a male visitor in her yard at night. While Mrs. Mason cannot see them from her bedroom window (and Sarah knows this for certain), she and her nieces can hear them. Sarah and Jane's denials are met with Mrs. Mason's full contempt. Jane is slapped repeatedly, and Sarah, after quite the fracas with Mrs. Mason, leaves her service.

De Lisser gives Sarah the last as well as the first word. She leaves the Mason yard loudly, victoriously, and she says to Mrs. Mason all the things she has said to Jane, but with more biting and colorful language, bringing into and upon the yard the "nagerness" Mrs. Mason works so assiduously to repel. The wall of middle-class respectability crumbles under the barrage of Sarah's tongue. In this final fight between Sarah and Mrs. Mason, the source of their disagreement and mutual discontent is revealed. De Lisser foregrounds these tensions as a commentary on race relations in twentieth-century Jamaica: Mrs. Mason pronounces,

"Every nager is a nager'" after the police officer requires that she pay Sarah the wages she owes her and Sarah retorts, "De mallata [mulatto] ooman vex because she can't tief me" (de Lisser, 1972, 58). In conversation with her nieces, Mrs. Mason blames the outcome of her fight with Sarah on "the education they getting... they go to free schools, an' we 'ave to pay for their schooling, and all they can do with it is to forge people's name and abuse their betters. That's what the Government doing now; educating all these people instead of teaching them 'ow to work" (de Lisser, 1972, 60). When the argument between Mrs. Mason and Sarah reaches a certain pitch, race comes to take a central place. If before, Mrs. Mason's protections are about class and respectability, and Sarah's rebellion is about her freedom and agency as a big woman, at the height of the confrontation this performance is abandoned, and racial terms are traded liberally. Mrs. Mason's fear of the "nager" yard encroaching on her yard is expressed through her frustration with the government's commitment to equal access to all Jamaicans.

Most instructively, however, it seems as though Mrs. Mason realizes that the Negro yard is already on her premises, as loud altercations and vigorous protestations are regular features of the space. There are disturbing things in her own yard that she chooses not to see because seeing them would acknowledge intimacy with the servant, or else her own negligence and incaution for the girls in her care. Mrs. Mason's marginality as brown matron proves what Belinda Edmondson argues about Jane's "brownification"—that is, that "blackness [is] latent in brown middle-class respectability" (Edmondson, 2009, 84). De Lisser very purposefully leaves Mrs. Mason's own story untold; she is merely *badmind*, cheap, and morally compromised. Finally, de Lisser's characterization of Mrs. Mason functions not only to present himself as supporting the cause of emancipation of the working classes but also to distance himself from his own class, both as he seeks to move into a higher color class and also as the female character helps to accomplish that distance (he is after all a man, not part of this domestic suss and stress).

Mrs. Mason's deliberate blindness to her nephew Cecil's lascivious behavior creates a space of collusion between Cecil's sexual surveillance of the girls in her employ and her own selective class, color, and gender surveillance. Cecil's brownness and maleness put him above his aunt's moral vision for her schoolgirls and maids. While Mrs. Mason has stringent rules about entertaining male company, even enforcing a curfew on her adult employees, within the walls of the Mason yard the rules do not apply to Cecil. Choosing not to see Cecil's antics may be another way for Mrs. Mason to deny her proximity to the ways and wiles of the "nager" yard. Cecil's surveillance of Jane, his studious attempts to find her alone and vulnerable, is evidence of behavior Sarah boisterously reveals as she leaves the yard. Sarah calls Cecil "mamparla,"[17] or effeminate, and at the same time condemns him as a man "who can't meck even... school girls stay in... employments in peace" (de Lisser, 1972, 55). She employs this seeming contradiction to describe his refusal to stand up to his aunt (effeminate) as he earnestly pursues the affections of girls in the family's service (de Lisser, 1972, 55). Sarah certainly understands the transactional nature of relationships; she openly admits to Jane that she is looking for a "friend" whose support will help her quit the Masons, but she does not see how the Masons might be part of this economy. While she condemns Cecil for not standing up to his aunt, she does not consider how the collusion between aunt and nephew allows Cecil to potentially have his pick of girls for free (or for insignificant gifts here and there), and certainly without anything as threatening as a commitment to a woman from the lower classes. The congruence of Cecil's sexual surveillance and Mrs. Mason's selective surveillance is enough to remove any glimpse of freedom and agency from Jane's career in Kingston, thus dashing her dreams of life in the city. In fact, the brown yard in its anxiety around its near "nager" identity comes to mimic the oppressive power of the plantation. And from this Jane must flee.

Jane flees the confinement of the Masons' yard for what is, in comparison, the full freedom of a tenement yard in East Kingston. The half-hour walk from the Masons to the East Kingston tenement is not just a walk through space—from "the little brick-and-wood single-storey house in Heywood Street" (de Lisser, 1972, 28) to Sathyra's room in an East Kingston tenement; from a lower middle-class street to the walled domain of Kingston's working poor. It is also a journey that reads like a passage through time.[18] Jane leaves the Masons' a servant, subject to the caprice of her employer-cum-guardian and the woman's nephew. On her arrival in the tenements, she is exposed to the possibility of being a free agent, via the prospect of a job that pays money, acquiring things of her own, keeping her own hours, and having a social life. De Lisser also means to signal the cost of Jane's freedom: her deep descent into the chasm of East Kingston poverty and Blackness. The yard described by de Lisser as "one of the innumerable yards in one of the numerous lanes in Kingston" (95) houses many, many residents. Living there is cheap—this is how Jane can flee the Masons with nothing, as she settles into her new life, borrowing her first few whiffs of independence from her roommate, Sathyra. Life in the yard is close and turbulent. Brutality and hilarity are neighbors, and sometimes they are twins. In the yard, Jane finds freedom swiftly, but it is complicated and often volatile. De Lisser's presentation of the yard cannot be read as an endorsement of its culture, ethical or otherwise, even as he mines that culture as literary aesthetic and ethnographic color.

At one level, the presentation is a form of romance that satisfies the audience's appetite for such. Through several narrative/plot moves de Lisser signals his idea of the yard as a mere holding area for his rural heroine come to town, pretty much in the vein of the fairy tale forest as the paradoxical space of adversity and freedom through which the heroine must pass on her way to a less equivocal and more conventional freedom among "higher" classes. The yard, including its cultural technologies of suss and sussveillance, often appears in de Lisser's rendering also as a form of vernacular entertainment. For observers of de Lisser's class, it may be a form of spectacle. In his ultimate containment of its dwellers in certain typologies and in certain spaces, the text supports the state's purpose in the wall as a structural attempt to keep some out by keeping them in. The project is then clearly double-edged; de Lisser's yard, dangerous and risible, is no celebration of proletariat power that rises unequivocally above the shenanigans of the brown petite bourgeoisie. Its practices make for good literary strategy, but, through the ethnographer's voyeurizing eye, it too is finally controlled.

This trajectory is most fully seen in the contrast between the characters of Jane, who is not presented as the typical yard dweller, and Sathyra, the muse of the yard. Jane is sheltered and her naïveté about yard matters in the early days of her arrangement with Sathyra causes the arrangement to end abruptly. Jane does not at first navigate the opportunities of the yard well because she is naïve and innocent. Jane's naïveté is particularly apparent when she fails to understand a crucial aspect of the systems of power that operate in the tenement yard: the arrangements by which male "friends" (also known as "meal tickets") of female yard dwellers become sources of economic and social support. Such forms of support may range from funding attendance at dances to, most ideally, engaging in relationships with the women that might even lead to marriage.

In a classic yard scene, Sathyra turns from friend to foe when Jane elicits too much attention from a potential meal ticket, Mr. Sampson. Sathyra understands the dynamic of the big yard, and when Jane refuses to leave their shared room so that Sathyra can have Mr. Sampson's attention all to herself, she expertly constructs a scene that reveals the generative power of sussveillance. Indeed, she chooses to rely on a deliberate plan of sussveillance instead of physically overpowering Jane with a "good beating" (de Lisser, 1972, 126). Sathyra sets upon Jane by performing an accusation that Jane has stolen her money. She expects that the loud accusation will attract the attention of people in the yard. As Sathyra throws herself against a table inside, so that to those outside it will sound like a physical assault, de Lisser writes: "Jane got outside, but Sathyra had achieved her object. 'Look how dis gal assault me!' she screamed out to the assembled people, 'and how she mash up me things!' Then she too bounced out of the room and called on everybody within a radius of five hundred yards to witness the wretched and mean advantage that had been taken of her. Jane in the meantime was crying and sobbing and calling upon God to be her witness that she had done Sathyra nothing and not even seen the colour of her money" (de Lisser, 1972, 128). Sathyra and Sarah understand the power of sussveillance. And Sathyra is already aware, from the way Jane left the Masons' house, that her new roommate has neither taste nor capacity for suss or its derivative power. Sathyra had been scandalized when Jane left in the dead of night, removing any possibility of creating spectacular drama out of her departure either by spreading suss on the Masons or by revenge "tiefing." "Is a long, long time she siddung pon di wall a watch you a watch she." In fact, in the early twentieth-century moment, Sathyra and Sarah see sussveillance as female-centered agency that can subvert those with power.

Sarah tells Jane of Mrs. Mason's plan to have them each report on the other so that she can maintain control, and Sarah, not Mrs. Mason, secures Jane's confidence. Similarly, Sathrya seeks the eyes and mouths of the yard to bring swift shame on Jane to ensure that she leaves her room and her "meal ticket" alone.

Sathyra's anxiety about social mobility and the establishment of her financial situation is partly responsible for her vehement expulsion of Jane from her room. Even more important, de Lisser's presentation of Sathyra (and Sarah and others like them) and his presentation of Jane as a counterpoint to her makes a distinction between Jane as a dweller in the yard and Sathyra, who embodies the yard as de Lisser sees it. Sathyra knows Kingston. She knows how to manipulate and mobilize suss, and she understands what the stakes are with or without a "friend" like Mr. Sampson. Jane, on the other hand, is presented as an outsider to the cutthroat ways of the urban working class. She is honest, and chaste, and good; she does not court drama. De Lisser's depiction of these types preassigns Jane and Sathyra to success and failure. As much as Sathyra manipulates her neighbors to believe her lie, they know her and distrust her, even as they enjoy the spectacle she provides. Conversely, they feel an affinity for Jane, whose only fault is that she is naïve. Jane's exceptional kindness to baby Jim— whom she cares for when she is home from work—and his mother is an opportunity to show the reader her maternal instinct. And her deep moral dilemma as she attempts to ward off the advances of Mr. Curden, her foreman, is more evidence of her virtue. Unsurprisingly, these qualities prepare Jane (or more importantly de Lisser's audience) for a fairy-tale ending; she marries significantly above her station, while Sathyra vanishes back into the maze of innumerable tenements.

It is important to note that de Lisser markets his book within a particular romantic tradition; it is a tradition into which Jane does not naturally fit. It is not surprising, then, that Jane's ending does not only erase the yard's power to confer a truly free selfhood as already discussed; it also domiciles her into a kind of associate middle-class whiteness. Her qualities read like a manifesto for middle- and upper-class womanly purity, which seems to become necessary for her to be an acceptable Black heroine. Jane as a "type" supplants Jane—and the yard—as vivid life. Even so, de Lisser's observation that Jane's parents and church elder had entreated her to stay pure indicates that the ideal of womanly virtue was not the monopoly of the brown and white classes.

Sathyra, in contrast to Jane, is relegated back to the tenements and becomes an emblem of the power of suss carefully controlled and confined. If Jane's marriage is her reward for being a good quasi-brown, quasi-white girl, it is also a way to fully extricate her from the tenements, which then appear not unequivocally as a road to freedom but as the seasoning required for a true heroine. We could say that while Jane "escapes," it is only to a marginal brownness that de Lisser grudgingly shares. He does not open such a space for Mrs. Mason, however, perhaps because she represents a type, present in the society, that poses a threat to his class position: she is near enough to the middle class to aspire to its echelons, and too near to the lower classes in behavior and education to be allowed into the ranks above. She therefore does not qualify for his condescension nor the concession of matronly respect. De Lisser is both sus(s)picious and ambitious.

Susan Proudleigh (1915), first appearing as a serial in the newspaper *Jamaica Times*, like *Jane's Career*, relies on the vernacular for its effects. There is a distinct difference—an escalation—in the second novel. Here melodrama and creole speech patterns are aspects of de Lisser's contributions to the story of Jamaica. The narrative voice, however, is not that of an ethnographer but that of a labrisher: an unrestrained gossip with a total commitment to "suss" out (discover through deep mining) and reveal every fine detail and hidden corner of the story. The tone is consciously lubricious and ironic, not only invoking gossip but playing to the audience's desire for intrigue. Intrigue is well supplied in the life led by the titular character, who, we know from her name, suffers from the mortal sin of hubris. The effects of serialization are apparent not only in the "excess" of detail and the tonal scale, but in the maze of plot twists, characters, and climaxes. If gossip, the stratagem by which people watch each other in close, confined spaces, is thought of as the form of *Susan Proudleigh*, the novel can be characterized as a Caribbean labrish text. De Lisser invests in suss and sussveillance not as mere "seeing" strategy but as narrative form. The voice of suss is the main narrative voice; there is no corrective narrative voice. The proliferation of dialogue, the massive gathering of voices (commenting on each other, parroting or mocking each other), is part of what animates the "suss" of the novel, the ways it performs in the arena of serialization. The narrator's sussing and "publication" of the small workings of Susan's and yard life both enunciate the volatile clashes in the yard as (spectacular) performance and as an absence of the desire for any kind of privacy. The latter, like de Lisser's treatment of Sathyra and his ultimate treatment of Jane, highlights the class positions that so often separate the people and the fictive chroniclers of their lives in this period.

It is possible to read Susan as a continuation of Sathyra with a more sustained examination of her story and its motivations. Susan's context, unlike Jane's, is purely urban, and unlike Jane, she is worldly and sagacious. Susan is calculating and direct: she wants the swiftest way out of poverty; she is neither sweet nor respectful of anyone—man, woman, or God—who does not support her plans. Yet she is the picture of decency and decorum because only a decent and decorous woman could have her life appointed in the way Susan's is, with a suitor lighter-skinned than herself, a little house with two rooms, plus gifts of furniture, dresses, and shoes. This is her vision and version of uplift—a small security—the Black good life.

Susan's attempts to "make life" in Kingston for her and her family are a response to the labor crisis facing the urban poor and provides the most convincing, albeit subtle, argument to excuse her prideful and self-aggrandizing ways. Susan left "the Government elementary school when a little over fourteen years of age" (de Lisser, 1915, 33). Her father was a carpenter, but was left infirm and unable to continue his trade after a severe case of rheumatism, and her mother, a washerwoman, earns but a pittance that barely keeps the family from starvation. Her brother is away in Nicaragua for work, but only sends a few dollars irregularly (de Lisser, 1915, 33). We are never uncertain about Susan's feelings for Tom, the meal ticket who begins the novel: it is simple, he has saved the family with his weekly gift of five pence of support in return for Susan's affections. The five pence pays for the little house they live in, and indeed it is through this questionable relationship that Susan is able to maintain the pride and position she viciously defends.

Most interesting for me is the centrality of sussveillance to Susan's sense of place, how her body signifies in that place, and her studied dedication to be better than and eventually out of the tenements. The story begins amid "Susan's Dilemma"—why it is people in the lane hate her, particularly Mother Smith and her bellicose daughter, Maria Bellicant, who have gone out of their way to "throw word" after her and laugh at her—their attack strategy in the feud over the suitor that Susan and Maria share. The complications of "watch [dem] a watch me" by which Susan's life is played out provide much of the narrative comedy. The mother-daughter duo are open and unapologetic about the fact that they have made it their occupation to closely watch Susan, assess her pretensions, and send back their assessment to her via throw word and derisive laughter. Susan makes sure to position herself where she can hear these assessments and signal her own counteractive "watchie-watching." Susan's favorite spot is in her house, on a chair by a window looking out onto the lane. This position suggests the vantage point of a barricade—a self-made wall blocking Susan in and away from the outer confines of the yard—and is well suited for word catching and word throwing. It is clearly as well a prime spot for watching the goings-on of others in the lane. Because Susan sees herself as superior to everyone else, even indeed members of her own family, she is committed to not having others interfere in her business, though she is content for them to see all the many ways she is superior to them. Watching everyone's business in full view of everyone, and particularly in full view of her sussveilling rivals, doubles her enjoyment as sussveiller extraordinaire. The situation may be comedic, but it is a deadly politics of survival in which not only the escape from numbing poverty but also the sense of self are at stake.

Tom Wooley, Susan's intended, also fears sussveillance and is perhaps the best evidence that it is powerful beyond women's spaces. Tom is not so concerned that Susan and Maria fight over him, drawing a crowd in the street. Nor is he concerned to right any wrong opinion Susan might have of his relations with Maria; however, what Tom is opposed to is Susan taking Maria to court because he does not want his name to be called, to be heard in such a matter. And indeed, he is right to be cautiously afraid, for when his name is called in court, the news finds its way back to his boss, who promptly dismisses him and gives his job to one of the many (suss carrying) young men who want his stable and coveted position. For both women and men, the stakes of suss are public—but while Tom engages (respects and fears) formal institutions, Susan is concerned with the yard community as the institution enacting judgments.

Suss and sussveillance are responsible for the movements in the plot in book 1 of *Susan Proudleigh*. They establish the space of the lane and the place of the protagonist in the space. Suss is part of the artistry of the telling of *Susan Proudleigh*. First, we know that this is not de Lisser's story, that is not a story he, a middle-class white-brown man, has lived, but that just as with *Jane's Career* his careful watching of the experiences and listening to the speech patterns of poor Black Jamaicans is the source of these Jamaican stories. That *Susan Proudleigh* was first serialized in the *Jamaica Times* is certainly partly responsible for the structural deployment of the seductiveness of suss, each chapter revealing some new turn, some new drama in her life. But more striking is the way suss, like the seven-foot walls used to demarcate the dwellings of Blacks in Kingston and Spanish Town and the surveillance of these dwellings, demarcates the place of the yard and the layers of power within the yard. Suss also functions as a barometer of social anxieties in early twentieth-century Kingston: suss, and in particular the brand of suss meant to appeal to de Lisser's newspaper audience, show that the general themes of scintillating interest had to do with the paths to social mobility, especially if there was drama or even romance along the way.

De Lisser's use of Jamaican Creole and creole speech patterns is one of the earliest literary examples of the recognition of Jamaican vernacular as entertainment, ethnographic social history, and cultural capital. Prior to the appearance of *Jane* and *Susan*, Claude McKay had published *Constab Ballads* (1912) using language somewhere along the continuum of standard English and Jamaican Creole. Many have criticized McKay's Creole as artificial and have cited the influence of his anti-modernist patron, Walter Jekyll, whose dedication to the idea of an untroubled native may have caused McKay to stumble around in his own dynamic tongue. De Lisser, though patroned, and though peripheral to the language community he represents, writes what reads to me as an accurate rendering of Creole and, as well, in his attention to the culture of suss, an acute apprehension of a creole or vernacular spirit in *Susan Proudleigh*.

I consider two examples from the novel. The first is an altercation between Susan and the police officer who is called to break up the fight between her and Maria. The officer is scandalized to find two of his own in such an ugly display of barbarity and asks the crowd and the fighters, whom he calls "ignorant" and "common,"

> "You ever see white ladies fight in de street?" . . .
> But Susan, though in trouble, would not even then allow herself to be classed with the policeman and others in the category of common folkses.
> "I am not common," she answered defiantly; "I am not your set!"

> "Silence, Miss!" thundered the policeman, scandalized. "I am the law! Do you know dat?"
>
> "I never see a black law yet," cheekily replied Susan. (de Lisser, 1915, 16)

Arguably, de Lisser is not simply representing Jamaican Creole here, but a vernacular moment. The officer's introduction of whiteness/rightness into his rebuke cuts all his hearers deeply, and when Susan responds she not only speaks up for herself; she speaks against the officer's power by using the officer's rhetoric. The structure of her retort is a statement with an embedded or implied question, "I never see a black law yet," otherwise meaning "Are you the law?" or "This is what law come to?" She plays with the concept of the law by racializing it and trivializing its human manifestation. Michael Bucknor's language on the oral and aural quality of Afro-Caribbean speech rituals as what he calls "tonal turbulence" is enlightening here. In this altercation, de Lisser "relies on the resources of Afro-Caribbean expressive culture—'kass-kass,' 'drop-word,' 'back-chat,' and the general use of a 'ceitful' tongue" (Bucknor, 2009, 55). Suss in its guise as "drop-word" and "ceitfulness" is integral to this many-layered vernacular moment, by its attention to the quotidian details of life in Kingston's yards and lanes.

The second vernacular intervention is de Lisser's presentation of the intrigue or the call of Colón, Panama, where many Jamaican men (1850s–1920s) went to work on the building of the canal. The story of Colón is colored by incomplete narratives of family members who have left but not returned; the rumors of life there are as thick as the tales of the deep jungle—fevers, injustice, and the possibility of acquiring great wealth. Rhonda Frederick's work on the Colón man argues that Caribbean literature and folk songs told stories of Caribbean life on the isthmus that were "largely silent" in contemporaneous histories of the canal. Her work, then, is concerned with bringing into discourse what she calls "imaginable and historical narratives of Colón men's experiences" (Frederick, 2005, 8). De Lisser's participation in the "imaginable," and here again with the corroboration of his ethnography (he had traveled to Panama several times and written about it in *Twentieth Century Jamaica*), puts him in a favorable position as teller of this tale. De Lisser is writing when Panama is hot on the minds and tongues of Jamaicans and embroiling the question of labor migration in family dramas, in "man and woman business," and even to frame escape. Subsequent to the first waves of migration, the suss is about returnees who have shows of wealth, especially in sartorial excesses and gold, but that wealth is tacky and unschooled, as with Tack Tally in McKay's *Banana Bottom*. Colón becomes another career for poor Blacks, a riff on the gendered "career" of finding a man, evidenced in de Lisser's sustained interest in the ways out of poverty available to young Black women—Jane, Sathyra, Susan in Jamaica.

Book 2 of *Susan Proudleigh* provides a more fulsome picture of life in Panama. The weather (the interminable rain in the jungle), American racism (the particular brand that is casual and cutting), the brutality of the Panama police and their batons, fires, and the tragic accidents common in the Canal Zone are all part of living there. The details of Susan's life continue to be dramatically featured via the men she is involved with: Sam Jones, her intended with whom she departs Jamaica; John MacKenzie, an old acquaintance of Sam's who becomes friends with the couple and later steals Susan from Sam; and Tom Wooley, Susan's first beau, who departs Jamaica for the Canal Zone ahead of her with the promise that he will send for Susan. When Tom discovers Susan with Sam and then meets her again as Mrs. John MacKenzie, he jealously makes trouble for her in Panama. Susan's father, aunt, and sister Kate also emigrate from Jamaica, surprising Susan first in Culebra and then settling in Colón. In the stories of Sam, John, and Tom, de Lisser proves there is more than one brand of Colón man and none of them—not Sam Jones, who is double-minded and fickle; not MacKenzie, who is solid and boring, dead before his actual dying; nor Tom Wooley, who is kept seething and slighted at the margins—is the Colón man of the stereotypes, decked in gold and ignorance. But then again, we see none of the three back in Jamaica after their tour in Panama; rather, how we see them is as Jamaicans in Colón. The multiple twists and turns of the plot and the seething convolutions of spying, (veiled) sexual intrigue, rumor, fictive imagining, and speculation circulated as news go beyond what we see in book 1.

Book 2, set in migrant space, and more specifically in the Canal Zone, allows for the narrative expansiveness seen in the addition of the very large cast of characters—a way of chronicling the reality of the great influx of people to the Canal Zone, the turbulences of contact, the many points of meeting, the many new stories generated. The serendipity of the Canal Zone as a meeting point that was topical and current is that it works wonderfully for serialization—by extension, for suss. It is in book 2 that suss as the main narrative voice becomes most apparent. However, Susan's convoluted relationships and the many stories elevated as main plot, not side plots, are more than serial entertainment: they become a way of signaling the importance of the Canal Zone at this point in Jamaica's and the region's history, and a way of imagining the untold lives of the men and women who went. The Zone as both migrant space and a vast economic enterprise brought a different set of dynamics for the working class. Susan and de Lisser's expanded cast of male characters are freed from constricting spaces such as the urban yard. There is greater freedom to pursue different relationships, the promise of a new path to economic solvency, and for women like Susan, more tracks to upward social mobility. She is also freed from her neighbors' watching. Freedom is not unequivocal, however. For one thing, she now moves under the shadow of U.S. racism, which is its own surveillance machine. For another, she is never quite free of the presence of suss—she constantly imagines eyes pursuing every moment of her progress or lack thereof. As a master sussveiller, she carries within herself the censuring eye of respectability that pushes her, for example, to pressure Tom into marriage and to choose to marry Tom's friend Sam MacKenzie instead—because he asks. Even if Susan does not perceive it, the unfreedom that Jacob Miller sings about—dreadlocks can't live inna tenement yard—is hers because of the moving potency of sussveillance.

De Lisser was one of the two most iconic literary figures[19] to emerge in Jamaica during the first decades of the twentieth century. Paying close attention to the intersections of suss and surveillance, he recognized their potential as literary capital at a defining moment in the nation's political, economic, and cultural life. De Lisser is keenly aware of the dynamic force of sussveillance as a Black technology of survival and resistance against the colonial state's containing walls. By extension, he comes to understand flexible power. In other words, de Lisser saw that these technologies had significance beyond the vernacular arts (performance artistry, anancy poetics/subterfuge) that he was able to mine for his literary productions.

There are several levels at which de Lisser's legacy can be estimated. Writing a story for the newspaper, even at a time when many could not read, meant a more diverse and inclusive audience, across location and class, than would have been possible via the traditional press or even the local and regional literary magazines. There is the clear probability that insofar as many of his readers would have been Black and not necessarily middle class, the experience of "seeing" Black spaces represented in a "real" (and therefore ultimately respectful) way in literary text, was impactful in terms of its psychic, social, and political consequences.

De Lisser's representational focus is the city, and specifically the urban yards of Kingston, the capital. As chapter 2 will show more closely, this casts a different searchlight than the focus on rural folk spaces and practices that predominated in literary discourse during the early to mid-twentieth century. The city was a space of contestation for scarce capital—whether economic, class-based, political, or living-space capital. The city was, crucially, a space of always implosive, underground rumblings of revolution and fear of revolution that emanated from the Black yards. This dynamic may have been birthed on the rural plantation, but its iterations in the city took new forms even as the containing walls around Black spaces were reconstructed to manage insurrections. De Lisser understood that the urban yard was a Black space. Today, the urban yard is still a Black space. *Jane's Career* and *Susan Proudleigh* (even with the latter's use of the Canal Zone as a double setting) are consequential yard novels, and more particularly novels of the city that reveal the powers and irrepressibility of the Black urban yard. This becomes especially clear when they are read in a diachronic scope that includes Roger Mais's *Brother Man* (1954), Alvin Bennett's *God the Stonebreaker* (1964), Orlando Patterson's *The Children of Sisyphus* (1964), Michael Thelwell's *The Harder They Come* (1980), and the genre of 1970s–1980s poetic and musical works that address the yard.

We begin to see in de Lisser's work a certain prescience, a spot-on reading of the political life of the colony. As Rachel Mordecai so persuasively argues in *Citizenship under Pressure* (2014), the continuing urgent contestation of the nation's life and identity was always centered around issues of Blackness and came to a head in the nationalism of the 1970s, which Mordecai reads not as a conflict around forms of government (democratic socialism versus capitalism) but around the hitherto unacknowledged public conversation on whether Blackness should be the face of the independent Jamaican state. De Lisser's clear understanding that the voices he was representing, and their "dangerous" technology of sussveillance, had implications far beyond the (walled) domestic spheres in which they arose, marks his work as a pivotal moment in Jamaican literary history. Sussveillance and the yard can be read as instances of a decolonial pressure that constantly exerted itself against the imperial state and that had a circulatory power beyond those that Foucault attributes to the panopticon. None of this, of course—as Tivoli and the later yard novels reveal—suggests any kind of triumphant entry into equality or privilege for yard dwellers over the years. Indeed, the contrary remains true, even if yard dwellers are increasingly able to move out of the yard into other socioeconomic spaces through such means as education and parallel economies. The "presentness" of de Lisser's Black women characters is made hypervisible not merely by the sensational medium of newspaper serialization or by their featuring as the heroines in fairy-tale romance mordantly localized (Jane) or questioned (Susan), but more so by their dwelling in the resistive cultural-political fields of suss-sur-veillance and the ways those fields structure the oxymoron of (gendered, political) power and literary authority.

2

"The Dungle Is an
Obeah Man"

• •

Spiritveillance in *The Children*
of Sisyphus

In this chapter, I turn from the urban yard to consider another area of exclusion, the slum that emerged on the back side of Kingston in the 1930s. While the yard was walled within the city, the slum emerged outside of the city in a no-man's-land. The slum was considered a squatter space, or in Jamaica-speak, *capture land* (usually land or space that is unoccupied because of its unideal location or because it is generally not believed suited for living but is then claimed or "captured" for living by the ultra-poor). In its most extreme form, the slum became the Dungle, as in dung heap or trash heap—the repository of human detritus. Because the slum was outside of the *regular* jurisdiction of the city (often this means all the usual civic benefits: garbage collection or sanitation, protection/safety by the security forces, access to working schools and medical facilities), the dwellers there were not considered by their betters to be citizens or even humans in the same way as other city residents.[1]

I engage the shift from the yard to the slum through another of the ground-breaking city novels depicting the pre-independence era, Orlando Patterson's 1964 novel *The Children of Sisyphus*. Together, de Lisser's and Patterson's novels provide some of the most powerful cultural studies of the period in the way they give access to a visual and conceptual cartography of the city in the making. "Visual" and "in the making" highlight that this is in effect a *moving* cartography, not only as these novels show us the ways the city changed physically and geographically under competing pressures, but also the widening circles of exclusion through which the city was being conceived and constructed: a steady movement outwards from the excluded inner circle of the yard to the slums of West Kingston, which chart the outer edge of the city's margins, a geographical and conceptual no-man's-land that threatens the pristine city.

Patterson's controversial, on the surface doom-laden, novel figures among the literary works that fell into obscurity throughout much of the post-1970s reading of Caribbean literature. In revisiting this difficult work, as several other scholars have done, I want to argue that while *The Children of Sisyphus* fell into literary obscurity because it could not fit easily, if at all, into the prevailing visions of the nation-state or West Indian national culture that engaged the critics, Patterson's novel is one of the most important reflections on the underpinnings of the modern nation-state that emerged in its contemporary moment. By extension, *Sisyphus* allows reflection on the ongoing neocolonial pressures at the heart of the postcolonial crisis that in Jamaica reached an actual and symbolic high point in the 2010 Tivoli incursion accomplished under the oversight of U.S. surveillance machineries.

The Children of Sisyphus engages newly independent Jamaica not as an experiment in imagining community but by its searchlight on the veins of exclusion that gave the state its lifeblood and without which it could not be imagined. The role of different machineries of surveillance that kept such exclusions in place is the subject of this chapter. The chapter shows how the great slums of West Kingston were established so that threats to the city's pristine face—the ultrapoor, the Black, those on the religious margins—could be kept at a distance and under surveillance. Patterson's novel is very much concerned with how independence was framed in the early years of the Jamaican nation; the novel uses religion and the social geography of Kingston as political epistemes that interrogate and reveal a nation concerned with advancing into the middle class. The project of exclusion that this push necessarily entailed, both in actuality and in the world depicted in the novel, was especially centered, beyond class or even color, around what might be termed the "spirit underbelly of Africa"—in other words, Africa, whether real or invented, was the greatest threat that the colony becoming a nation felt that it had to overcome.[2] There were those whose fear of Africa stemmed from Western values, but the more complex reality included the fear that the new nation would be typecast and would come under pressure from the West. The specter of Haiti's punishment by economic embargo, diplomatic isolation, and general exclusion from the community of nations after declaring itself a Black republic was not a distant image but a living reality as versions of these exclusions were still in place in the 1960s.

My core argument surrounds the novel's adumbration of a practice that I term spiritveillance, which like sussveillance was a countervailing yet ironically complicit power generated from within the slum itself, had some say in the ordering of the city. Taking the utterance by Patterson's female protagonist, Dinah, "The Dungle [is] an obeah man" (Patterson, 1986, 20) as my point of departure, I show how the slums exerted a pull on their residents from within that did not easily give them over to the ultra-colonial quest for middle-class respectability that signaled the nation-state. Above the humble shacks of Back O' Wall flew the proud flags of Jamaica's African-based trinity: Rastafari, Revival, and Obeah, proof that many on the other side of the tracks—in Kingston's hinterland—were not simply waiting to die or disappear, but were creating new visions of self and imagining alternative futures. Patterson's view of these religions is neither idealistic nor integrated into a project of indigenous national culturation, however.

Instead, the religions are intertwined in a complex theorization of the concept of the most denigrated religious practice—obeah. I consider how *The Children of Sisyphus* uses religion and religious practice as central to the experience of those in the Dungle (slums) and how religion and religious practice effect what I have termed "spiritveillance," a pull or strategy with the efficacy of obeah, as a means of the slum holding on to its own. This happens in deeply ironic ways: the slum dwellers are both practitioners and objects of religious surveillance (spiritveillance) from the inside, and this practice in its effects resonates with the state's practice that ensures the survival of the slum as a category indispensable for the construction of the state's pristine urban face, free of detritus.

The project of the slums, as obeah man, however, cannot be reduced to complicity with the official powers, but rather is a claim to *a different legitimacy*. When Dinah, as she prepares to escape the Dungle, engages in this rumination "the Dungle [is] an obeah man," she connects the space of the slum with spiritual power, and moreover with the power of destiny. Taking Dinah's lead, I am suggesting that a grounding part of this power is surveilling, both in the ways the relationship between poverty and Africa-based religious practice attract surveillance by the state in 1950s/60s Jamaica and in how surveillance is essential to practices within Africa-based, Jamaica-grown indigenous religions. Surveillance as a spiritualist or metaphysical technology—the form of oversight that I term "spiritveillance"—works from seemingly antithetical sources to produce the meeting with the state's apparatus that looks like complicity. But obeah's function as the metaphor for these spiritual forces, and its power to see/read and fix, emphasizes the endemic and ubiquitous power of the spiritveillance Patterson explores in the novel. Obeah is the pull of the slums (Dungle) on their denizens (working through religion and other means), and the power of the slums to encroach on the city. The encroachment on the city has a specific intent: to call their escaped residents back to a reckoning with what the escapees have failed to confront or understand, which is the Dungle itself. But obeah is also the power of the Dungle to undermine the city's attempt to separate slum and nation-state.

I show the close parallel between Patterson's representation and the actual practice of city planning that can be deduced from contemporary archival records and observations. The feverish nature of the city's attempts to ban the terror of "the Dungle," and Patterson's close attention to these sociopolitical events are remarkable. Patterson enacts for us the cartographies that are referenced at the beginning of the chapter. Patterson knows the city well, first as a regular visitor to his grandfather's home in Jones Town and then as a student at Kingston College who traversed the terrain and informed himself about it. (If Patterson had come into Kingston—from Clarendon, his original residence—by train he would have passed the Dungle. The train station in Kingston is a stone's throw from the Coronation Market and the eastern edge of today's Tivoli Gardens.)

Making Kingston, Making the State: City Planning in 1950s–60s Jamaica

I begin with the history of the real city that Patterson drew. The sound of bulldozers grumbling through squatter communities in West Kingston in October 1963 represented only one strain, but a highly significant one, in the cacophony of voices and opinions on what the new, independent Jamaica should become.[3] Jamaicans at independence were concerned about how the new nation would look, and in the process of nation building, the question of whether or not the country would appear *ready and competent* at the independence experiment was a source of particular anxiety. Spatially, the process of readying Kingston as the flagship city involved two crucial interlocking strands of action and ideology that Patterson's novel rehearses.

The first was the need to shine the searchlight of respectability on the city newly in the making and show that the nation's capital could withstand the glare. Kingston became the capital of Jamaica in 1692. Its location against the deep wealth of a natural harbor that had from the sixteenth century attracted buccaneers and privateers as well as being in the shadow of the Blue Mountains made it for some an ideal city-space. But Kingston was not "made" in 1692. In moving the capital from Spanish Town, the emphasis was more on commerce than on shaping the idea of a city; as a concept it was unfinished. In fact, in true British fashion, very little was invested in making it grand, and whatever architectural beauty there was, was subsequently destroyed or compromised by earthquakes and fires. Ian Thomson in *The Dead Yard* describes Kingston as an unattractive city that the "British [had] allowed . . . to grow in ugly parallel streets down to the sea's edge" (Thomson, 2011, 17). After emancipation and in the face of significant migration into Kingston from rural areas, the city grew rapidly. Colin Clarke outlines that, to accommodate this growth, by 1848 new houses were constructed and new settlements developed at "Rae Town, Brown's Town, Lindo's Town, Hannah Town, and Smith Village to which were added Fletcher's Town, Kingston Gardens, Allman Town, Franklin Town, and Passmore Town" (Clarke, 2006c, 34). These might be said to have been the habitations of the respectable poor, the possible up and coming lower middle class in 1962.

The second strand of the nation-city project was about deciding the future of the "darkest" and "ugliest" parts of the capital. The most extreme offenders were the slum communities on Kingston's western edge. From the city's earliest days, western Kingston, where Patterson's Dungle is located, lagged in development behind the rest of the city. The geometrical plan of Kingston that took the orderly shape of a parallelogram, according to Clarke, never extended to the west of Princess Street (Clarke, 2006c, 8), perhaps because "[t]he marshes at Delacree Pen and Greenwich Farm deterred the expansion" (9). This location on marshland was of course critical, symbolically as well as in actuality. As Clarke tells it, "By 1920 several of these districts were composed of densely populated tenements," but up until this time "little development had occurred along the Spanish Town Road in West Kingston" (Clarke, 2006c, 34). Clarke goes on, "On the periphery of the city in general and near the city rubbish heap in West Kingston, the majority of buildings were described as poor" (Clarke, 2006c, 41). And it was here on the periphery, along the rubbish heap, or Dungle, that the most depressed social groups remained.

In Moore and Johnson's *"Squalid Kingston" 1890–1920* the chapter "Squalid Kingston: How the Poor Live" is based on articles in the *Jamaica Gleaner* in February and March of 1893 by an anonymous correspondent who traveled all over Kingston documenting what she/he saw. As the writer travels westward, one set of observations is consistent with the argument I am making about West Kingston.

> Our route lay further over to the West and we drove along the railway station and on to what is known as the Kingston Penn [*sic*]. Here the city authorities are establishing another refuse ground and as we passed there were some 20 or 30 persons grubbing among the dirt for anything they could find which would bring them a few coppers. . . . Right in the centre of the refuse ground was a dwelling. It had three sides and a roof and a short man might have been able to stretch full length from one end of the room to the other. . . . Passing along the brick yard we were soon in the midst of little plots which combined to make up a greater portion of Kingston Penn. The Penn is quite a little town in itself and few persons who have lived in the city for many years are aware that such a place is in existence. Here the people, amongst whom are included Creoles, Chinese, Coolies &c. pay 9d to 1s. a week for a little plot of land upon which they have to build their own house. The result is that there is no regular form of architecture, each man erecting according to the dictates of his fancy or according to his ability to work. Every conceivable material has been used in the construction of these tenements which for variety cannot be equaled. (Moore and Johnson, 2000, 34–35)

The anonymous writer's perspective is certainly different from that of Patterson's Dungle historian, the prostitute Rachael whom I discuss later in the chapter. But their experiences with Kingston slums in 1893 and the 1960s are not significantly different. West Kingston it seems had always been poorer than the average poor. The writer's observation that few others in Kingston knew of the abject poverty in West Kingston confirms just how geographically marginal and socially peripheral slums like the Dungle were. Certainly, one difference between Kingston Pen in 1893 and how it and other great slums developed into the twentieth century had to do with who was resident there. Jamaicans of Asian heritage were not among the residents in the middle of the twentieth century. This suggests that by the time of nationhood, the slums had become a filtration device in which poor Blackness had been flushed out as the detritus left behind.

Notwithstanding the terrible conditions, as the city's population grew (more than doubling between 1921 and 1943), the largest concentration of residents settled in West Kingston. "Squatting persisted and even intensified after 1944, and 3,752 persons were enumerated in four camps in West Kingston in 1951. The four areas together represented *'the worst example of slum life in the island'*" (Clarke, 2006c, 139). The largest squatter settlements were at Trench Town (2613), Dung Hill (285), and Kingston Pen, Back O' Wall (844). The camp at Back O' Wall had been in existence at least since 1935" (Clarke, 2006c, 139). What we see overall is that West Kingston was not a community or set of communities that experienced decline: the marshes of 1692 became the squatter settlements of 1962 and then the tenements of today. West Kingston's only development was industrial, even though the factories and their waste had an uneven relationship with the slum dwellers. What we are also seeing is that "the largest concentration" of new dwellers in search of economic independence and concomitant social uplift was relegated to the independent nation's waste. The Dungle was therefore not a minority space synonymous with its geographical location as periphery: it represented, in origins, the rural folk—in numbers, a large slice of the city's demographic; in aspiration, a majority. As a sociologist, Patterson was no doubt aware not only of these significant facts but also that West Kingston's "patterns of residence dated back to slavery" (Clarke, 2006c, 42). West Kington more than any other space emblematized the historical angst that the envisioned city could not escape in the moment of national self-making. This history of Tivoli as Back O' Wall's descendant remained integral to how Tivoli was perceived by those who carried out or lauded the incursion.

The importance of the dilemma posed by the slums in the 1950s–60s, the decades in which *Sisyphus* is set, cannot be overemphasized. These were crucial decades for national development, first, as the colony looked forward to independence and, before and after the event, as the nation in the making sought to craft an identity very much concentrated in the urban concept of Kingston. That the great slums—Kingston Pen, Back O' Wall, and the Dungle—existed in these decades of nation building is one of the single most important factors that highlight the generic requirements for achieving a nation-state, at least as the nation-state is conceived in modern times. The slums were not just physical eyesores—miles of poverty and underdevelopment, the ugly side of Kingston, and unequivocally Black—they were as well ideological hotbeds, subversive, and frightening to the other striving Kingstonians who would live anywhere but there. There, as I have suggested, for many would have been akin to a return to Africa, that is to say, a return to an ugly past or a step into a threatening future.

These urban plantations (city versions of surveillance zones) were too objectionable physically and ideologically to attract the panoptical surveillance machinery such as would have been deployed on the slave plantation. To put it another way, it could easily be said that no urban overseeing power could consider them as anything more than a spectacle to be turned away from. Yet surveillance was the inevitable means by which the slums were governed. Given the slums' spectacularly unsightly ugliness, surveilling was accomplished by its opposite—a turning away of the gaze from them. The idea of the city was accomplished by keeping slum dwellers confined in such ways that they did not have to be seen—that is, where they could not encroach upon the boundaries of the nation or the nation's consciousness yet were easily accessible for containment raids in case of any signs of attempted encroachment. Surveilling therefore *required* ensuring not only that the slums did not grow geographically toward the east, but also that the slum dwellers remained in the slums, not part of the defined city's demographic. In this context the names were symbolic: Kingston Pen, a section corralled off, as in a cattle pen; Back O' Wall, encoding the area's extramural status; the Dungle, in Jamaican Creole, the trash heap.

This strategy recalls Didier Bigo's concept of the banopticon. As Simone Browne points out, Bigo defines the banopticon as the effect that is achieved when "those whom the state abandons are profiled and then banned on the basis of specific categorizations of risk. An example is 'the racialization of risk'" (Browne, 2015, 38). In contrast to Foucault's panopticon, which supposes that all members of a society are equally subject to surveillance and control, and further that both those who surveil and those who are surveilled inhabit a common space, "the banopticon . . . deals with the notion of exception and the difference between surveillance for all, [and] control of only a few" (Browne, 2015, 6).[4]

Profiling and banning of slum dwellers in Kingston in the 1960s was indeed both racialized and marked by class—a slum address would almost always mean these two. While this exclusion was ostensibly orchestrated by the state, it was effected via a more intrinsic, or imbedded (and therefore more extreme) set of social apparatuses: dwellers are locked in (not expected to find work or life on the outside), and this is ensured not only by the police, but by the cycle of poverty and by citizens for whom contamination by poor Blackness is a threat to their own uncertain identities. The great slums were understood as the places where criminals and the abject poor lived and hid, and thus even though the all-seeing eye of the state was not always on the slums (police were not posted at their gates and high walls were not a requirement), the slums were summarily targeted by the state apparatus whenever there was any outbreak of crime. Used to demonstrate the state's power of surveillance, they were where criminals were to be found, whether or not any slum dweller was responsible for the crime. Indeed, the absence of high walls and a constant police presence emphasizes the banopticon as it operates here: where walls and police postings might have suggested a constructed effort for which the state was liable, the absence of such visible permanent markers suggests that the slum is a natural phenomenon, another country that has produced itself outside the borders. At the same time, this absence signifies the turning away of the gaze from this unremitting eyesore, surveilling it from a dissociated distance.

The extreme and unsettling poverty of the slums allowed for a clear interpretation of what was understood to be the middle class, as the slums' existence created visible outsiders, and by extension insiders. I find Bigo's explanation of who are insiders and outsiders, in his discussion of detention sites at EU border crossings, very useful for my reading/understanding of the role of slums in Jamaica in the 1960s. Bigo contends that "[t]he detention camp for foreigners is for the banopticon the equivalent of what the prison was for the panopticon of Michel Foucault" (Bigo, 2007, 4). To those on the inside, detention camps are holding spots for foreigners; for those on the outside, waiting zones on the inside:

> Thus the priority in these camps is not to detain people indefinitely but to send them back to their points of origin as soon as possible. The priority is to prevent people from settling, denying them the possibility of staying and living inside a country not considered their own. The aim of the centers is not to jail persons to correct behavior or to defend society against them. The purpose is not disciplinary, even if in some countries the two ideas (discipline and removal) are merged and work together upon the same populations and in the same sites. The rationale is not one of punishment but of keeping the detainees at a distance from a certain territory and, sometimes, inside the given territory, from certain welfare benefits. (Bigo, 2007, 23)

In the nascent postcolonial context, scarce resources, the poison of well-entrenched self-hatred and fear of the erstwhile colonial masters' surveilling judgment, made it easy for the progeny of the field slave population to be lodged in camps/slums on the margins of the city. The slums became holding places for the steady stream of rural poor migrating to Kingston in the hope of socioeconomic uplift but, lacking either community or jobs within the borders, were forced to join the urban poor who knew many decades of this brand of destitution. While slums are not detention camps containing foreigners, and while there was no official policy of placing the new arrivals in these areas, slums contain Jamaicans who are so marginal that they are often treated as foreigners. Philip Curtin argues in *Two Jamaicas* that full emancipation in 1838 only exacerbated the differences between Jamaicans: "Instead of growing closer together in the end of freedom, the two Jamaicas had grown further apart. They were not only separate in caste and race, but to varying degrees had separate economies, separate religions, and separate cultures" (Curtin, 1955, 158). In the case of the slums, the administering of law rendered their separateness ineluctable: separation by race and class can be seen as social practice, but the police selecting out these communities for surveillance and blame whenever a crime occurred makes exclusion a legal category. And it is in this context—where exclusion is linked with the operation of law—that the idea of the slum dweller as foreigner gains credence.

Patterson's setting in *Sisyphus* gives us some insight into life in the Dungle, which not only was one of the actual slums but also became the generic moniker for the ultra-slum. But more than its insight into the Dungle, the novel gives insight into the society that produces the Dungle. The relationship of tension between the privileged and the aspiring citizens inside the border and those on the outside highlights the contradictory porosity of the border. In defining itself against the Dungle, the city is already shaped by the Dungle. At the same time, the Dungle residents do not stay within the "camp" area or treat it as a "waiting zone" but as a threshold space from which they actively attempt to escape across the border. But most important, the Dungle as an obeah man exerts a spiritual force that challenges the city's surveillance machinery at all levels.

Interestingly, the concern over the slums began not with demolition but with talk of housing rehabilitation. Terms used to describe the plans and outcomes of the rehabilitation program included words like "upliftment" and "renewal"; in fact, one arm of the program was called "Operation Friendship."[5] (The irony of this kind of language, which is more appropriate to exercises of détente among rival or hostile countries, resonates with Curtin's two Jamaicas.) Yet there remained palpable tension between the tone used to describe the hopes of the program, especially with regard to space, and the language used to describe the residents who would be impacted. In an article in *Public Opinion* dated December 3, 1960, a photograph of the slum area called Kingston Pen, popularly known as Back O' Wall,[6] is included with the caption: "[t]he sprawling shanty town which is Kingston Pen, one of the many 'eyesores' in the Corporate Area which the government plans to eliminate under the land acquisition and house building program" ("Housing Rehabilitation Programme," 1960).

In the same article, Premier Norman Manley voices his concern about restoring these spaces and giving people access to "humane and decent living conditions" ("Housing Rehabilitation Programme," 1960). The contrast between this rehabilitative language around city renewal and beautification and the language used to describe Back O' Wall residents is exemplified in an article in the February 14, 1962, issue of the *Star* newspaper, arguing for police involvement in Operation Friendship. The article, which is, instructively, one of the very few that even noted the presence of the people of Kingston Pen, declares, "[B]ehind the notorious Coronation Market to the west a group of hard-core, grim-faced, hard-jawed young and seasoned hooligans wreak havoc on the rest of society as they transform that bloc leading from Darling Street to Back O Wall into a living Hell on earth" ("Operation Friendship," 1962, 6).

This type of language would have primed the reading public for a page of photographs that appeared in *The Star* a year and a half later, beginning in the top left corner (*The Star*, October 14, 1963) with a photograph of police and bulldozers as they crawl into Back O' Wall. Two of the frames show altercations between demonstrators and the police and a thick crowd of people holding signs with statements such as "Bustamante Down with the Bulldozer"—a plea to the prime minister and his party asking for kinder measures ("Squatters Clash with Police," 1963). More brutal than the altercations between angry crowds and the police is the final photograph, of a family returning to the rubble of their belongings after the bulldozers have had their way ("Squatters Clash with Police," 1963). There is a curious voyeurism in the line of pictures marching across the top of the page, with the innards of squatters' homes smashed open by the iron jaws of bulldozers presented as shameful spectacles. Here too is evidence that the machinery of urban renewal is multipronged: renewal and erasure and spectacle and surveillance work hand in hand. In the case of Back O' Wall, the hope of some future greatness/renewal must be preceded by the work of erasure/the bulldozer. The language in *The Star*, which, in effect, makes invisible any justifiable motivations of the hard-jawed hooligan, convinces its readership that brutality is necessary.

Similarly, surveillance of these communities, most fully realized in the shattered, exposed dwellings and belongings, is an implicit necessity to ensure that no (eye)sores remain on the body politic. Those readers who are not Back O' Wall dwellers are made complicit as impelled voyeurs; those who are Back O' Wall dwellers see their shame, and the living conditions to which they are subjected, spread out as good evidence why Back O' Wall (which, according to the novel's historian, Rachael, gave way to the Dungle) cannot be tolerated.

The page of photos in *The Star* suggests that there was indeed an appetite for this kind of display of poverty and destitution. The slums of West Kingston were not just poor dwellings with leaking roofs, they were shacks made of cardboard and other waste material. They stretched the meaning of the Jamaican folk song "Dry Weather House"[7] to its furthest limits—"house" was too sturdy a noun for these dwellings. That the dwellers were neither owners nor renters, but instead squatters, itinerants of the worst order, made the spectacle all the more satisfying, and their protests more outlandish, without visible or legal justification in the eyes of the respectable.

Saidiya Hartman's treatment of the slave coffle as spectacle, where even well-meaning whites agreed the coffles were something to see even as the spectacle was deeply disturbing, is a useful parallel. Hartman argues that

FIGURE 2. Slum Removal, 1963: Squatters in Kingston Pen demonstrate against impending removal from their homes. *The Star*, October 14, 1963. © The Gleaner Company (Media) Ltd.

"this circumscribed recognition of black humanity itself becomes an exercise of violence" (Hartman, 1997, 35). The parallel, though not a precise one, captures a dimension of race relations in Jamaica which Henrice Altink has called a "public secret" (Altink, 2022). Cultural critics Rex Nettleford and M. G. Smith many decades earlier named the denial of Blackness, or Black people's legitimate *presence* (*presence* in the ultimate sense) as part of the definition of Jamaican identity. The fact is, there were no "brown" people in the slums—and here I mean "brown" in the sense of socioeconomic positionality.[8] In the squatter communities of West Kingston were to be found the fullest convergence of all that Black signified in independent Jamaica. In Jamaica, "goodness, beauty, even God" (quoted in Nettleford, 1970, 32), and certainly wealth, were racially indicated, and they never signified Blackness. Nettleford notes that "[t]he heaviest concentration of these alienated and unemployed poor was to be found in West Kingston" (Nettleford, 1970, 49), and the masses crowded into Kingston's ghettoes were not imagined in Jamaica's reverie of racial harmony. Put another way, a West Kingston slum address was a mark of Blackness, and in the independence moment Blackness like this was not part of the ideal new nation.[9]

Surveillance in *The Children of Sisyphus*

The push toward greatness in the independence moment was not simply a spatial consideration. Belinda Edmondson (1998) has argued that the model of the "English gentleman" and "Victorian Literary Man" framed the way many West Indian writers of the nationalist generation saw themselves and their work. Orlando Patterson's intervention in the nationalist debates via *The Children of Sisyphus* does not represent such a quest for greatness. Rather, it addresses the grit and squalor of the ultra-poor, and how the alternative, hermetic power of spiritveillance was a source of terror and obsession for both the ultra-poor and the aspiring city that set itself against them. What separated *Sisyphus* from the yard novels of the period was its uncompromising refusal to participate in the national project of gentility. In Roger Mais's *Brother Man* (1954), for example, we have the saving graces of the nation from below embodied in the idealized figure of the Rastaman in the lane. Interestingly, the eponymous Brother Man is pitted against the ultimately defeated obeah spirit of Bra Ambo. In C.L.R. James's *Minty Alley* (1936), a couple of decades earlier, James's middle-class teacher-voyeur inserts himself into the lower-class urban yard and obliquely, or symbolically, as the novel's narrative focal point, takes on a status equivalent to the writer "elevating" the proletariat to their "true status of personality."[10] If the yard in James's novel has its own organic life separate and apart from Haynes, there is a sense in which Haynes as a middle-class protagonist-observer remains central to the narrative politics of bringing the yard into literary respectability. James's yard dwellers may be seen as the urban equivalent of Claude McKay's rural folk in McKay's rambunctious celebration of primitivist folk negritude in

Banana Bottom (1933). McKay presents his rural folk as a high form of gentry that is the best articulation of the nation in becoming. Indeed, McKay's presentation could be seen as emblematic of the general treatment of the rural peasantry in literature up to the independence period.

On the other hand, we have *The Children of Sisyphus*, which arguably has had a significantly more limited afterlife than any of those mentioned above, precisely because of its refusal of a discourse that focused on the nation as center. By this I mean that the novel "failed" to attract and sustain kudos in nationalistic literary criticism because it could not be read to fit an ideal of the nation as an ultimately inclusivist category. Neither could it fit an ideal of community (rural or urban) as a microcosm to which the nation could look for its enabling referents. Patterson's novel, by focusing on detritus, the concept of human dispensability as a necessary element in the imagining and construction of the nation, calls nationalism to account as a failing, not a redeemable ideology.

This is crucial—the nation is envisioned as possible only on the basis of an exclusion, and in this case the exclusionary foundation is the Dungle. Patterson's Dungle dwellers are existentially, of necessity, extramural, outside the nation, just as was demonstrated in the treatment and situation of the real-life Dungle. For Patterson's characters, there is neither escape from the confines of Dungle space nor relief from its existential hold, whether through education, religion, resistance uprising, or migration. *Sisyphus* is a hard, determined stare at poverty in West Kingston without the deflection of humor or romance. In fact, some have read *Sisyphus* as a tragedy, especially in its vision of the independent nation. But to read *Sisyphus* as tragedy is to misread the novel. It is to miss Patterson's voice among the many who were dreaming of a new Jamaica.[11]

Patterson's choice to tell the story of slum dwellers in independent Jamaica is in itself an act of counter-erasure. It is an instinct different from the work of bulldozers, an engagement with the cast-off and an independence vision very different from the performance of male-centered greatness. Patterson, a sociologist, was roundly criticized for writing soulless novels and instead roughly stitching together his sociological research into plastic, "Barbie-doll" fiction (Hearne, 1972, 79). By Barbie-doll fiction, Hearne means to suggest that Patterson is an intruder on the artistry of fiction writing. But as a descriptor of *Sisyphus*, his critique strikes an off chord, particularly because of Patterson's protagonist Dinah, who, to this reader, is carefully and complexly rendered— anything but a Barbie doll.

And indeed, it is her forays in search of escape, and the inevitability of her return, that most centralizes the Dungle (as opposed to the nation) as the novel's thematic center. Dinah's return in particular raises the question of the sentient life of the Dungle as a space with powers and identity in and of itself, as complete a human space as the nation-space from which it is cut off. Ultimately, though the character of the nation emerges only as secondary foil—as antagonist, if you will—the novel may be read as an exploration of how the nation-state and the Dungle overlap. Patterson addresses their interdependence and their osmotic character, as well as their insistence on control. Above all he exposes their regulatory apparatuses at the core of which are the machineries of surveillance and spiritveillance that I am discussing here.

The pivotal phrase, "The Dungle [is] an obeah man" appears in the second chapter of the novel. This phrase captures the social history of subaltern space, the negative demarcation of the urban slum, and of Jamaican popular religious practice. Dinah, a prostitute from the West Kingston slum, the Dungle, seizes the opportunity offered her by Special Constable-cum-customer Alphanso to have a new life with him in a room in the "respectable lower-middle-class" not-slum Jones Town (Scott, 2014a, 115). The event that is Dinah's taking leave of the Dungle is a locus for expanded readings on West Kingston, in particular the Dungle, on gender(ed) relations, and on religion (Rastafari and Revival), and the concept I am terming spiritveillance. Inside the shack that Dinah shares with her man Cyrus and her son Nicholas, Dinah is alone with her thoughts. As she temporarily hides the small box into which she will stash all her worldly possessions in preparation for leaving, she considers how the paltry and fragile and dastardly came to be her life, and she concludes that the Dungle where she lives has the potency, fearsomeness, and knowledge of an obeah man. Dinah's intent to defy this power is the source of conflict and the perspectival center in the novel.

Dinah is every slum dweller who seeks to defy the rules of the banopticon—yardie style.[12] As I have discussed, Bigo's concept of the banopticon suggests that the terms of surveillance are not the same for all, and the exceptions in society—those banned from full admittance into the citizenry—are subject to extra scrutiny. Dinah as a figuration of individual agency allows us to see the push and pull factors at work in keeping her in and returning her to the Dungle. The push of standard surveillance, the oversight, power, and control usually wielded by the state is certainly present in newly independent Jamaica. Most prominently, surveilling power is evidenced in the anxious brutality of the police, in the actions of the politician and the civil servants at the Labour Office, and the "very pale" (Patterson, 1986, 113) upper-middle-class housewife who employs Dinah as a domestic.

There remains the lingering surveillance by colonial England as well. Aspects of the formal relationship remain, such as the overseeing power of the governor general, but also a culture of being overseen. The new imperial presence of white American sailors and the dangerous powers they wield, especially as their basest desires, legal and illegal, are supported by the Jamaican police, are also noted. Dinah, Mabel, Mary, and the other Dungle-dwelling prostitutes are intensely surveilled, while the American foreigners are protected and accommodated. The means by which Dinah and the other prostitutes must ply their trade in the interstitial space between the Dungle and downtown Kingston highlights the ways the disciplinary apparatus functions in the subjugation of poor, Black, female bodies. By virtue of their trade, the women must attire themselves as spectacle. Their spectacularity is not for sale but for free voyeuristic sampling; the sampler may choose to buy or not to buy after he has enjoyed this free preview. At the same time, as spectacle, the women are more visible to the authorities and therefore more open to surveillance and to being pushed back to the Dungle.

But I have spoken of a pull from within the Dungle as well. Indeed, part of the significance of this argument is that the most effective "veillance" presented in the novel is practiced by local Jamaicans in slums like the Dungle. This "veillance" is largely radical in that it often works to undo and undercut the power of the state for the purpose of liberating believers and followers. In the Jamaican context, this is a power that is distinct from political power. Rather, it is rooted in the regulatory apparatus of religious practice—spiritveillance. Spiritveillance emerges through the "seeing" and "reading" power sourced and inspired by the teachings and practices of Africa-based, Jamaica-grown religions. "Seeing" implies a more deeply informed spiritual perception and discernment, not simply the process of experience or witness generally understood to be the domain of two-eyed vision. "Reading" is spiritual insight and the actual process of attaining deep psychic knowledge of a person or situation.[13] I argue that this extra-sightedness, spiritveillance, is not only used to liberate, but also to control. Dinah's escape from the Dungle and her prophesied and feared return are orchestrated via spiritveillance.

An important foreshadowing of the power of spiritveillance is seen in the moment that Dinah becomes aware of the ubiquity of the Dungle's presence from which this power is later seen to emanate. As Dinah attempts to hide her flight box, she must "dig away a part of the floor so that the box would fit underneath the bed. A stinking stench of stale dung and debris stung her nostrils and she had to move away her head until she became used to it" (Patterson, 1986, 19). Immediately below Dinah's feet, in fact, the packed earth that is the floor of her home carries the stench of the history of West Kingston, particularly the Dungle. The Dungle is the ramshackle community where the main characters live, a place alive with the smell of waste, at once cast off on the margins of Kingston and at the same time the very essence of Kingston combined with its waste. Rachael, the old, wise prostitute, tells the story of how the Dungle came to be home and refuge for Kingston's discarded poor—a version corroborated by social historians. Rachael's telling describes how urban renewal projects inspired the razing of Back O' Wall and the migration from Back O' Wall to the Dungle: "An' when di dirty police dem raid de squatters dem in Back-O-Wall when Backra ready fe buil' 'im factory, me was di firs' person fe hit 'pon di idea fe come an' live ya. Yu can't run a man from off a shit, dat is wha' a say. Dem laugh after me firs'. But when later ah see dem comin' over one by one, two by two, as de police drop dem baton 'pon dem backside an' burn dem out, I 'ad de las' laugh" (Patterson, 1986, 23). According to Rachael, when the most iconic of the great slums, Back O' Wall, located behind the Coronation Market, across the train tracks, back behind God's back, became contested space and was considered as part of Kingston that could be renewed, those who squatted there had to vacate. Rachael's move to the dung heap was an attempt to secure more permanent refuge: "you can't run a man from off a shit," she contends.

Patterson's portrayal here is consonant with the history of the development of Kingston. And when Dinah digs the earth beneath her and Cyrus's bed and the stench of old waste and debris fills her nose, Dinah's engagement with the Dungle is historically inflected: below the earth is evidence of the story of the Dungle told to us by Rachael. Indeed, as on the surface, which is littered with garbage and human waste, below the surface teems rot. Rachael's history of the Dungle is not just history, it is as well ontology. She contends that Kingston's wasteland is so unlikely a domicile for humans that it is the best place for castoffs—prostitutes, Rastamen, obeah men, and the abject poor—to live undisturbed. Rachael believes that living on wasteland will exempt them from the surveilling eye of the powers that be. She makes no comment on the spectacularity of living in the Dungle, and she seems unaware of what Bigo's concept of the banopticon brings to light: that the gathering of Kingston's castoffs in one place arguably makes surveilling simpler. There is evidence in the novel, such as when the police come looking for Mary, the prostitute who retrieves her daughter from the state, that the Dungle is where they find all criminals and that the details of guilt or innocence do not matter. Patterson makes a major case of this: surveilling the Dungle is an imperative of the state, and gathering the castoffs in one place ensures the ease and effectiveness of the project.

Dinah's experience with the historical dirt of the Dungle is very much lived in the novel's present as well. The first chapter of the novel describes three garbage men who journey into the slum to dump Kingston's waste and relates how these deposits are crucial to the Dungle dwellers' survival. The garbage men and their carts are drawn by donkeys, not horses, and there are three, not four of them. Still, I read them as versions of the apocalyptic horsemen of Revelation 6—messengers of death and damnation for those not clothed in white. The slum dwellers' ravenous descent on the discarded scraps from the rest of Kingston is the picture of an apocalyptic dystopia, and in this we see the repetition of Sisyphus's stumbling journey joining the past, present, and future of West Kingston in an unending cycle of poverty. Here poverty, twinned with and orchestrated by the statecraft of making (human) waste, may be read as obeah, producing an inability to escape the Dungle. The stark contradiction within this "reality" is that this "obeah" from the state is what the people depend on for survival—so it both feeds and kills. Such a contradiction is what the city entering independence seeks to escape by relegating a category of people to the margins, yet obviously, it is precisely what it cannot escape since the Dungle as waste heap is fundamental to the city's "public health," image, and survival. Both the city and the Dungle depend on the construction of the Dungle, and the city and the Dungle are interdependent.

So far in my analysis of Dinah's digging away the dirt in her hut, I have only considered the Dungle as the earth on Dinah's hands, which is also the land that was first settled by Rachael and other refugees from Back O' Wall. But I want to suggest that the surveilling obeah as presented in this scene is not only visible, touchable power, it is an encompassing sensory power as well. The stench of the Dungle is so alive and undoing that Dinah must turn her head until she gets used to it. The smell of the Dungle is also used to identify its residents in a multi-sensory matrix of surveillance[14] and expulsion. Keturah, the destitute mother of seven, tells the Rastafari elder, Brother Solomon, of a latest slight. Keturah loses a job washing clothes the same week she gets it when a woman passing by sees her working: "'Me see you a'ready,' she say, 'is wha' yu doin' in dis part o' Kingston?', so me ask her if is any o' her business an' same time she say, 'Ah 'member whe' ah see you now, you come from de Dungle, you is a Dungle pickney, ah can smell it 'pon you, wha' yu ah do in good people place?'" (Patterson, 1986, 43). The woman reports Keturah, who is dismissed by her employer and returns to the Dungle unpaid and hungry. The smell or essence of the Dungle becomes another locus for surveilling slum residents: "ah smell it 'pon you." There is also the embedded notion that if Keturah never "wrenk" (meaning "evinced a rudeness that stank") with the woman, the woman might not have escalated her identifying attack.

Similarly, when Dinah unfortunately meets Mabel in the Jones Town yard where Dinah has just settled with Special Constable Alphanso and is disturbed by Mabel's loud identifying of her, it is not a coincidence that Dinah is at a washbasin scrubbing clothes, ostensibly committed to a clean transformation. Before they fight, Dinah warns and begs Mabel for her discretion and identifies the Dungle as more than a physical place, but as an essence of a thing. She says, "Ah done wid what ah lef' behin' an ah don't wan' to hear 'bout it. It look like yu still livin' in the Dungle, though yu out of it in flesh" (Patterson, 1986, 62). Both examples indicate that the Dungle has a presence beyond its physical location and is capable of "traveling" backwards and forwards, into the city-space from which it has been ostensibly expelled. Keturah is the Dungle, Mabel is the Dungle, and though she battles it, Dinah confesses to Shepherd John when she first has audience with him that what haunts her "Is de Dungle" (Patterson, 1986, 139). She explains, "Yes, Shepherd. Ah running from it. Ah try hard as ah can. But it not outside o' me. It inside" (Patterson, 1986, 139). "Inside" speaks to the internalization of the dwellers' belief in the Dungle's power. If we read the city's version of "obeah" (feeding the people on garbage) as an attack on the spirit of the Dungle dwellers, and as a concomitant undermining of the city's ability to discern or evaluate itself justly, we could also almost see the feeding of the people on waste as not just a banoptic mechanism but also a bizarre form of spiritveillance (distinct from the Dungle's version), an invasion of personal agency. Indeed, the slum dwellers' enforced abjection recalls the Jamaican aphoristic saying, "Smaddy musi obeah yu"—a reference to inescapable bad luck that can only be explained by powerful, *unfathomable* spiritual forces.

Woman Luck Deh a Dungle Heap

The Children of Sisyphus highlights the double subjugation of the female by surveillance machineries in more ways than one. One such way is that male characters, whether in the Dungle or out of it, practice their surveillance techniques on women. Even the men who lead religious orders that are expected to be liberating use woman-objectifying surveillance strategies that are complicit with the surveillance by the state. The Rastafari bredren, Cyrus; the Revival leader, Shepherd John; and Special Constable Alphanso, two religious men and one man of the state, are all ultimately concerned with controlling Dinah's body, perhaps more than they are with the material and spiritual accommodations they offer her. That Cyrus and Shepherd John are able to use their powers of "reading" and "seeing" in a negative "obeah" of control highlights the fact that if the Dungle is in the city, the city is as much in the Dungle—gender oppression exists in both, and in the broad spectrum of human failings, if the city is not an ideal, neither is the Dungle idealized. Rastafari and Revival, like Bedwardism before them, arose out of the rubble of poverty and degradation with a stubborn and powerful pride. The novel suggests, however, that the practitioners never gained anything more than symbolic ascendency in their anti-colonial fight. As Cyrus and Shepherd John work to undo the forces of oppression, they also begin to enact power and surveillance using these same models. This seems like a harsh judgment, but it does serve to highlight the ways gender as a category of oppression fell through the cracks of liberation movements.

Patterson's choice to make the novel about Dinah, and arguably his choice to privilege the woman's point of view, offers a critique of the patriarchal traps and institutions Dinah and the other women find themselves in and cannot escape. That Patterson points to the misogynist and physical violence of Rasta men also undoes the romanticizing of Rasta and its transformative power in the moment, in the same way he questions how women's bodies are used in Revivalist ritual. Patterson's focus on women was central in the conceptualizing of the novel and in its earliest editions also quite important to the way the novel was marketed and read. At one point in its early publication history, *Sisyphus* was titled *Dinah*, with the curious subtitle *Body and Soul She Was Trapped in the Nightmare World of Voodoo*. The cover (Pyramid Books, 1964) features the naked outline of a Black woman in the foreground, theatrically set to signal both struggle and resilience, with religious symbols flanking her on either side.

As well, the first edition of *Sisyphus*, published by New Authors in 1964, uses the face of a Black woman with dominant eyes and lips and black splotches marking and almost obscuring her. The black and the brown of her face and torso are the same black and brown of the setting behind her. The choice of art for these earlier book covers is certainly in contrast with the Longman Caribbean Writers edition (1986), which features a red-eyed, bare-chested, dreadlocked man staring, and the latest version reissued by Peepal Tree Press (2011), which seems most anxious to literally interpret the Greek myth referenced in the title via an Africa-inspired interpretive lens. The cover photo is of a sculpture by Edna Manley, and it features a matri/patriarchal figure crowded around by her/his progeny. The shifts in the titles and subtitling of the novel and the choices made to market it prove that in its earliest iterations Dinah was significant in the reading of the novel, while later versions and readings made her less central. In his 2013 interview with David Scott, Patterson reveals that as he wrote the novel he was grappling with women's issues based on his own family experience. Whether the shift away from Dinah was an indication of publishers responding to the concerns of the postinde-pendence period in which male narratives were dominant is a moot point.

The image of Dinah stooping on the ground in her hut digging the earth to hide her box can also be read as a performance of the proverb, "ooman luck deh a dungle heap, fowl come 'cratch it up." The well-known proverb is used centrally in Louise Bennett's poem "Jamaica 'Oman": "'Oman luck deh a dungle, / some rooted more than some / But as long as fowl a scratch dungle heap / 'Oman luck mus come!" Bennett's poem underscores the fowl's role in unearthing woman's luck, while in *Sisyphus* Dinah is the one scratching the earth with the hope of flying the coop of the Dungle. Carolyn Cooper in *Noises in the Blood* provides a reading of the poem and proverb that I find useful here: "In that body of Jamai-can folk wisdom transmitted in proverb, Anansi story and riddle, is the genesis of an indigenous feminist ideology: the paradigm of a submerged and fated iden-tity that must be rooted up, covertly and assiduously. The existential dungle, the repository of the accumulated waste of the society, becomes in the folk iconog-raphy the locus of transformation. It is the dungle, and the dehumanizing social conditions that allow it, which are the enemy of woman, not the male" (Cooper, 1995, 48). What Cooper names an "indigenous feminist ideology" that projects success for the Jamaican woman, despite the historically inlaid social condi-tions, is evident here. Dinah turns her face from the stench, fixes her nose, and completes her task. But to suggest that the Dungle is the only enemy of woman is to elide the full range of Dungle power, including the aspect concen-trated in masculine "spirit" power alluded to above.

The power of Rastafari is first witnessed and felt by Dinah in the opening pages of the novel. When Dinah decides to wash her body—two weeks dirty—in the sea by the Dungle, Cyrus, who is cleaning his fishing nets, sees her. Cyrus's gaze is lustful and all-consuming. Dinah, who is well acquainted with the ways of men, has a vague suspicion that "he is casting some kind of spell upon her" (Patterson, 1986, 15). Later she calls this spell "a terrible piece of obeah" (Patterson, 1986, 15). Cyrus's power begins in his eyes—"His eyes were dark, glazed and bright, like lakes in the moonlight jungle" (14); "He stared through her with a kind of mocking condescension" (15); his gaze makes Dinah naked in a way she had not been before; it is presented as consuming and masculinist. Cyrus declares Dinah his Eve and himself her Adam, and yet here and throughout their rela-tionship, he must actively forget that he shares Dinah's body with her paying customers. After a powerful sexual encounter that is not definitely either rape or consensual, Cyrus takes the naked Dinah to live in his hut with him as his wife. And there she abides until six years later when Rachael finds her escaping to Special Constable Alphanso and a new life in Jones Town.

Dinah is not tricked by Cyrus. In their first encounter she resists him by declaring that Rastas "treat dem 'oman too bad" (Patterson, 1986, 14). She knows very well what it will be like to be his woman. Mabel (another Dungle prostitute) knows too. Mabel's boisterous stint in the Jones Town yard comes to a dramatic end when her Rasta man finds her, beats her, and takes her back to the Dungle in a donkey cart (Patterson, 1986, 130). The "oil a fall back"[15] that Mabel sprinkles on Dinah's doorstep to obeah her back to the Dungle finds Mabel in another way, not through the obeah she intended for Dinah, but in the will of Mabel's Rastaman/lover. In the novel, both Mabel and Dinah are subdued and surveilled by the gendered power of Rastafari. The power is called obeah because of its mysterious efficacy, which finds the women in their places of hiding outside the Dungle. The fact that the city cannot escape the Dungle any more than the Dungle dwellers can, is seen not only in Mabel and Dinah's encroachments into Jones Town, but also in the Rastaman's being able to find them, driven by the same rabid imperatives of disciplinary/domiciling control as the police excursions into the Dungle. Cyrus's Adam and Eve simile may suggest that he sees Dinah as an equal mate (the idea of male-female equality in the biblical "male and female created He them" in which as a Rastaman Cyrus would have been well versed); however, in the novel what comes to the fore is the contradictory idea in the trope, of woman as the source of man's downfall and the one therefore needing constant surveillance and control.

Dinah's unofficial counselor in the Jones Town yard, Mrs. D, informs Dinah of Mabel's ill will toward her. It is Mrs. D who suggests to Dinah that she find Shepherd John at the "Revival Zion Baptist of God"—as he is a renowned Revivalist whose powers are stronger than obeah. As with Dinah's experience of Rastafari, the Revival church is a place of surveillance and exposure. And as with her experience with Rastafari, the process of being "read" is both spiritual and sexual. The shepherd's first reading of Dinah involves him looking at her so completely that he appears to "stare through her" (Patterson, 1986, 139). As in her first meeting with Cyrus, she feels naked, exposed, and surveilled: "He studied every detail of her soul with his piercing black eyes. Yes, she was sure he could help her. But what was he thinking? The intensity of his look was beginning to frighten her. She was bare. She was ashamed. She wanted to fall at his feet and burst out her soul. Never before had she felt the way she did towards any man" (Patterson, 1986, 139). Dinah must be fully exposed to the shepherd and her sins laid bare before him for her to join the Revivalists. The process of purification is not just the washing and beatings she endures with water and blood and whips, she must also endure the shepherd "[washing] her with his eyes again" (Patterson, 1986, 141). Just as with Cyrus who veils his desire for her in religious terms (she will be his Eve), so does the shepherd sheath his desire in the ritual cleansing and processing of a new sister of the First Order. "Order" is significant here, as a term that reveals the structural ethos of religion as a societal system and a frame for keeping (women) under patriarchal containment. This is something that the Dungle shares with the city that seeks to banish self-knowledge by relegating its underbelly out of view.

Patterson's focus on eyes (black eyes and brown eyes, severe and piercing eyes, "wild and frightening") (Patterson, 1986, 108) and their work in seeing and staring are a motif in *Sisyphus*. Seeing and staring function in the ways we expect in religious practice; that is, this watching is a mode of achieving conformity and most especially, as the above shows, the power of the male gaze. Yet, as with Cyrus who makes a grand though obviously compromised claim over Dinah, the shepherd's seeing power is also limited. He ignores his de facto equal in the Revival band, the Elder Mother, who watches him watch Dinah when Dinah first arrives at the compound. "Quickly, he walked over to Dinah. The Elder Mother took two slow steps forward so that she was in full view of them. She folded her arms and eyed them silently. The eyes were black and wide, the lips more tight and severe than the bolted door of a store-room" (Patterson, 1986, 138).

Henceforth the mother is described in masculine terms: Physically, she stands "straight and erect and with her arms folded"; she rarely speaks and is greatly feared because, it is said, "her spirit strong" (Patterson, 1986, 148). It is the Elder Mother who trained Shepherd John, and though John is beloved because "is 'im an 'im spirit dat keep de church together . . . she still hold de purse-string" (Patterson, 1986, 148). The reader perceives that despite the language used to describe her, the Elder Mother, as one of the women who lives with the shepherd, feels jealous of the shepherd's attention and affection for Dinah. The Elder Mother's womanhood is overlooked, but like Dinah she too is scratching up her luck. The shepherd's lack of discernment of the mother's needs and his refusal to acknowledge her as a threat, even with Dinah's warnings, is true blindness, not sightedness, and it costs him his life. The Elder Mother as a countersurveilling force curtailing the disciplinary power of male sexual desire emphasizes Patterson's feminist discourse as much as his choice of Dinah as a protagonist who refuses submission as her last word. Here overall Patterson is deconstructing received ideas of obeah as a spiritual force that is suprahuman; he is identifying forms of intentional human activity as a form of obeah. In doing so he casts a searchlight on institutionalized structures such as misogyny, domestic abuse, and the oppression of women through religious systems.

Obeah as Spiritveillance, Spiritveillance as Obeah in *Sisyphus*

The left-leaning paper the *Tribune*, first published in Jamaica in 1937, fills in many of the silences around the surveillance of certain groups. In an article titled "Security Watch on Rastafarians, Reds" in January 1961, the writer suggests that "among those being watched are persons suspected of being in sympathy with the Rastafarian movement, persons known or suspected to be extreme leftist adherents, and certain other people entering the island." The identification of a surveillance culture in Jamaica was not to be found in any mainstream dailies such as the *Jamaica Gleaner* or *The Star*. There was already close surveillance and control of Rastafari, often reported as clashes with the police, destruction of squatter communities, and many, many (Miss Mollypolslike)[16] reports of the peculiar ways of Rasta. This article, however, suggests that others/outsiders/foreigners (Rasta sympathizers and communists) are also being watched at a level that suggests a voyeuristic fascination beyond the "necessity" of exerting control. A public service ad/announcement taken out in the *Jamaica Star* on January 17, 1962, warns the wider society and tourists to be respectful of "Picture Shy Rastafarians." The announcement asks tourists to "not take pictures of Rastafarians walking on the streets without their consent" and states that "Rastafarians are strongly opposed to such conduct" (*The Star*). The tourists' gaze on Rastafari, like the state's gaze, in these early days is resisted by Rastafari.

Diana Paton argues that even though the legal status of obeah, which was outlawed in 1898, has not changed over time, the general perspective on obeah as mysterious, potent, and dangerous was eclipsed by more visible and easily surveilled African religious practices that became popular in the first decades of the twentieth century. According to Paton, "obeah was coming to be seen as something exotic and quaint, rather than dangerous. . . . Rastafarians were instead targeted through laws about dress, drugs" (Paton, 2015, 280). Dinah's perspective in *Sisyphus* challenges this thesis in that neither Rastafari nor Revival generates the palpable fear that obeah engenders. Rastafari and Revival, by appearing through the sexual and surveilling practices of *men*, are revealed not in their efficacies but their limitations. Patterson's phrasing of Dinah's final return to the Dungle as obeah indicates his sense of obeah's larger grasp and power.

When Dinah calls the Dungle an obeah man, she simultaneously acknowledges the power and the mystery of the most feared African-derived religious practice in Jamaica and its efficacy in the physical world. Dinah's attempt to encapsulate in words the spirit power of the Dungle by associating it with the spirit power of obeah has anchored my discussion so far. Do we read Dinah's statement as solely metaphorical, or is naming the Dungle an obeah man an attempt to confront and flee the arational, outsized fear the spirit power of the Dungle has over her? The novel does not present an actual obeah wo/man, a telling absence in a text so ardently concerned with the complexities of second indigenous or Africa-derived, Jamaica-grown religions and the experiences of believers in independent Jamaica. While we do see the working of obeah, albeit secondhand, as Mrs. D tells Dinah of Mabel's sprinkling the stinking and potent oil of fallback powder and we witness Mrs. D's counteractive sprinkling of protective powder, we never see who prescribes these treatments. The fact that obeah power is alluded to, evidenced, but never actually seen performed in the novel amplifies the unknown quantity and the fear it engenders.

This fits into some obvious dimensions of how obeah is perceived and practiced in Jamaican culture. Obeah is generally feared, yet it produces fascination. Nathaniel Murrell's discussion of perceptions of obeah in the Caribbean reveals some of this. Murrell's choice of language including Western terms that have been used to "other" and persecute practices generally assumed to have provenance in Africa and his reflection on the impact of community are worth our consideration: "Obeah operates with coded magic and healing pharmacopeia and also may deploy esoteric artilleries of sorcery, prescience, and witchcraft to accomplish its purposes. Practitioners work undercover and at nights because they are seen as evildoers working against the harmony and welfare of community life and dabbling in iniquity" (Murrell, 2010, 230). Murrell's language—obeah practice is "coded," "esoteric," "undercover"—confirms it as an entity/practice that is surveilled because of its contradiction of European, Judeo-Christian norms. Obeah is seen as a direct link to Africa, and it is witness to how Africa is perceived as the original continent of darkness.

In the experience of the descendants of the enslaved, obeah is a link to "history" that is unwritten and unknown in the annals of "History"; there are no monuments, no ancestors, and very few stories from the Middle Passage, but there are stories of how culture was lost and obscured on the plantation. At the same time, obeah is part of the evidence that recognizes Africa as a corridor of spiritual arts. In obeah practice there is evidence and recognition of retained knowledge despite the violent and deep ruptures of the slave trade and slavery. This recognition places obeah as part of African spiritualist cosmogony, which always assumes that though spirit action takes place in the world of "man," it also supersedes, transects, and infuses the world of human action. In the long view of independence, part of "obeah identity" is that it is both visible and hidden, so that the language Murrell uses of code and esotericism is apposite.

"Darkness," therefore, such as the darkness in obeah practice, is ultimately impenetrable. Ironically, this resonates with the dimension of the cosmos that astrophysicists refer to as "dark matter." Simone Browne's fascinating discussion in *Dark Matters* is certainly important here. Browne thinks about the concept of dark matter in these ways:

> what might bring to mind opacity, the color black, limitlessness and the limitations imposed on blackness, the dark, antimatter, that which is not optically available, black holes, the Big Bang theory, and other concerns of cosmology where dark matter is that nonluminous component of the universe that is said to exist but cannot be observed, cannot be re-created in laboratory conditions. Its distribution cannot be measured; its properties cannot be determined; and so it remains undetectable. The gravitational pull of this unseen is said to move galaxies. Invisible and unknowable, yet somehow still

there, dark matter, in this planetary sense, is theoretical. If the term "dark matter" is a way to think about race, where race, as Howard Winant puts it, "remains the dark matter, the often invisible substance that in many ways structures the universe of modernity," then one must ask here, "invisible to whom?" (Browne, 2015, 9)

Browne's discussion of dark matter helps us think through just how much Dinah perceives the power of obeah as existing all over and within the Dungle. In the independence moment, Patterson, through obeah, which in the novel is active but untraceable, re-creates ground zero of dark Africa on Jamaican soil, imagined via all the stereotypes in and about the Dungle, yet complicating the stereotypes through obeah's associations with the ineluctable.

Paton argues that the term obeah "has always referred to multiple phenomena. At the most obvious level, it describes practices involving ritual attempts to manipulate a world of spiritual power" (Paton, 2015, 1–2). Paton's discussion of obeah historicizes the practice and its respected and feared power famed in the history of Jamaica. For instance, obeah power was said to be critical to the maroons' dominance in the Maroon Wars against the British (Paton, 2015, 35), perhaps most popularly known via Nanny's magical posterior power. As well, Paton finds evidence that the maroons' "sense of collectivity was produced at least in part through religion" (Paton, 2015, 35), so that obeah is effectual in strategies of war and also in the formation of community. In later rebellions, such as Tacky's Rebellion (1789), obeah becomes more easily surveilled and thus begins to take its place in the legal history of Jamaica. Prohibition laws against the practice of obeah began from as early as 1789 in response to Tacky's Rebellion, but the actual Obeah Act was ratified in 1898. Paton traces how heavily violators were surveilled and persecuted in the ten years following its enactment. As time passed, however, surveillance and prosecution became less and less and the Act remained a symbolic statement against African retentions such as obeah that did not fit the picture of modernity in pre-independence and postindependence Jamaica.

Beyond the fact that obeah and the Dungle can be read as a paradigm of unknowable, threatening power is the possibility that they can be read from a different angle via the Sisyphus myth. Here, obeah and the Dungle as obeah, which appear at the center of a principle of trickery, are connected to Sisyphus, who had a life before his unending punishment on the hillside. The Greek myth reveals Sisyphus as a cheat and trickster. According to *Britannica*, "In post-Homeric times [Sisyphus] was called the father of Odysseus through his seduction of Anticleia. Both men were characterized as cunning. Sisyphus was the reputed founder of the Isthmian Games. . . . Later legend related that when Death came to fetch him, Sisyphus chained him up so that no one died until Ares came to aid Death, and Sisyphus had to submit. . . . Sisyphus was, in fact, like Autolycus and Prometheus, a widely popular figure in folklore—the trickster, or master thief" ("Sisyphus," n.d.). Sisyphus's life before his confinement to the repetition of the hillside, his outperformance of the gods, his athletic ability, and his success at cheating death, the lore about him as "cunning," "trickster," and "master thief," changes him from simply a punished figure in Greek mythology to a very familiar figure in Jamaican cultural life—Anancy, ginnal, samfie, scammer.[17] And knowing that figure much more than I do the punished Sisyphus (and his children) offers many more possibilities of reading his punishment. One such reading is to consider the punishment as a technology of surveillance. Sisyphus is best monitored on the side of the mountain—his cunning is best controlled, and the equilibrium of all the gods best maintained. In essence, Sisyphus's banishment to the futility of the hillside and the weight of the big rock acknowledges his power even while he is there; it is in his punishment that we see his worth.

The ginnal Sisyphus and the trickster obeah man/Dungle are connected. Obeah men are often perceived or imagined as frauds such as Wumba in Claude McKay's *Banana Bottom*, Bra' Ambo in Mais's *Brother Man*, and certainly Antoinette's husband in Rhys's *Wide Sargasso Sea* if we read him as a wannabe worker of obeah, who does not have the wisdom in pharmacopeia or access to mystery and power of Africa, but who succeeds in undoing his wife via hate and badmind. Their power and cunning are often connected to place as well, not necessarily in the way that the place, the Dungle, becomes the obeah man in *Sisyphus*, but in that their tools and technology may be place- or culture-specific. We have seen that Dungle/obeah power is multidimensional. But Dinah's statement that the Dungle [is] an obeah man recognizes the Dungle's energy in itself as a reservoir of power. It is highly surveilled, but it is invisible; it is marginalized and ineluctable.

Dinah, as an escaped Dungle denizen, fails to read the codes of right and proper city behavior when she is employed as a domestic by Mrs. Watkins. Here is evidence that Dinah represents something dangerous, dirty, and unsettling to the independent and advancing nation. Her disdain for right and proper behavior in other domestic workers is further evidence that her presence uptown is potentially polluting. Both literally and figuratively, Dinah assumes that she can enter Mrs. Watkins's house through the front door; when Mrs. Watkins exclaims her displeasure, Dinah must ask what she has done wrong:

> "What it is, ma'am?"
> "What it is? You dare to ask me what it is? I can see that the chances of your staying here for any length of time are very slim. Will you kindly walk around to the back entrance. And if you don't mind I'd be happy if you used that entrance in the future." (Patterson, 1986, 113)

Dinah's life in the Dungle makes the line between the Dungle and uptown unfathomable. The social and cultural differences between the two places prove

Dinah and Mrs. Watkins a world apart, and while this distance does indeed fulfill Mrs. Watkins's prophecy (that Dinah won't stay employed for long), it also confirms the power of the Dungle to hold on to its children. Dinah's lack of literacy in the social and physical geography of Kingston is also in a way a sign of the Dungle "essence" that does not deal in boundaries, and which therefore mocks the city walls, inviting strategies of expulsion.

Back to the Dungle: The Dungle as Obeah Man, a Counteractive Spiritveillance

The ending of the *Children of Sisyphus* has been read as evidence of Patterson's "tragic vision" of postindependence Jamaica[18]—the most profound disappointment being Dinah's return to the Dungle, Patterson's interest in the experiences of poor Jamaican women via Dinah and her interactions with other slum-dwelling women like Rachael and Mabel, with women like Mrs. D who have barely escaped and now live in Jones Town, with wealthy, near-white women like Mrs. Watkins, with Ruby her servant, and finally with the Elder Mother of the Band of Seventh Fire, seems from one perspective to fall short of its promise of revolution or at least resistance. For why must Dinah return to the Dungle? And what does her return signify, if not a tragic pessimism that focuses on the Sisyphean stone rather than the trickster demigod? Is spiritveillance to be perceived merely as a machinery of "spirit thievery" that complies with and fulfills the state's surveillance project? The Elder Mother, the great visionary behind the Band of the Seventh Fire, murders Shepherd John and in a moment orchestrates full blame to fall on Dinah. The last time Dinah is conscious, "they turned their eyes on her . . . their eyes were wild and frightening" (Patterson, 1986, 180) and they use hands, teeth, and feet to pummel her and tear her apart. Spiritveillance becomes surveillance, or spiritveillance and surveillance converge against Dinah's audacity. In this final moment, holding on to her life with a frayed thread, Dinah becomes conscious that "she had to get back. She knew she had to get back. There was no longer pain, for there was too much for her to feel. The life was almost gone. But she knew she had to be back there in the Dungle. She knew she had to taste the filth again. She knew he would be there waiting for her" (Patterson, 1986, 180–181).

In the Dungle, Cyrus awaits Dinah's return. For Cyrus, she has but a few hours to show up before the repatriating ship to Ethiopia docks to take the Rastafari brethren home to Africa. Cyrus imagines that Dinah's timely return would not mean a return to the Dungle she left, which was a constant reminder of his inability to provide for her and protect her, but rather a return in time to experience the fulfillment of his radical hope. But the language at the end of the novel suggests that return *to the Dungle*, not Cyrus, is imperative—"she had to get back"—and as well that her return offers some fulfillment—"she had to taste the filth again" even if it is presented in unsavory terms. This is the ubiquitous filth in chapter 2, where she first perceived the Dungle as an inescapable power. Edouard Glissant's discussion of reversion in *Caribbean Discourse* is helpful here. Glissant argues, "we must return to the point from which we started. Diversion is not a useful ploy unless it is nourished by reversion: not a return to the longing for origins, to some immutable state of Being, but a return to the point of entanglement" (Glissant, 1999, 26).

Here Glissant suggests that excursions to "elsewheres" become meaningful only where they cause us to confront or become alert to the need to confront what we had run away from in the first place. The "point of entanglement" is the point where the self and self-understanding are birthed, since it constitutes a reckoning with the whole life, the untidy, the unsavory, the ambiguous, the contradictory, and even the transformative possibility that was previously undiscerned because one was always in a state of (panicked) flight or somnolence. Until this "return to the native land" (Césaire, 1969) of the self, its places and origins, the moment of self-realization is delayed. In Haitian Voudun cosmogony, the trickster stands at the crossroads with the riddle of life, and the riddle is answered, wrongly or correctly, by the road one takes at the crossing.

A return to and close analysis of Dinah's departure from the Dungle is useful in conversation with Glissant as I close. Dinah's flight box contains "two dresses, one panty, a pair of pedal pushers, indispensable to her profession, a bra, a pair of rubber slippers" (Patterson, 1986, 20). Her belongings can be read as a physical archive of her life up until she leaves Cyrus and the Dungle. She was poor, for sure, and she was a woman of industry. Her decision to move to Jones Town with her pedal pushers suggests that this might not change or that she sees her move to Jones Town as part of her industry—her fulfillment of Man Man's investment/belief in ambition. But the archive of Dinah's life is not just material. Her recall of her six years in the Dungle with Cyrus, and her memory of old Rachael's stories, combine to extend the physical archive to a set of experiences of deep psychic and emotional weight. On the one hand, Dinah attempts to be fully liberated from the Dungle, and on the other hand Dinah sees her Dungle identity as specially equipping her with a radical and unfettered liberty. The Dungle in effect is transformed into midden, that is, an archeological mound where the fowl foot has dug up Dinah's luck, her discovered sense of self and its enabling genealogies.

The best evidence of this is her wonderment about the servitude of Ruby, Mrs. Watkins's maid who has served the Watkinses for three generations and whose ethereal invisibility is shocking to Dinah. In Ruby, she sees some of the self-effacement of the young, just-come-from-country nanny who walks her little brown charge with no concern for anyone else, not even herself. Dinah is completely out of place in this world, and she is so because she perceives herself as a whole radical person, influenced by the Dungle and perceived or known because of her past, her living archive there. In the Dungle, she is liberated to be her own self. There she need not lower her voice, nor prove herself; in the Dungle she need not be washed and transformed. "The Dungle is a obeah man" might in this moment be read as a wry and accepting but also welcoming acceptance of the "veillance," the pull from the inside, that has called her back to this moment of recognition. The Dungle in this moment is akin to a seeing, reading eye and an inexorable power that one does not easily escape because in the end it is a principle of spirit or "dark matter." There is no evidence that Dinah's return to the Dungle has anything triumphal about it. In fact, the brutal context in which revelation comes to her (she is being beaten almost to death) invokes more of the sense of a descent into an abyss, with all the abyss's contradictory, frightening, and enabling asymmetries.

Patterson's look at the Dungle—the lowest point of the emerging nation, the dump outside the city—is of critical importance. The literature of cultural nationalism had in the main valorized the folk and given a place to the urban poor. Scholars, if they looked at the Dungle at all, tended to present it as tragedy. By choosing the Dungle and inhabiting it with prostitutes and 1960s (not yet accepted) Rastafari, Patterson takes us to the surveilled-excluded edges of the city and the nation. Like Miss Mollypolls, the light brown woman from uptown in *Sisyphus* who in essence exclaims, "Look, a Rasta!" we are made to see the Dungle.[19]

The Dungle doesn't appear again in Jamaican fiction until two decades later in Michelle Cliff's *No Telephone to Heaven* (1987). Cliff's 1970s Dungle breeds the bare life of Christopher, who is (kept) destitute and desperate. If within the city the Dungle is feared from a distance in Patterson's novel, Cliff's novel in stark contrast allows the Dungle to traverse the boundaries of the city and comes intimately close to the main. The imagined nightmare of the Dungle becomes a reality for Paul H and his family in their own bloody beds all the way uptown in Stony Hill. Christopher's slaughter of his wealthy employers is driven by his sense of a spiritual calling to right the wrongs of his immiserated past. As in Patterson's novel, though in a different way, Cliff's Dungle character is closely linked to the veillance of the spirit. At the moment that he lifts his machete to strike, "A force passed through him. He had no past. He had no future. He was phosphorus. Light-bearing. He was light igniting around him. The source of all danger. He was the carrier of fire. He was the black light that rises from bone ash" (Cliff, 1996, 47). Here as Christopher enters into the sense of his name, spiritveillance becomes an apocalyptic force. Cliff asks us to look at the Dungle at another critical moment in Jamaica's history: the 1970s attempt to remake the nation as a Black socialist democracy.

Twenty years after Cliff, journalist and writer Diana McCaulay published an environmental protest essay (2018) in which she addresses the environmental threat posed by the literal present-day dungle, the famed Riverton City, which is Kingston's main official garbage dump. Statements on Riverton City, and indeed images of the poor and destitute foraging in the dump, are common in Jamaican media and public discourse. Even so, most Kingstonians don't think about the dump until it burns out of control or they make the sobering connection that the dump is also a community where people live. McCaulay plaits these strands (dump and community) together to tell the story of how zoning produced Jamaica's twenty-first-century dungle. In the language of urban planning and design, zoning is familiar-speak. In my studies of West Kingston, slum clearance was often carried out to make slum lands into industrial zones. And many West Kingston neighborhoods shared space with commercial and industrial zones, making them less and less appealing as places to live. McCaulay takes note of the fact that the fumes of the dump migrate beyond the dumpsite into these nearby lower and lower middle-class parts of the city: "Seaview Gardens, Riverton City, Riverton Meadows, Callaloo Mews, Duhaney Park, Cooreville Gardens, New Haven/Riverside Gardens remain within the sacrifice zone" (McCaulay, 2018). This phrase, "the sacrifice zone" which reprises the essay's title, is particularly laden. The title flags McCaulay's focus on the people of these neighborhoods, especially little children, who live in the toxic fumes from the proliferating dump. "Sacrifice Zone" in obvious but sobering ways speaks to the long genealogy of "civilization" by exclusion carefully surveilled: in ancient religions, the practice of human sacrifice in the interests of the clan's survival; in the modern moment, the secular authorities of race and/or the imagined nation. Patterson has been the first to remind us in fiction of the ways exclusion, surveillance, and the unyielding watchfulness/resistance of the spirit pose the riddle of nation-making in Caribbean spaces.

3

Smile Jamaica, for the Camera

• •

Performance and Surveillance in 1970s Jamaica

"Dreadlocks can't smoke him pipe in peace / Too much informers and too much beast" (Miller, 1975). The distinctive style of Jacob Miller's music and these words in his hit song, "Tenement Yard," have had some resonance in the critique of the state's surveillance of Rastafari in Jamaica. In particular, the use of ganja/herb as a sacrament that works to enhance meditation, what Miller calls "penetration" in the song, is in question here: "Caan penetrate inna tenement yard." Meditation and penetration are especially crucial to the creative process, and thus the interruption of the dread's peaceful pipe smoking is the interruption of the creative process. It is also potentially the interruption of the work of overcoming. Pipe smoking is interrupted, the dreadlock's peace is disturbed, and all in the space of the yard which is a semiprivate and semipublic space for the dreadlocks, but never a safe space. Who is doing the interrupting is significant too: informers and beasts, the song says. Informers are often neighbors turned spies and those close enough to smell the smoke of the ganja pipe and then to waft the smell beyond the yard (suss), that is, to inform the authorities. *Beast* was a colloquial term for the police, who because of their partisan nature in the 1970s were feared as much as the gunmen. Miller's song, which was first released in 1975, became an instant hit in the roiling political climate of 1970s Jamaica. Miller's lyrics

FIGURE 3. Smile Jamaica Poster: Poster Advertising the Smile Jamaica Concert. *The Gleaner*, December 1976. © The Gleaner Company (Media) Ltd.

resonate perhaps even beyond the experience of Rastafari. If Jamaica is the tenement yard and the dreadlocks refer more generally to Jamaicans who, like Rastafari, upset the status quo, the informers and the beast can also be extrapolated outward. "Informers," with the cultural suggestion of an insider who snitches, can be read as Jamaicans ideologically opposed to radical political trends in the country. "Beasts," on the other hand, usually refers to an oppressing outsider, whether local, governmental, or international, and so in the context of this chapter can be interpreted as international surveillance agencies with stakes in

Jamaica duly anxious about ideological shifts in the ruling party. Whichever way we read the tenement yard, as a literal tenement or figuratively as the nation, the song suggests that surveillance is ontologically and socially disruptive; it is as an attack on agency and the right to free citizenship.

Miller's song, like much of the music of the 1970s, is political in that it bemoans the hypersurveillance of Rastafari by the powers that were, and the general abuse and surveillance of poor Black citizens. This anti-Black, anti-Rastafari surveillance occurred even in and precisely because of the push to establish Jamaica as a Black nation,[1] and the song intimates what many in Jamaica believed to be true at that time, that there were bigger, more ferocious beasts than the local police, in the form of international intelligence agencies. There were three kinds of responses to the charge that the Central Intelligence Agency (CIA) had been sent into Jamaica to upset the direction of Michael Manley's "democratic socialism." The first and most common was silence. During the period in question there is little or no mention of the CIA in any of the major, mainstream daily papers. The conservative *Jamaica Gleaner* and *The Star*, its affiliated tabloid, are both deafeningly quiet. The second was the substantial work being done internationally to uncover the activities of the CIA in destabilizing countries considered unfriendly to the United States. Former agent Philip Agee published his book *Inside the Company* in 1975 and did a book tour, of sorts, in hotbed places like Jamaica. As well, left-wing publications report on the situation in Jamaica. In 1976, Socialist International circulated a fifteen-page booklet of essays titled *Jamaica Destabilised: British Guiana Repeated?* which presents a close analysis of the CIA's covert work in Jamaica (*C.I.A. Briefing*, 1976). The booklet was published by the Agee-Hosenball Defence Committee, a British-based committee that was formed to deter Labour Home Secretary Merlyn Rees from deporting Philip Agee and Mark Hosenball to the United States. At the time, both the British Labour Party and Jamaica's ruling People's National Party (PNP) were members of Socialist International. The booklet includes an article by Andrew Pollack, "Under Heavy Manners," one by Ellen Ray called "CIA and Local Gunmen Plan Jamaican Coup," and "Media Operation in Jamaica." Locally, there was significant tenement rumination on U.S. interference in Jamaica's political affairs. Michael Manley's book, *Jamaica: Struggle in the Periphery* (1982), is an example of a local response.

Third was the response from the political right. Most notable is a report given by Edward Seaga, then leader of the Jamaica Labour Party (JLP), right before he was elected as prime minister, at a conference sponsored by the Center for Hemispheric Affairs of the American Enterprise Institute. In his talk, Seaga charged that Cuban agents had infiltrated Jamaica. "To use Jamaica as a particular example, Cubans are involved in training our security forces both in Jamaica and in Cuba. Indeed, it was only in June of this year that we uncovered the involvement of Cuban D.G.I. agents in the training of the Jamaican Special Branch, which is the intelligence unit of the police force" (Seaga, 1980, 140). Seaga goes on to say, "It is true by the way, although not necessarily in the mainstream of what I want to say, that Russian K.G.B. agents are also involved in the training of Jamaican Special Forces and, in particular, the Special Branch Unit" (Seaga, 1980, 141). Seaga's claim here sidesteps the left-leaning claims that the CIA was interfering and disrupting life in Jamaica and suggests instead that the Russians and KGB had sway in Jamaica, especially in the training of Jamaican intelligence. This turning on its head of the claim of American surveillance not by direct refutation but by seeding another narrative into the space—that is, pointing a finger at the ideological enemy of the West—was not only evidence of the complexity of the time, but an indication also of the high stakes around "intelligence." For some, the CIA was the only possible culprit, given the evidence produced by the left.

Bob Marley confronted the reality of such surveillance in the watershed "Smile Jamaica" concert of 1976. The concert is the main textual focus of this chapter. Smile Jamaica is known to be the first of Bob Marley's late 1970s concerts in Jamaica. The better known "One Love Peace Concert" followed in 1978, and in the context of a discussion on political surveillance, it is significant that that concert was organized by Claudie Massop and Bucky Marshall, the leading bad men (precursors of the garrison dons) of the two opposing political parties, the Jamaica Labor Party and the People's National Party.[2] There was very little to smile about and almost no peace in Jamaica in 1976 and 1978, and certainly not much of either in the rest of the decade that is the focus of this chapter. My research is based in part on written accounts of the concert in biographies and memoirs about Bob Marley, mainly in the sections that recount the attempt on his life. In addition, I have interviewed people who were close to Marley or who were at the concert; these oral accounts, along with newspaper articles, work to fill in all the many sounds and voices around the concert. The chapter also considers footage from the 1976 concert and Marlon James's 2014 novel *A Brief History of Seven Killings*, his fictional representation of the attempt on Marley's life in the days before the concert.

In the two chapters preceding this one, I have discussed culturally inflected elements of surveillance in Jamaican literature. The Smile Jamaica concert allows me to bring another lens to the examination of this issue, first, because of the particular dynamics associated with performance of this kind, and second, because relationships around the concert allow for a close-up look at the involvement of government and geopolitical relations in surveillances of the postcolonial state. The "suss" of CIA involvement was not the only linkage with concerns about high-level surveillance. The concert, because of its proximity to the general elections of 1976 and Bob Marley's seeming association with Michael Manley and his democratic socialist politics, became a deeply watched political moment within Jamaica itself. Further, the concert proved the singular power of reggae music in the making of a significant national moment, and in this sense could be said to reveal and harness the "threat" of the music as a people force that could destabilize or build a political agenda. Smile Jamaica, as Marley had hoped, gathered thousands of Jamaicans to the National Heroes Park, formerly known as Racecourse. The assembly, just two days after Marley and his company were attacked by gunmen, was a powerful statement against interfering outside forces and fearmongering. A second crucial factor was that the concert, as well as the drama attending its staging, confirmed for many the public secret that U.S. surveilling agencies were on the island and actively intervening in Jamaica's political story.

Yet a third factor was that the concert was being staged during a government-imposed state of emergency in a declared attempt to address politically motivated crime. On Saturday, June 19, 1976, Governor General Sir Florizel Glasspole, acting on the advice of the government, declared a state of public emergency for a period of one month. The period was extended three times and then terminated by proclamation on June 6, 1977. According to Ministry Paper No. 22, "an important aspect of the State of Emergency was that it gave to the Security Forces powers in excess of those available through the Suppression of Crime (special provisions) Act" (Ministry of National Security, 1977). In essence the Act gave the security forces extended powers of surveillance and significantly reduced the freedom of movement and agency of citizens. The overwhelming attendance at the concert, then, could be read, at least in part, as resistance to the lockdown/surveillance dynamic, even if the officials in charge of the curfew were themselves present and even though the government was seen by some as the movers behind the concert. In this context it is worth emphasizing that under surveillance regimes, some are less equal than others: while the curfew impacted everyone, it was targeted mainly at persons from the kinds of communities that Marley wanted to share in the concert, communities similar to the one where he himself had been brought up. And while many uptowners were present, the fact that huge numbers were also from the common people serves to underscore this dynamic of resistance and the people's sense that Marley "belonged" to them and that his involvement in the concert could be trusted.

The impetus to align Marley with a more than partisan affiliation is also apparent in the major attention that has been given to the iconic photo of the later One Love Peace Concert, of Marley joining the hands of Prime Minister Michael Manley and the opposition leader, Edward Seaga. The dreadlocked superstar and "One Love" ambassador stands in the middle, signifying his role as peace broker, in direct opposition to any idea of him as a supporter or either left or right. The One Love Peace Concert was an attempt to curate the power and magic of Smile Jamaica two years before, highlighting the ways it transcended partisan politics and the perceived necessity to surveil Marley's choices as an artist.

I come closest to analyzing surveillance in its traditional sense in this chapter. By this I mean the kind of watching that reinscribes traditional power relationships: surveillance that is disciplining. Smile Jamaica serves as a crucial entryway into considering the politically and socially fraught 1970s Jamaica. More and more, there are texts that consider the period with great depth and range from several perspectives.[3] For the purpose of this discussion, I am most concerned with how state and international surveillance had an impact on the decade and, in this context, with the close and dialogic relationship between surveillance and performance. Performance here refers at one level to the literal event that took place when Bob Marley occupied the stage at Heroes Circle on December 6, 1976. As the chapter reveals, however, the experience of the concert was not confined to that evening of December 6; it was a protracted drama touched by the embroiled politics of the decade and in particular the critical impact of gun violence in that politics. Further, the drama began to be enacted from the moment the performance was announced, and reverberates long after it ended, in the form of large sprawls of narrative speculations that circulate and become more important in our understanding of the concert than the concert itself.

So, first, I am concerned not only with the visible moment of performance but also with the ways social and political contexts affected the concert and its reception. Second, I am concerned with how narrative contexts were active within that performance, in the same way that the backdrop of a stage might be crucial to the act and the audience's reception. James's blockbuster novel with its choric cast of seventy-plus voices, each narrativizing from a different perspective the attempt on Marley's life that preceded the concert, performs a meta-discursive turn in ways that are helpful in theorizing this latter aspect. Taken together, the various strands of the chapter's argument elucidate a complex network of acts, performances, and narrative that attenuates the hegemonic powers of state and neocolonial surveillance.

James's approach to the telling of his Bob Marley story resonates with my methodology in doing the research for this chapter: sifting through the many different firsthand perspectives on the concert and navigating existing versions of the same story has meant that my concern is not with the pursuit of "objective fact," but rather with the ways factors such as vantage point and vested interest create the substantive narrative through which a historical event is ultimately perceived. Some facts about the concert are so different that they are in conflict. Many facts are personal to eyewitnesses and observers, especially now that they have been filtered by the passing of time. Many facts, because they are personal, were in this very loaded 1970s moment politically informed. Suss is a useful framework here, as it captures the importance of culturally inflected (sur)veillance to the work of U.S.-based organizations primarily dependent on "intelligence gathering" in support of a U.S. doctrine committed to American-style regional stability. In conversations with eyewitnesses, I often encountered generative stories, little forests of rumor in the concrete jungles of Kingston, that grew other stories and questions, and because of this I came to see in

90 • Inside Tenement Time

published accounts a similar trend. Indeed, the surveillance by the CIA and the local police relied heavily on tips found in hearsay and the interpretation of how things appeared. There are, then, multiple strains or types of material that exist about the concert: the written, official, mainstream, oral accounts, and the video footage.

These multiple strands and types of material highlight the dialogic and contestatory nature of performance, with its multiple speaking voices/I/eye-narratives, as well as the extent to which in the volatile political milieu of 1970s Jamaica a nation entering into remaking its independence compromised and challenged the efficacy of surveillance technologies. I want to distinguish this operation of narrative from the operation of suss that I dealt with in chapter 1. My concern is not with how gossip and rumor as culturally inflected resources create alternative stories that challenge the status quo, but with how the actual experience of all involved, and the psychic powers of their individual vantage points, come together in rhizomatic narrative networks within which the surveillance monologue forms only one of many competing strands. Further, my analysis of the actual concert allows me to think through the ways in which the formal stage as a convention mutates in the Caribbean context, and the ways such mutations amplify codes of resistance. And this is crucial: that performance and narrative, each in and of itself always a multiple field of signification and "play" (in the Derridean sense) do not only undermine monoglossia; they also undermine the possibility of a history of surveillance that allows it panoptical power. As I have argued, this is particularly the case in the Caribbean, where performative modes such as Carnival, dance, and other vernacular arts are historically linked to resistance and where suss is an uncontainable strategy of making and influencing meaning.

"Smile Jamaica": The Song and the Concert

Bob Marley's song "Smile Jamaica" was never included on an original LP, though it was added to the album *Kaya* when it was rereleased in 2001. It is likely Marley's encouraging Jamaica to smile (in the 1970s) did not fit the roots-rebel, lover-boy persona that record company executives chose for his albums. Considering the context of Jamaica at the time, smiles would have been difficult to come by. In fact, the song acknowledges the call to smile as part of the plight of being on an island in the sun where the idea of the place and its people does not necessarily match the reality they live in. The verses of the song shift between stereotypical notions of Jamaicans having soulful fun in the sun, being called on to smile, and the assertion, "we're gonna help our people / help them right; / oh lord, help us tonight / Cast out that evil spell / throw some water in the well / and smile" (Bob Marley and The Wailers, 1976). Here there are other implied meanings: smile as a way to persevere through trouble, smile as resistance because evil has been cast out and there is a fresh installment of hope in the well. Most important is that the smile is not for the tourist's gaze; the song is for a Jamaican audience, especially with the pressure of the CIA watching.[4]

The Marley song and a now quite popular song with the same title by preeminent reggae crooner, DJ, and star Chronixx suggest that in the 1970s and in the second decade of the twenty-first century, some reggae artists have understood their art as intimately tied with their relationship to their home country, Jamaica. Chronixx's version of "Smile Jamaica," a lyrically more advanced song than Marley's, is a love song for Jamaica. In his song, Jamaica is personified as a beautiful girl who is treated poorly even though she does not deserve it. "Oh I met a girl this morning / she was love at first sight." Like Marley's, Chronixx's Jamaica is a tropical beauty with all the qualities that outsiders often see and are drawn to. Jamaica's beauty and talent are the subjects of potentially dangerous attention and watching. The subsequent verses of the song expose that attention in historical and present terms: "She has a rich history / A beautiful woman with the sweetest gifts / Beautiful sunrise and an evening kiss / I find a nice sunset on the evenin' seas / But she told me that she's tired / Tired of exploit and liars / She gave them reggae, beaches, flowers and ferns / All she got was abuse in return" (Chronixx, 2013b). The chorus, like Marley's, offers comfort ("smile for me Jamaica, don't cry," etc.) and a commitment to his love for Jamaica ("don't you cry, here am I"), suggesting a riff on another Marley love song, "No Woman No Cry." Chronixx's contemporary version of "Smile Jamaica" is certainly one way to come to terms with what Marley meant when he, according to his manager, Don Taylor, wanted through the Smile Jamaica concert to give some ease to the "screw face" and a reason for the people of Jamaica to feel hopeful.[5] Chronixx's 2013 song is written in and for a Jamaica that is not so different from Jamaica in 1976. Certainly, the trajectory many would have imagined for Jamaica in the 1970s—that is, a continued entanglement with political and social violence—is realized in contemporary Jamaica, except for one thing: in the 1970s there was a more heightened understanding that people were being watched, not only by neighbors and those inclined to be inquisitive, but very keenly by the state and the eagle-eyed Big Brother from the north.

First, it is significant that over 40,000 (by one estimate, 80,000)[6] people decided to assemble at the mouth of downtown Kingston four-plus months into a curfew and at the height of the political turmoil, bearing in mind that it would seem the curfew was not lifted. This gathering of huge numbers can be read in multiple ways: for example, as the expression of relief from the mind- and body-numbing containment imposed by the curfew; certainly as the occasion for suss (the opportunity to tell, invent, or extrapolate stories of what happened and why or to claim knowledge of the real and hidden powers in attendance). I want to suggest that in the collective will of the people to gather in unprecedented numbers a stone's throw from the angulated maze of working-class downtown's streets—King Street, Gold Street, Matthew's Lane—is the spirit of resistance.

Other aspects of the concert's geographies are important. National Heroes Circle is located not only at the mouth of downtown but also at the lower end of Cross Roads, an area sandwiched between uptown and downtown and therefore constituting a kind of intermediate space between class zones. The Circle, then recently named, encloses National Heroes Park, then also recently renamed from its original moniker of (King) George VI Memorial Park.[7]

The prime minister and the commissioner of police were both at the concert, so this is clearly not a case of law-breaking. Rather, the concert's master of ceremonies, Elaine Wint-Leslie's comment that the massive crowd was an indication of "people standing up in rebellion against what was happening" in Jamaica at the time (Elaine Wint-Leslie, in discussion with the author, August 2018), made manifest in the attempt on Marley's life, resonates here. The crowds in treetops, on top of car bonnets, spilling over in forbidden spaces across containment ropes, the sea of spectators spread out as far as the eye could see, became, visually, a single massed (mainly Black) body insurrecting against the mandated controls of the curfew, but also indicative of a refusal to be intimidated by whichever surveillant had organized the shooting, whether the suspected CIA or other (insider or "beast") interests that might have objected to Marley's association with the PNP or his espousal of "let us unite" values for the political parties. Of course, we may also reflect on what it means in the toppling of containment that some of the enforcers of containment and surveillance were themselves on stage or had joined the crowd in spectating.

Equally important, as Wint-Leslie's comment points out, was the fact that on stage Marley could barely move, as over two hundred members of the audience crowded around him on the stage from the beginning to the end of the concert. The two hundred people were those willing, should the gunmen return, to use their bodies as a distraction from him. They stood with him so that they could shield his body while his lyrics went free. Two hundred people would have had the assurance and perhaps the insurance that so many bodies made it difficult, if not impossible, to focus on any single one. Not only might we consider how the bodies on stage both became a single body, metonymic of the larger crowd, but also how they *diffracted* the stage lights away from Marley and onto themselves, a tightly knit communal grid, performing the national spirit of resistance. In my interview with her, Wint-Leslie said that many attending the concert were "committed to the sense of independence" that so many Jamaicans felt slipping away, so that the crowd and stage could be read as a community response to excessive surveillance and in-security. As an attempt to take back fun, open space, and nighttime vibes in Kingston on the eve of what would be a bloody election, this act was also clearly resistant. And, with reference to the unique Caribbean investment in performance as a way of stretching identity (self-aggrandizement, self-making), many onstage were people wanting to share in the spectacle of the moment, to be caught on camera as resisters. We are reminded of Carnival, in which "spectators" become performers as they join in the road march bridging the gap between those on the stage and those on the street.

The Smile Jamaica concert furthermore allows a consideration of the nexus of surveillance and performance in spatial terms. The politics of the concert were first worked out with the move of venue from Jamaica House lawns to Heroes Circle. This was done to allow both more spectators and a broader swath of ordinary citizens to attend, and to obviate the impression that the concert was tied to the government or a political party. For Marley, the people's reception of the concert as an act for Jamaica and Jamaicans was paramount. This move immediately became another kind of dangerous signal that could energize the CIA's attentions in a different way: surveilling a crowd at the headquarters of the government that was perceived as a threat to U.S.-style democracy is a different ball game from surveilling an amorphous, unruly, and unpredictable crowd in a space that many perceived as "belonging" to them.[8] In the case of the Jamaican government, finding the resources to oversee and control such a massive crowd would have been a challenge. And then, of course, the concert itself moved Kingstonians through spaces that had been cordoned off by politics.

First, then, the concert as a staged national event endorsed by the government and conducted in a space far more open than Jamaica House (audience members in trees, on rooftops, and spilling out into the streets) posed a problem for the government to effectively conduct the surveillance required by a state of emergency. Second, for the CIA, there was the riddle of how to read the dynamics of the location, given the multiple fields of (culturally and politically marked) signification at work in a reggae concert performed in Heroes Circle. How, for example, to disaggregate strands of motivation in a way that would make legible to the outside surveiller's eye the extent to which presence and participation signaled allegiance to the government or resistance to the government? How to read the mood of the country in a context where the audience inevitably moved beyond watching and hearing to the active participation of bodies in dance and sing-along, often in an exalted state, and in a space where such huge swaths of the populace were congregated? It seems to me that nothing short of spiritveillance would have helped the CIA in this case. And if CIA operatives were present moving through the crowd, how might the transmission of kinetic energies, as well as the need to disguise as other in order not to be outed, have affected the project of surveillance? Considering this question, it is fascinating that it was reported that one of the videographers who filmed the concert was the son of a CIA operative.[9]

Marley's agreement to do Smile Jamaica causes his own space to change—a U.S. intruder, "a white bwai," according to Marley (Salewicz, 2014, 297), walks into his yard, delivers a warning that is perceived to be from either the U.S. embassy or the CIA, and the Echo Squad, a special police contingent, takes over his gate, whether as a constant and unremitting eye trained on his movements to ascertain where his allegiances lie, or as protectors to guard him against similar or more sinister invasions. And yet, on the day when Marley was shot by unknown intruders at his own home, the Echo Squad was missing in action. Perhaps more interesting than the actual facts of who or why, which we do not so far know, is the swirl of Jamaican speculation as to the possible perpetrators and their relation to other watchers. In other words, the received narratives surrounding the facts, whether these facts are hidden or overt, to a large extent determine the hold—or lack thereof—that the mechanisms of control have on the populace.

I want to think as well about the cultural-political implications of the two hundred bodies on the stage within a larger Caribbean context. Theorizing performance in the Caribbean has tended to center on traditional performance expression including masquerade, Carnival, Jonkunnu, and various forms of dance. All these expressions in some way represent the impact of surveillance on everyday life, where acts of cultural resonance and enjoyment under pressure needed to bifurcate and rely on double entendre to continue to be allowed to be in civil society. Songs of resistance disguised in beautiful melodies, body memory of defiance, and insurrection choreographed into entertaining dance are examples.[10] At the root of any yoking of this tradition and the formal stage is the question of whether the two ideas of staging and insurrection can coexist—that is, to what extent and in what ways is it possible to "stage insurrection" on the formal stage? This question arises only in light of the contexts of the formal stage, by which it is already automatically co-opted into official conventions that may limit such stagings.

Of course, when I use the word staging here to talk about these traditional performances, I am referring to the moving stage of street performance, which as a space for group performances in service to a local community has gradually disappeared from the contemporary scene in some Caribbean countries. I do wish to note that this change is partly due to the pressure or threat of surveillance from the respectable classes or the state under pressure from external powers. Harnessing vernacular theater onto a formal stage and making it work in a different way had to do both with surveillance to keep ordinary people under control and with making money for the government (in the case of Carnival, for example), but also for the economic elite or power brokers. While the perceived need to use the formal stage as a surveillance mechanism may be attenuated at different points in the nation's history, the economic imperative has remained powerful and constant. Certainly, though, in the politically mistrustful moment of the Smile Jamaica concert, it was the surveillance pressure, not the economic, that was uppermost in the minds of many. In our present post-1990s moment, the formal stage as a surveillance access medium has been superseded by yet another interpolative technology: the ubiquitous cell phone, which allows state authorities, neighbors, and even virtual strangers deep interior access to the most private communications and acts and provides evidence in cases where crimes against certain (unheard and silenced) communities and individuals would previously never have been recorded or taken seriously, and justice never won.

Mann, Nolan, and Wellman discuss wearable technology as personal empowerment, and they see this kind of sousveillance as akin "to holding a mirror up to society, or the social environment" by allowing "a transformation of surveillance techniques into sousveillance techniques in order to watch the watchers" (Mann, Nolan, and Wellman, 2002, 336–337).

Regardless of whether the performance was the uncorralled street theater or the formalized stage, Caribbean performance as we know it is generally at some level produced for, or understood to be open to, surveilling eyes; thus the stage or any notion of formalized performance represents an interpretive intervention not necessarily in harmony with the expression or the "visible" performance. For instance, commentaries on and criticism of the white planter class were bound up in many traditional costumes of pre- and post-emancipation Trinidad. In its original presentation or manifestation, the element of ingenuity in mimicry and critique was part of the masquerade's power. While we know that the surveilling eyes and laws of the planter class stopped the drums and purged the rebellion out of the costumes, not so much is made of the impact of preserving masquerade by putting it on the formal stage. "Putting performance on stage," or the middle-classification of traditional folk performance, created opportunities for citizens anxious about respectability politics to enjoy these expressions without being constrained by social surveilling pressures. The stage changed the relationship between performer and audience.[11] With the mediation of the stage there is no way to preserve the full range of natural, unscripted interactions between audience and performer. Not only do audiences constrained by social surveilling pressures clean up in deference to those same pressures, but access is limited to those who can afford to pay.

The stage puts space between performer and audience and may in fact inscribe or maintain critique, a distancing space of judgment, that is opposed to the insider-participant ethos of the local community carnival. There is a way in which the audience's positionality shifts toward, though it does not necessarily become synonymous with, that of a surveiller. Yet again, all of this is mediated by the kinds of pre- and extra-performance relationships audiences may have with the actors: in the case of the Smile Jamaica concert, it was very clear (and James makes this a major part of his text) that there were surveillers in the audience, but also that for the majority of those attending, drawn widely from the populace, there was some sense of affinity and shared identity both in terms of their felt connection to the country and in terms of their sense of Marley as "one a we"—a son of the Kingston yards who had made good representing their own experience in music and song. This is crucial in thinking about the fact that the two hundred people who went on the stage with Marley breached that distance between performer and spectator in unprecedented ways. This was different from the typical Caribbean way of shouting back to the actors at certain moments, inserting their own dialogue in the script (this often resulted in actors inserting the audience's intervention in the next night's performance).

Whether the crowd that went on stage was primed by Marley to do this before as part of the act, or this was a spontaneous decision, or something a particular group planned on their own, the point is that the defiance against surveillers, attackers, and all other invaders was performed in plain sight by this breach of the conventions of the formal stage. In a real sense, the performers moved away from the tradition of masquerade or hiding. Arguably, Marley's performance was impacted by the power of that breach: while he had less space to perform his characteristic moves, he seemed to my view to have shifted into an almost exalted space, perhaps a channeling inward of energies that could not be physically expressed. In a very real sense, the performance had the feel of a "chanting down Babylon."[12] The sustained hum of voices in the background was also remarkable in the footage—this is not something usually picked up, or if picked up, left unedited. It does work (serendipitously) to emphasize the crowd's support for Marley and their pushback against the controls.

In that context, lyrics such as those from the song "So Jah Seh," a pronouncement of the immutability of God, must have taken on deeper, more present meaning to Marley and the situation in Jamaica. The song, which functions as a kind of benediction at the end of his performance, is a protracted meditation in which Marley seems to grapple with the attack on his life, using Rasta metaphysics to suggest that his life had been saved by the intervention of powers beyond flesh and blood. From the concert footage, it is clear that the words of this song move Marley to a place where he finds intimacy with the closely pressed audience. Over and over he repeats the words "So Jah Seh,"[13] sometimes with the I-threes responding "I an I, gonna hang on in there, I an I, I nah let go," sometimes with Marley singing this response, or alternatively the words "puss and dog they get together, what's wrong with loving one another?" as pleas, exhortations to the crowd, to the country. At the end of the long song where Marley falls into a deep meditative reverie (what Jacob Miller might call "initating in the tenement yard"), evidenced by his closed eyes and swaying body. He emerges from that meditative space on stage as he stops singing and passes the microphone to someone else on the stage. The moment may be read as a small ceremony to mark the change of focus that he is about to enact; thereafter, Marley removes his shirt to expose where the bullet grazed his chest and lodged in his arm. This action, along with Rita Marley's performing at the concert dressed in a hospital gown attains a deliberate spectacularity: it put their hurts on display for those who wanted to see, and served as testimony that they, with Jah's approval (so Jah seh), would carry on in their work against the powers of Babylon. Bob and Rita's open and embodied performances signify as evidence that the surveilled and attacked bodies of the nation would also testify and stand against these powers. By performing the concert, the Marleys chose not to hide from the attackers, but rather to present an open display of the body as both accusation and transcendence. The moment shifts from the political plane to the spiritual.

Reading the Backdrop

If the exposed bodies of the Marleys, together with those two hundred bodies on the refracting stage, serve to attenuate the hegemony of surveilling machineries, the narratives that form the backdrop and afterlives of the performance further inscribe this break. That is to say, the multiple, contradictory perspectives on all the key aspects of the concert destabilize any notion of a single, undisputed (factual) narrative about the concert and its lead-up or its implications. In this section, I entwine perspectives from very different narrative groups writing and speaking about the concert and its contexts. The narrative threads from memoirists, biographers, and historians include Timothy White's *Catch a Fire* (1983), Chris Salewicz's *Bob Marley: The Untold Story* (2009), and Anita Waters's *Race, Class, and Political Symbols: Rastafari and Reggae in Jamaican Politics* (1985). In conversation with these narratives written by journalists and researchers are the books written by family and close associates of Marley who were often eyewitnesses (or close enough) to key moments in their and Marley's life. Don Taylor, Marley's manager from 1975 until Marley's death, wrote *Marley and Me: The Real Bob Marley Story* (1995), and Rita Marley, Marley's wife, penned *No Woman No Cry: My Life with Bob Marley* (2005). I spoke with Marley's road manager and friend, the footballer Alan Skill Cole, with Colin Leslie, who managed Marley's Tuff Gong group of companies, and with Elaine Wint-Leslie, media personality who was called on to be master of ceremonies at Smile Jamaica. Arnold Bertram was minister of culture and state from 1974 to 1976. Bertram is the only politician I interviewed. I also read Marlon James's novel *A Brief History of Seven Killings*, which helps us imagine the many different dramas unfolding concurrently with Marley's performance at Smile Jamaica. I focus specifically on one fictional thread in the novel: the story of Bam Bam, a young man recruited to kill Marley, who, when he fails and is on the run, watches the concert from a bench in National Heroes Park, the former Racecourse.

The provenance of the concert is recalled differently in four of the main works on Marley's life. Taylor suggests that the idea of the concert came from Marley himself, who wanted to treat the politics-torn Jamaican people after several months of the state of emergency, and several years into the churning belly of the turbulent 1970s. As emphasized in the context that Taylor provides, violence was rife in Trench Town and Jones Town, and the nation was still traumatized by the Orange Street fire of May 1976, where political thugs kept adults and children inside a burning building and held firemen hostage in the fire station to prevent rescue. These are just two examples of the social and political decline of a nation already in economic meltdown, but they are enough to explain why a socially conscious artist such as Marley would have felt driven to offer some kind of intervention. Don Taylor suggests that the actual advertising of the concert and the initial venue for the concert were a clear indication that Manley and/or the PNP had gone back on their word and were attempting to manipulate the concert for political ends. White and Salewicz tell a different story. In their versions, Prime Minister Manley approached Marley with the idea of a free concert for the people and Marley readily agreed based on the assurance that it would not be politically construed. So while Taylor argues that the concert was eventually politicized by PNP bullying and manipulation and against Marley's will, White and Salewicz's version suggests that the event was in its genesis political, solidly in the hands of the PNP and certainly the higher levels of the party.

These two opposing versions of the concert continue to be firmly held, though not necessarily on political lines. Despite their differences, both accounts suggest that various interests, including not least the PNP echelons and government, had a vested interest in overseeing or surveilling the concert for potential political fallout as well as to identify specific lines of political currency that might unfold. In interviews conducted in August 2018 in and around Kingston, the question of the provenance of Smile Jamaica elicited equally different and passionate responses, depending on the relationship with Marley and Manley, respectively. Leslie and Cole's stories corroborate Taylor's. For both, it was common knowledge in the Marley camp that Bob, like everyone else, was concerned with the preponderance of trouble in Jamaica. Cole noted that on tour in 1975 across Europe and North America, Marley lamented that he had not done a show in Jamaica in a long time, and it was while he was on tour that the germ of the idea for the Smile Jamaica concert grew. In *Marley and Me*, Don Taylor includes great detail about how the concert came to be. Bob wanted a Christmas morning concert that would fit with "traditional merrymaking at Christmas" (Taylor, 1995, 137). He didn't want to "tek weh the little man food" so he proposed it as a free concert and an opportunity "to relieve the pressure on the people" (Taylor, 1995, 138). Taylor goes on to describe how Bob called Prime Minister Manley to propose the concert and how Manley responded to the idea with enthusiasm (Taylor, 1995, 139).

For these close personal associates of Marley, the issue of power is obviously extremely important: for them, the posthumous narrative as legacy had to emphasize Marley's sovereign *agency*: his control over the decision to speak. This resonates not only in terms of how Marley was seen as a ghetto youth who had torn through the veils of power that kept persons of his class and race in subjection, but also in terms of how people power, the power of the dispossessed, had achieved presence and voice that would be visibly and vocally displayed in the choices of governance. In that sense, the people were becoming the nation, and the government was acknowledging and acquiescing in that accession. Of course, this is not to say that Cole and Leslie saw the arrangement of the concert or its genesis through the lens of competition for power; clearly, though, they saw it as an expression of Marley's free choice to express his concern for the people he was singing about, and almost certainly their statements seek to perform within the narrative of Marley's legacy, not within the (sensation-making) narrative of the surveillance intervention.

Like White and Salewicz, Arnold Bertram, former minister in Manley's government, maintains that he, on behalf of the PNP, approached Marley with the idea of the concert. Bertram suggests that with elections on the horizon, the success of the 1972 Bandwagon campaign, in which musicians were enlisted as the soundtrack of the PNP's campaign, came back to mind. The Bandwagons, performed in 1971, were the first time music and popular musicians were used as part of Jamaica's elections, and Bertram argues that Smile Jamaica in 1976 was an attempt to follow this successful model (Arnold Bertram, former minister of local government, youth, and community development in discussion with the author, August 2018).

The significance of Bertram's connection of the concert to the Bandwagons is brought sharply into focus by a work such as Anita Waters's *Race, Class, and Political Symbols*. Waters gives a full description of the role of the Bandwagons. "Once a week during 1971, the PNP held a bandwagon in some parish capital or country town. With the help of Clancy Eccles, the musician who was hired by the PNP and who wrote several songs used in the campaign, the party hired all the major artists whose songs expressed dissatisfaction as well as many of the other popular artists of the day. Of fourteen artists listed in a bandwagon advertisement, eight were among the top 25 artists for 1971 or in the top ten in the month preceding the election" (Waters, 1985, 131). Max Romeo's "Let the Power Fall on I," Delroy Wilson's, "Better Mus Come," and Junior Byles's "Beat Down Babylon" were key tracks on the Bandwagon. It is not difficult to see how the Bandwagon model worked for all involved. Romeo, Wilson, and Byles were already topping the charts, so crowds would have been drawn to see them perform, and Manley sought "mass voter appeal among urban and rural wage workers, the own account workers, the peasantry and the unemployed who make up the majority of the national electorate" (Stone and Brown, 1981). Being on the Bandwagon would have taken them on tour across the island, and this would have increased the artists' and Manley's appeal, which was already quite considerable.

There was also an ideological consideration. According to Bertram, this would have been many of these artists' first exposure to "liberation politics." The PNP's 1976 election manifesto outlines the party's commitment to "human development, economic justice, economic independence, and foreign relations," all begun in the 1972 campaign, so the Bandwagon would have convened ideas afloat in the popular realm, many of which took their inspiration from Rastafari and the PNP's radical political trajectory. Bertram's perspective, however, ignores that many of these artists were embroiled in ideological arguments of their own. Many of the songs, even before they were on the Bandwagon, were viewed as criticism of the JLP or in dangerous support of Black power. Waters explains: "The reaction of the government and media institutions to this onslaught of ghetto criticism was one of repression on several fronts. First, every song mentioned in this chapter so far was forbidden radio play. Even indigenous music that was not banned received very little broadcast play on the two radio stations, one of which was government-owned and the other independent" (Waters, 1985, 102).

So even before the Bandwagons, the music had an insurrectional life of its own that worked as counterculture by what Sylvia Wynter calls the "subversion of the signifying chain that constitutes our now hegemonically institutionalized normative respective psyches . . . functional to the dominant order" (Wynter, 1977, 25). Waters's naming of this subversive fighting power as ghetto criticism is important: the suggestion is that there is a ghetto *school of thought*, a vernacular academy from which reggae emerges. Clearly, the evidence shows that the music, along with other artistic products of the time, was being closely surveilled and was, not infrequently, proscribed.

Significantly, Marley had been one of the artists on the Bandwagon, though his popularity in Jamaica had not peaked then. In suggesting that Smile Jamaica was Manley's 1976 Bandwagon, Bertram may be seeing Smile Jamaica as a reprise of Marley's apparent "affiliation" with the PNP. Yet what we know for sure is that not all the artists on the Bandwagon were in support of Manley or the PNP, nor was the music written in support of his campaign. The coincidence of the radical lyrics and Manley's (for the time) extraordinarily radical message of social justice and Black equality worked to fuel the largest voter and spectator turnout in Jamaican history, and both Manley and the artists, regardless of any separate and individual agendas, benefited from this exposure. Obviously, the artists made their own calculations regarding the capital to be gained from the Bandwagon relationship—there is no evidence that they planned to go all the way with Manley or to give him their votes. They were savvy in negotiating a space of power for the exposure of their music through this collaboration with the potential authorities (the PNP, as expected, won a resounding victory in the subsequent elections) that could of course at any moment turn against them. Their participation could be viewed as a mutual benefit scenario—a paradoxical co-optation.

Bertram's perspective on Smile Jamaica placed alongside Waters's history of the Bandwagon suggests that not only was Manley (and the PNP) aware of the huge political power quotient that could be harnessed from popular music; they were also experienced in the exercise of a certain kind of control over popular music (and by extension other cultural products).[14] They had recognized how damaging JLP surveillance of such products was, as almost certainly the crass censorship by which the JLP had banned political lyrics from the airwaves had helped to fuel the vast groundswell of popular discontent with JLP governance that swept the PNP to power in 1972. As a result, PNP surveillance was, if not more subtle, certainly in a more conciliatory mode, choosing co-optation (part of which was a rhetoric of Black equality in which the musicians felt they had a stake) over ruthless domination. The PNP in requesting the Smile Jamaica sequel to the Bandwagon was harnessing lessons learned to this drive to curate music into political message—this was a success they felt they could repeat, with the will of the people as co-drivers.

The departure from the JLP's more draconian form of surveillance was in theory a masterstroke as it was so far removed from the slave-plantation version that was more in plain sight as an offense to the people. Smile Jamaica as political surveillance and control of the people's mood was arguably something the PNP needed at this point, on several levels. One was the way it might work to "appease" a nation that felt itself to be under siege from escalating violence and economic fallout from the government's loan agreements with the International Monetary Fund and the World Bank. Another was the geopolitical optics of assuring the surveilling superpower that the people and their government were at one; disaffection, whether orchestrated from outside or born from local experiences, was not the full story. Many citizens had started fleeing the country, fearing economic collapse and what they saw as ideological radicalism. Indeed, Bertram's viewpoint leads us to contemplate the ways this concert was for the government at the time a crafted performance of national health and wellness aimed at particular audiences, including but not limited to skeptical citizens.

Perhaps the most striking difference in the versions of whose idea the concert was, is how they are grouped. The White, Salewicz, and Bertram version is what would be read as the official version. Whether intentional (as possibly in Bertram's case) or inadvertent, the official version works to place the spotlight on the most major political intervention in Jamaica's history, the PNP's experiment with democratic socialism. The continuing intrigue surrounding this experiment and its aftermath has shaped multiple analyses of the period, and inserting Marley, and by extension reggae music, as a political player in this scenario heightens the intrigue. Unlike these writers, Taylor, Cole, and Leslie were all close to Marley in ordinary, everyday ways. Taylor was Marley's manager, Cole was his close friend and personal manager, and Leslie managed Marley's Jamaican companies. It is no surprise that one version leans in one direction and the other in another direction. For these close associates, the driving imperative is to present Marley as a goodwill ambassador and preserve his image unsullied by political partisanship. This perspective delinks Marley from any possibility or necessity of surveillance by either the local political sides or the U.S. intelligence machinery. The image curated by this uncoupling is the iconic artist, the romantic reggae superstar who instantiates the best of the Jamaican nation, not its threat. In an odd kind of way, Rita Marley's memoir *No Woman No Cry* works to underscore the nonthreatening image. Concerned to portray Marley in his persona as husband, father, and son rather than as a political "operative," Rita places the idea for the concert firmly in the hands of Bob's multitude of advisers. In her version, Bob took some bad advice, resulting in his decision to do the concert.

Clearly, the unseen Babylon powers referenced by Marley at the concert never delinked either Marley the artist or reggae music from the ghetto school of thought—that is to say, they identified both Marley and reggae with a radical political quotient that they saw as eminently dangerous. The announcement of the concert mobilized a new layer of surveillance of Marley and his art as well as of Jamaica and Jamaican politics. Marley himself was not as limited as the average citizen, not in his uptown residence at 56 Hope Road, where an extended world grew up around his fame as an international rebel star. Still, when the concert was announced, watching of Marley increased in two very specific ways previously mentioned: surveillance by the U.S., via the "white bwai" who paid a visit to Marley to threaten the revocation of his visa if he "didn't tone down his lyrics" (Salewicz, 2014, 297), and watching by the Echo Squad.

Don Taylor and others saw the "white bwai's" threat as a manifestation of the CIA in Jamaica, a persistent "more than rumor" that many Jamaicans believed to be probably true. The September 14, 1978, issue of the left-wing newspaper *Struggle*, in a piece called "CIA on Trial: Jamaica Gives Evidence," presents evidence that over the period 1962–1972, "U.S. imperialism worked hand in glove with the pro-imperialist JLP government to heap oppression on blacks of Jamaica" ("CIA on Trial," 1978, 6). The piece also states: "In 1963, the JLP Government signed a Military Treaty with U.S. imperialism giving them the right to intervene anytime they saw fit in the internal affairs of Jamaica. . . . In 1967, the JLP declared a State of Emergency and used the army and police to step up repression against the poor people of Kingston. . . . By 1968, . . . they banned all progressive people from entering the island, banned all progressive books (even 'Black Beauty,' a children's book about a horse) and seized the passports of anyone who visited Cuba" ("CIA on Trial," 1978, 6). The article goes on to suggest that when the Jamaican people resisted, the CIA resorted to even nastier tactics, sabotaging the economy and arming the undereducated. The "white bwai's" visit to threaten visa revocation is a more personalized precursor to the development in which many artistes and entertainers were taken off planes and denied U.S. entry after Tivoli 2010 and the extradition of Dudus Coke.[15]

Still, the image of a white American man walking into Marley's residence with this threat implies a very singular watching of Marley's moves, or more accurately, his words. His lyrics are what are cited as his transgression. The "white bwai's" visit immediately after the concert was announced suggests that not only was Marley's art being closely watched, but perhaps that it was considered more dangerous, more potent in a live show in Jamaica. Certainly for the U.S., any perception of a threat to U.S. influence in the region came not only from Manley's democratic socialism policies, explicitly linked to the emergence of a Black nation, but also from the rise of the Black power movements that had spilled out of the U.S. and found large accommodations within the Caribbean region—the Trinidad Black Power uprising of 1970 must have been fresh in CIA political consciousness and may have provided part of the context in which Marley's radical lyrics were viewed.

The high political stakes involved in the concert can be seen from the fact that Marley at this time was "assigned" a heavy security detail. White describes the Echo Squad's arrival on the Monday of the week of the Smile Jamaica concert in this way: "PNP vigilantes calling themselves the 'Echo Squad' mounted a twenty-four-hour guard at Hope Road" (White, 2006, 287). Bigger Ford, a veteran police officer, takes to task White's description of the squad, noting that they were politically affiliated police officers who had their headquarters on Trafalgar Road and not a squad of vigilantes (Bigger Ford, veteran police officer, in conversation with the author, August 2018). The September 5, 2000, issue of the *Jamaica Gleaner* carries an article supporting Ford's description of the squad. The article, entitled "13 Squads in 24 Years," lists the Echo Squad formed in June 1976 as the first of twenty-four groups of Jamaican police for the purpose of fighting crime. The squad was said to allow only band members on or off the property without permission. Marley wasn't a stranger to political musclemen, but this close surveillance of his residence and his society marked a different moment. The Smile Jamaica concert upped his local profile significantly, so even as Marley refused the political association, he was clearly seen as associated.

The Echo Squad, then, not only imposed protection on Marley, but their surveillance also imposed political positioning or affiliation. In essence, they made him and his household more vulnerable by performing surveillance as spectacle. The Echo Squad used surveillance as a statement of power and a marking off of territory, not necessarily over Marley, but rather over those who might seek to claim any of the influence his person and his music garnered. It is difficult to interpret the squad's absence on the night of the shooting at Marley's residence. I-Nancy Burke (I-Nancy Burke in conversation with the author, August 2018),[16] who arrived at the residence that night before the shooting, confirms that there was no security at the gate. She notes, however, that the gate was closed, an unusual way to find it, and that it was dark even though she heard a band rehearsing. Here rumor, speculation, and suss substitute for certainty.

The squad's presence at 56 Hope Road, viewed within the dynamic of surveillance, was disruptive on a number of levels, none more so than the ways their interrogations ran counter to the well-established ethos and atmosphere of a Kingston yard that Marley's residence had become, even as it was also an international space and indeed courted an air of internationalism. Various accounts indicate that the residence was always crowded, not just with international or famous visitors but with friends, acquaintances, hangers on, and so on from Marley's previous community of Trench Town, and the house had become not only a place for Rasta "groundings" but also a place of reunion and a space where Marley's continuing hunger to stay close to his roots and to match his lyrics of social liberation with practical largesse toward those less fortunate was constantly played out. From this perspective, 56 Hope Road was yard come uptown, with all the implications of the "ghetto school of thought" and the resistive, restless, polyvocal, irrepressible populace noted from differing perspectives by de Lisser and Patterson, and all the ways these perspectives fracture the ideological hegemonies of single-family dwelling or middle classness that held sway at this time. Physically, the property evinced this impression of the tenement yard migrating: it had mushroomed beyond the main house as Marley had added other buildings that often housed these itinerant and sometimes semipermanent visitors.

Watch, See, Wait: Fracturing Hegemonies in James's *A Brief History of Seven Killings*

Marlon James's novel *A Brief History of Seven Killings* imagines a history of 1970s Jamaica that reinterprets the very concept of history while it muses on the relation between history and narrative or history as narrative. In presenting the multiple ways a historical event is played out simultaneously and differently in different people's consciousness, James's novel is a contemporary offering of how narrative shows hegemonies to be flexible and fractured. The novel brings together narrative as memory, forgetting, personal history, testimony, futures imagined, suss, voices from the dead, and so on as it presents not only the concert or the attempt on Marley's life but the wide cast of persons, biographies, and personal and political concerns that populated the context in which Marley lived. Many of these were tangential to the actual events but absolutely crucial to understanding the events, and more so the emergent nation in which the events took place and in which the crime remained "unsolved." The book as a choric drama emphasizes the performative aspect of narrative power. James's choice of multiple voices, many of which were from the underclasses, underscores his investment in the voices of people from the yards.

James recounts the experience of the Smile Jamaica concert from the perspective of the young shotta Bam Bam,[17] who is orphaned in a garrison community, groomed into a gunman, and is one of the men recruited to kill the Singer. Bam Bam, who is near the end of his short life, is James's only audience member at the concert, so to experience the concert from the perspective of his tattered mind is to experience a perspective that stretches the terrain of analysis covered by biographies and historiographic sources. From Bam Bam's perspective, surveillance is not specific to life in the fractious 1970s Jamaica, it is part of the reality of being born poor and Black in an inner-city community in Jamaica at any time. In his life there is no distinction between private and public, between inside and outside, and free will is obsolete; this is the result of hypersurveillance in and across the communities where he lives. In the first Bam Bam chapter, in the December 2, 1976, section of the novel, the first sentence of the third paragraph reads, "In the Eight Lanes and in Copenhagen City all you can do is watch" (James, 2014, 8). In this section of the boy's recollections, Bam Bam's watching is presented as a powerless thing in the face of the very powerful, all-seeing eyes of dons, shottas, police, and politics. All he can do is watch and yet Bam Bam's perspective, that is, his watching, is at a certain level a counter to surveillance, or it can be read as resistance to crippling surveillance, and this appears through veils of contradiction such as are evident when Bam Bam says, "Sweet talking voice on the radio say that crime and violence are taking over . . . and if change ever going to come that we will all have to wait and see, but all we can do down here in the Eight Lanes is see and wait" (James, 2014, 8). The affixed "all we [in Eight Lanes] can do" colors the reversed phrase "see and wait" with the same impotence as Bam Bam's "watch" and the announcer's "wait and see," like verbs with limited "do." But the reversal—"see and wait"—conveys a doubleness that inscribes agency: in Eight Lanes, one "sees"; that is, one has perception, insight, awareness, understanding of what is going on, even if one also must wait for the outcome of what is seen. Reversing the order of wait and see suggests that there is some act of "undoing" involved in the seeing, though something inevitable—perhaps a destiny—is already demarcated in their situation as denizens of the yard. The announcer's wait and see, by contrast, brings into ken a history of journalistic commentary on places like Eight Lanes, Tivoli Gardens, or any other garrison community. Such spaces are perceived as hotbeds of poverty, crime, and lawlessness, places that could easily empty out the hope of the nation, and so the nation can only carefully watch and wait for the outcome. The clichéd phrasing of the announcer's perspective conveys both the superior positioning of the ideological majority that watches with a jaded eye, and a kind of Judeo-Christian fatalism that ironically gives the objects of their watching (the criminals from the yard) over to anonymous greater powers.

The distance between the surveilling eye of such "powers" and the accelerated "seeing" into which Bam Bam is propelled by life in the yard is sharply focused in the narrative structure. Immediately following this statement, Bam Bam catalogs the deepest pains and disgraces of his personal life, things he witnessed despite not wanting to: "And I see my mother take two men for twenty dollars each" and "I watch my father get so sick and tired of her that he beat her like a dog" (James, 2014, 8). Bam Bam's seeing (because his eyes have vision) and watching (because he can't shut them) here show key moments in his life as orchestrated by someone else or situations beyond his control. The one person who loves him cannot protect him without silencing and hurting him, and his father, even though he tries, cannot prevent him from seeing the most brutal parts of life in the slums. Bam Bam recalls that the last time his father tried to save him was the evening of a gang war. His father convinces the ten-year-old Bam Bam that they are playing a game by going about the house on their knees. Tired of this, Bam Bam stands up to an immediate barrage of bullets, "[a]nd he grab me and try to cover my ears but he grab so hard that he don't realize that's digging into my eye. And I hear the bullet and the pap-pap-pap-pap-pap-pap and the whoooshboom and feel the floor shake" (James, 2014, 11). Despite his father's covering weight, Bam Bam hears woman, man, boy scream a death scream and thinks he will die under his father's weight. His father's protections save him, but they do not prevent him from hearing or later from seeing the worst. His father's fingers accidentally tearing into his eye signals painful hyperawareness of the realities of the Eight Lanes and Copenhagen City pressing in on them. Bam Bam's witnessing of his neighbor's death is also painful to him, but neither his nor his father's witness are enough to resist the powers that be.

Bam Bam watches the next scenes from under the sheet where his father puts him to hide "just in case bad man come in the night" (James, 2014, 12); from there he sees his father beat and violate his mother with a broomstick. The next day, from under this covering he watches his mother return with three gang members and Funny Boy, who beat, rape, and shoot his father and then shoot his mother in the face. Just as with the previous scene, Bam Bam is shielded, indeed his life is saved because of the crushing and covering weight of a parent: first by his living father and in this scene his murdered mother, who falls dead on top of him. Here again Bam Bam is a witness to murder, though unlike in the previous section, Bam Bam's eyes are the only witnesses to Funny Boy's taunting, and his acts of rape and murder. While Bam Bam's seeing and watching are largely impotent, Funny Boy's are not. Funny Boy understands that his donship would be compromised were his community to know that he is queer. Arguably this is why Funny Boy shoots both father and mother and significantly indicts the mother by shooting her in her mouth (a death meant to mark an informer). This silencing of the woman's tongue, like the shots that ring out when Bam Bam gets off his knees on the night of the gang war, together work to complicate the impotence of watching and seeing. Funny Boy and other gang members know that there is power in witnessing, so they use surveillance to make what Bam Bam and his mother see ineffectual, to rinse the power out of what they see. By the end of the first Bam Bam chapter, we come to know that there is nowhere in the Eight Lanes where Funny Boy does not have oversight. The don's power is in surveillance, and so Bam Bam flees the Eight Lanes.

Bam Bam, the boy's, seeing from under the protective curtain of his father's making—the sheet/blanket from where he watches his early life bleed away from him—can be juxtaposed with the older Bam Bam who watches or notices changes in Copenhagen City where he flees after his parents are killed. The curtain, of course, has theatrical resonance, and as my analysis above indicates, it is a flimsy protection in that even as it saves his life it functions as the place from which he witnesses the brutality of life in the inner city. It is under this curtain that Bam Bam loses his innocence, and where he begins his transformation from son to shotta.

Free from his father's protective curtain, Bam Bam watches men "bring guns to the ghetto" after they bring "corned beef and Aunt Jemima maple syrup" (James, 2014, 33). And here Bam Bam's watching takes on a marked sophistication, a shift from forced awareness of events over which he has no control to a dawning political consciousness that allows him to assess the larger issues of globalization and national power/lessness that frame life in the yards. There is a doubleness here: obviously, Bam Bam's capacity to "see" in this way is based on the brutal experience living under Funny Boy's donship; at the same time, it is the "freedom" provided by his flight to Copenhagen City that allows him space to think through these other, supraordinate contexts. His observation of the goods of the American empire being brought to Jamaica and given to inner-city dwellers—guns, corned beef, and Aunt Jemima maple syrup—is not merely documentary. He narrows whatever distance we imagine between the importation and distribution of weapons that will take many lives, and foreign tastes that will dull the appetite for Jamaican self-reliance and arguably cripple the Jamaican economy. Bam Bam notes that the food items come first and then the guns follow, to signal the desperate trap that is poverty, partisan politics, and inter/multinational economic imperatives.

Bam Bam's coming of age in watching is a strange kind of tango with surveillance, countersurveillance and deep, perceptive-seeing. His active "affiliation" with raw surveillance, the contradictory result of his status as one of the surveilled, comes as he is made part of a crew that watches the Singer, in open sight, at the Singer's residence at 56 Hope Road. Bam Bam is stationed there on order from don man Josey Wales, giving stark meaning to the line in Mutabaruka's poem "Siddung on the Wall": "Is long long time I siddung on the wall a watch him a watch me." Bam Bam's watching is watched not only by don man Josey Wales, but also, in Bam Bam's perception, by the Singer. "And I know we watched your big house on Hope Road for days now, and at one point you come talk to us like you was Jesus and we was Iscariot and you nod as if to say get on with your business and do what you have to do. But I can't remember if me see you or if somebody told me that him see you so that me think I see it too" (James, 2014, 7). At this point we see that he has an intimation that his watching/seeing is more than what it is supposed to be, but he is not yet quite sure what it is. Certainly he is aware of the shifting and convoluted terrain of watching and surveillance networks that he must navigate, and the precarity of his own position or capacity to see clearly within and through these networks, especially given his drug-induced confusion, a metaphor for the controlling situations, narratives, politicians, and dons that rule his life ("I can't remember if somebody told me that him see you so that me think I see it too").

The doubleness of Bam Bam's "coming of age" as shotta and seer is marked as well by his relationship to his most notable and transforming prop: his gun. To be assigned a gun is to be admitted to the high fraternity of shottas; to be assigned to surveil and take out the Singer is to attain notoriety widespread and long lasting enough to become a form of legacy, even if he is never identified as the killer. Bam Bam is fully aware of his fraught position as putative gun owner, owned by the gun: he notices how "when a gun come to live in the house it's the gun, not even the person who keep it, that have the last word" (James, 2014, 72). Yet at one level this comment on the style of the shotta and how people in and out of his ken respond to the weapon is in deep contrast to what his wielding of the gun actually comes to mean for him on the night of his attempted murder of the Singer. The attempt fails because he and his fellow shottas are high on cocaine and transformed into frantic maniacs not capable of shooting straight.

In the end, the gun does not have the last word, both because of Bam Bam's inability to wield it and because he has no fervor for it except when he is in a cocaine-induced stupor. This lacuna in his affiliation to the gun—his lack of real appetite for it—is one of the several ways James fractures the national image of the criminal. In James's representation, the criminal (Bam Bam) arguably replaces the Caribbean literary and cultural image of the madman or madwoman as community seer.[18] Bam Bam—named in part to signal dread, even apocalyptic conclusions (what a Bam Bam!), in part to signal the vulnerability one associates with an infant, in part again to inscribe the onomatopoeic echo of a gun blast—inhabits the contradictions of his person (a boy too early a man; a child who loved to read, outside of the benefits of schooling; a co-opted outsider in the criminal-cum-surveillance networks) as much as he instantiates the astonishing trauma of the postcolonial Jamaican state that James envisions in his rendition of what is seen by many as the most hopeful period in Jamaica's reaching after a truly independent statehood—the 1970s.

Because the guns do not have the last word on the night of the attempted murder, the Singer's performance is especially poignant. Bam Bam imagines himself to be the Singer's main audience, and in this moment his perception is indeed correct. Arguably, the Singer turns up to Smile Jamaica to show his attackers that he survived and to launch his attack via his art. And yet Bam Bam does not look like an audience member, he has not donned the full suit of admiration or curiosity that many of the crowd wear. The crowd neither watches nor sees the raggedy man, risen from the garbage lands in wet filth and crowned with the muck of dog saliva. What does it mean then that James makes him the audience? What does it mean that at this moment when he becomes the Singer's single audience, Bam Bam has apotheosized from a denizen of the yard to the figure of the Dungle as apparent in his uniform of rags, garbage, saliva, and wet filth? What does it mean that we see the concert from his eyes? We, the other audience, understand that Bam Bam is not the enemy. We know that he is a boy *seen* into the style of the shotta to survive and that in his final chapter (he will not make it out of 1976) he will wish for his daddy and "a kisko pop and lollipop and a tootsie pop" while dirt is shoveled onto him by the men he worked for (James, 2014, 268).

Bam Bam's perspective, as the main audience of the concert, limits the goodness in the superstar. The Singer's chanting down Babylon, his own search for justice and smiles, excludes the likes of Bam Bam. The Singer's reach is limited, his artistic hopes appear shallow and generic to his audience of Bam Bam. Positioning Bam Bam as the only viewpoint and the only narrator at and of the concert undermines the Singer's superpower presence—the hegemony of fame, one might say—and this elevation of the stripped man to the level of seer achieves special poignancy as Bam Bam's life ends with him being deliberately buried alive under the weight of dirt. This also becomes a key moment for James to call into question the hype of independence, the solid construct of the post-colonial state, and the literary tropes through which Caribbeanness is imagined.

James's representation engages the multiple levels at which surveillance infects the societal and sociopolitical networks of the city and reproduces cycles of exploitation: the dons occupy the "leadership" vacuum left by politicians' neglect, but not only do they negotiate power with the political echelons (maroon-like, in a way, though in plain sight); they also build their empire on the subjugation and close scrutiny of their own people. James presents in Bam Bam the lowest of the low on the social and even psychological scale, so that the personal devastation we see is almost complete. But by layering this hegemony of violence with even the limited form of resistive "watch power"—fractured power—exemplified by a character such as Bam Bam, James taps into a distinct Caribbean reality that "seeing," watching, and even surveilling are never unidirectional events in which the poor and powerless are only poor and powerless; rather, these processes operate reflexively in complex matrices of oppression, resistance, and co-optation in which all powers are fractured.

4

Bongo Futures after Tivoli

• •

The Reggae Revival and Its Genealogies

The Reggae Revival emerges out of the ashes of Jamaica in crisis. The crisis I refer to here has its epicenter in the Tivoli incursion of 2010, and so the book ends where it began. This chapter takes us back to the surveillance issues raised in the Tivoli incursion and asks us to reflect on the inherent contraindications of power implied in reggae as both the establishment's (global and national) adoptee on the one hand and the disrupter of Babylon on the other. The revival's address to surveillance and the Tivoli incursion were for the most part oblique rather than frontal, and the shape of this response directs my approach in the chapter. At the same time, however, I want to note the fact of other important responses from within the music industry. As I have discussed, following the Jamaican government's first refusal to extradite Dudus on the grounds that the U.S. surveillance methods were not legal, the U.S. had moved in swift rebuttal to revoke the visas of high-level politicians and musical artists. While no formal charges were made against persons targeted in this way, evidence of U.S. surveillance findings was most visible and dramatic in this act of withdrawing U.S. entry privileges. Revoking the visas was, of course, among other effects, a major economic strike against both the country and the musicians. In the case of the musicians, not only were they now unable to do shows and concerts in the U.S., but their travel within the Caribbean and to Europe became that much more fraught and expensive, since the U.S. was a frequent and convenient transit point between these locations.

It is therefore not surprising that the Jamaican songwriters and performers, usually swift to respond to topical events, were very silent on the issue throughout 2010. The silence, though obviously self-protective, like all silences cannot be unequivocally or linearly read, especially in a society with a history of underground and submarine resistance. There is ample evidence in the emergence of the Reggae Revival and other popular music acts that a deep response to U.S. surveillance was brewing in what, extrapolating from Fred Moten, I might call "the break"—that space-time between an act and the force with which it collides, or that collides with it at the opposite end of its trajectory. The force on the other side is never simply "equal and opposite" in the Newtonian sense. It is part of the paradox of impact that what is opposite is also product—therefore part and parcel of the act itself. It is also principle in the sense of existential reality, and therefore already, then, a fracture—a creative aporia—in the "initiating" force. And so, even though what we heard in the moment of the U.S. sanctions was silence, it soon emerged that the U.S. surveillance had a direct repercussion in the Jamaican music scene for a time. In 2011, the year after the incursion, king of the dancehall Beenie Man released the song "I'm OK," which, both in its timing and in its lyrics, presents in plain hearing a cloaked response to U.S. interference in the singer's livelihood and art.

The song engages in the kind of creole "language games" that are a staple of Caribbean Carnival and the everyday mas' of people-speak: "A serious ting a gwaan inna Jamaica / Mi can tell you something?" Beenie's introduction suggests a speaking in the audience's ear, a suss that is nevertheless out in the open, in the lyrics and resistive instrumentals of dancehall. "I'm OK" goes on to recount a story of losses in the music industry including the revocation of Beenie's U.S. visa. "After Bounty go a jail / Mavado crash offa bike, / Me lose me visa, but everything nice." The refrain follows: "I'm OK, because me clean every day / Clarks dem a beat / me change three times a day / Buy out any bar / cause me have money to pay" (Beenie Man, 2011). First, Beenie is repudiating any belief or rumor that somehow he is suffering as a result of U.S. surveillance power. The song also declares his innocence through the Jamaican preoccupation with cleanliness: "because me clean every day." "Clean" here references U.S. colloquial legalese, meaning innocent, but it is also proof that he is financially secure. He can afford to bathe and change his clothes three times a day. His body, his lyrics, and his reputation stay fresh even in this rumored tough time.

In the final stanza, Beenie Man comes closest to directly addressing the politics of U.S. efforts to censor him: "A me a di doctor / A Smokey Vale mi have mi house / But mi haffi live like a boxer / Yuh haffi live inna di garrison in Jamaica / Don't August Town next to Mona, oh / Standpipe and Papine a di surrounding area / Di US embassy jus round di corna / So how dem a worry bout me and visa / When US a mi next door neighbour?" (Beenie Man, 2011). Beenie's defense is first against those who have made assumptions about how surveillance has impacted his ascendency—when all is said and done, don't worry about me and this visa; the U.S. (embassy) is still close. But more than this, Beenie addresses the political relativities inherent in Kingston's geography and its incorporation of surveilled space. Though he has a house far uptown in Smokey Vale, he is somehow constrained to live in or be proximate to the garrison. Though clean, he has been implicated in garrison dealings. Indeed, the entire Jamaican populace had had their lives upended in one way or another by the Dudus affair. Beenie signals this with geographical facts that have always troubled attempts at separations in urban Jamaica: the working-class community of August Town is next to the middle-class community of Mona; the U.S. embassy is across the road from Standpipe, another poor community, and a stone's throw from Papine, a transit hub and intersectional space bridging uptown, inner city, and rural St. Andrew. If the U.S. embassy compound is U.S. soil in Jamaica, not only is Jamaica (the perceived garrison) shadowed by the U.S.; equally, the force (and dangers) of the garrison or its close cousin the yard or inner city are a potential threat to U.S. hegemony.

Beenie's potent declaration and cuss-out brewed in the yearlong silence under censorship and sanctions is both direct and slanted and addresses the rumormongers who are spreading suss against him as much as it addresses U.S. surveillance. In the case of the Reggae Revival, while some musical and visual artists did use their lyrics and paintings to address surveillance, the larger scope of their attention was Jamaica in crisis and the creation of an alternative, a community model that bypassed the entanglements of local and state politics and control by neocolonial and neoliberal forces. "Bongo Futures" therefore takes a different tack from the other chapters as its focus on the issues of surveillance is slant, marked more in the background contexts that fuel the revival's emergence than in the revival's direct engagements and expressions that are the main subject of the chapter.

Though the revival is popularly conceived of and critiqued as a revival of reggae music, it is more accurately understood as a social movement that in its initial stages saw the congress of young artists and thinkers (under the broad umbrella of Rastafari) as the occasion to imagine an artistic scene in Jamaica that was not beholden to powers of the establishment, nor subject to its disciplining machineries, whether of direct surveillance or of the economic and professionalizing structures more broadly referred to as "Babylon." The language of crisis is very presentist language. David Scott calls this moment "the postcolonial nationalist-modern in Jamaica," and he asserts that this state "is in profound crisis" (Scott, 1999, 190). Yet what Reggae Revival artists, musicians, and protesters of this particular moment did, in imagining bongo futures, was to situate the present moment of crisis, in relation to both a complex past and a complex future that recast "crisis" in more ambiguous terms. Here "crisis" is not only an occasion of terror but a space of heightened contestation in which the creative impetus has a particularly dynamic force against Babylon's hegemony.

When I first wrote about the revival it was in its early stages. The moniker revival, even if unintended in this context, assumes a discrete period in time and not a constant state of reawakening, upness, or emergence. In 2023, the group of artists, musicians, and thinkers I had once written about as emerging reached the top of their careers. Chronixx, Jesse Royal, and Protoje have received Grammy nominations in the best reggae album category, and Kabaka Pyramid won best reggae album, also in 2023. International approbation through the Grammy nominations and win have set music artists in the revival distinctly apart from other artists and thinkers in the movement who, though they have achieved various planes of success, have not quite the influence and money stamp of a Grammy Award. The success of the Reggae Revival has moved its artists from the margins to the center, from below the radar to the full shine of the video light, from up and coming to *out and bad*. How these shifts in the position of revivalists play out against the early idealism of the movement is part of the chapter's discussion.

The chapter is also concerned with the ways the revival's creative imaginary and lifestyle emphasized a version of community based on an idealization of the yard. By this I mean to signal how the revival's alternative drew on yard elements: Rasta spirituality, communal economic structures, reggae *as a concept*, to produce a space that was not so much the yard as a new possibility: not a yard they had seen but one *imagined*, that reflected their own cross-class, cross-space positioning. This was in effect the yard without walls.

"Reggae Revival" is a term coined by Dutty Bookman, a young man who traces his path to enlightenment through the Rastafarian faith and through Babylon in his self-published book *Tried and True* (2011). In history, Dutty Boukman was a Maroon leader and Voudun priest from Jamaica who also happened to be enslaved. Boukman presided over the Bois Caïman ceremony that began the Haitian Revolution in 1791. In adopting this name, Dutty Bookman of the Reggae Revival signals a wider swath of Caribbean revolutionary histories of freedom, to which he links both reggae and the new reconscientizing in which he is involved. In Bookman's experience, working against Babylon for the young, creative person in twenty-first-century Jamaica is making one's way through the once antiestablishment establishments (the Bob Marley empire and nontraditional media houses that have been co-opted by globalization and "professionalizing" mechanisms as well as the more tried and true sites of corruption and downpression in Jamaica: politics and a social structure that have favored the wealthy and near-white). "Reggae Revival," according to Bookman, is used to describe a response to the diminishing "cultural product" (Bookman, 2011) coming out of popular music; that is, dancehall and the culture it promotes. Bookman, in a June 2013 interview, explains, "Many people have lost interest in our cultural products, simply because they don't have access to the positive elements. I want to spread the news that consciousness is rising again in Jamaica, and it is being given expression through various artistes and art forms" ("Reggae Revival Discussion," 2013).

I am interested in the broad strokes Bookman uses to characterize this moment and movement and his desire to locate the revitalization of Jamaican music and arts in reggae. I am also interested in what the Reggae Revival yields in a Jamaican cultural experience. Does the genealogy of the term *reggae* bespeak cultural authority and success? What is the nature of the relationship among reggae, dancehall, and the revival? I consider as well the ways in which this conscious re/turn to vernacular culture functions as a way to revitalize how Jamaica figures within the discourse on neoliberalism and the Jamaican nation. Given the revival's own inherent ambiguities, discussed later in the chapter, there is ever the fear that the futures they seek to present intersect with the reified structures that they are combating and replacing.

Bookman describes a number of friendships with young artistes and thinkers like himself who moved away from the mainstream and toward another cultural incarnation, artists who moved (back) to the live sounds familiar in the late 1960s and the 1970s when reggae was first gaining ground. He coined the term "Reggae Revival" to describe and name the young musicians, artists, and writers who have returned to the "roots" sound and who have embraced Rasta as the spiritual center of their art, but the term itself is contested. For one, first-generation reggae artists have suggested that reggae never nearly died and therefore never needed a revival. They argue that the so-called Reggae Revival is an uptown idea, with all the attendant privileges: access to the media, education, and a fan base that blooms everlasting from social networks. Two, even more recent than first-generation reggae artists is what Donna Hope has called "the First Wave of this movement," which came on the scene at the "turn of the millennium" and which has had a significant impact on the Reggae Revival moment (Hope, 2013). These singers of "culture," often billed alongside dancehall artists but never subsumed by them, are ideologically grounded in Rastafari. This wave includes artistes such as Sizzla Kalonji, Fantan Mojah, I-Wayne, and Turbulence, among others. The first wave of the movement joins a long genealogy of singers of "roots and culture" that, though never present as a movement so markedly inflected by class and access as the Reggae Revival, has never been absent from the Jamaican music scene.[1] Three, others have questioned whether the term *revival* indeed captures the phenomenon that these artistes perform and have considered *resurgence* as a term that denotes the reemergence of reggae or of the popularity of the music, not as what reggae was but perhaps as a twenty-first-century retake and as especially distinct from the themes popular in dancehall. Whatever it is called, there is no doubt that in the second decade of the twenty-first century, a growing number of young musicians have produced a corpus of music that resembles the reggae of the first generation in its return to live sounds and the theme(s) of Rasta, social justice, and rebellion (the revival's themes fall on the continuum of conscious music from the 1960s to the present) but differs from it in some major specifics, such as who the players are and how they perform critique of the national and global sociopolitical terrain.

In exploring the roots of what has been called the Reggae Revival in Jamaica, I consider what it means that the revival is not singularly located in music and sound, but that revivalists imagine an artistic community and aesthetic that includes several other art forms as well. While for many the reggae aesthetic began in a very specific religio-cultural experience—Rastafari—not all revivalists see Rasta in the same way. In my close analysis of revivalists, I posit that while the revival suggests a reaching back to a defining cultural form, reggae, that has been localized and perhaps even nationalized, it is globalized in its commitment to engaging sounds and forms from different cultures and traditions. The result is that although the term "Reggae Revival" presumes a certain genealogy, it just as readily implies an uncertain future. The word *uncertain* suggests the revival's engagement with two political issues of the present moment, specifically, a redefinition of Babylon in terms of U.S.-Jamaica relations and in that context the rejection of neoliberalism. The Reggae Revival has also embraced fresh forms of artistic and social community that go far beyond what reggae as a distinct historical phenomenon had embraced. Ultimately, they re-create reggae as a principle rather than a music or a music industry, and in so doing suggest a new genealogy for reggae that is both epistemological and ontological.

This brings me to the idea of bongo futures and the Tivoli incursion as a major turning point catalyzing the revival. The incursion is prominent in the work of a number of revival artists such as Protoje, Chronixx, and Kabaka Pyramid, which I discuss later in the chapter. Ultimately, the Tivoli Gardens incursion connects not only with the global awareness of the revival but, as I will show, with the concept of bongo futures that I explore here. By *futures*, I mean to hear Lee Edelman's caution in *No Future* (2004) that any future that does not repudiate sameness and is simply a reproduction of the past is no future. I also hear David Scott, who sees a part of the way forward for Jamaica as a "future constructed on its own vernacular image" that is a contested image and an unauthorized image (Scott, 1999, 219). I use the term "bongo" futures to highlight the crucial part played in the revival by its genealogy in the vernacular arts and in particular the Rastafarian resistance to Babylon. "Bongo" first signifies as a drum, the voice of ancestral Africa retained in the New World, a sonic intervention in new world soundscapes. Bongo is also in Jamaica speech an adjective attached to Rasta, to signify a connection with Blackness, a full embodied embrace of Africa, and simultaneously a vigorous rejection of Europe and the Global North. "Bongo Futures," then, addresses an opened-out space in which Blackness is not under siege. This is an idea of the future the revivalists gesture toward with their imagining of a Jamaica and a Jamaican art scene not subject to Babylon powers, whether from outside or within. This idea is one of the ways that the revivalists sought to distinguish themselves not only from dancehall but also from reggae without the revival.

Yet unraveling how Reggae Revival differs from reggae is a thorny affair that I approach via what may be termed a history of the "death" and "resurrection" of the genre. According to Lloyd Bradley and Dennis Morris in *Reggae*, "Just after Marley died, in May 1981, it was announced in sections of the media that this marked the end of reggae. But that was never true. His death didn't mark the end of roots reggae—that had been happening without any outside help for a number of years . . . what it marked was the end of an era in which reggae was a bona fide part of mainstream music, occupying its own space on its own terms" (Bradley and Morris, 2002, 75). However, the notion of the space that reggae occupies in the Jamaican imagination and as part of a "Jamaican aesthetic" is crucial to this discussion. In *Natural Mysticism*, Kwame Dawes argues that "it was the emergence of reggae in the late 1960s that provided Jamaica (and the Caribbean region) with an artistic form that has a distinctively postcolonial aesthetic" (Dawes, 1999, 17). This aesthetic reveals the momentum gained by throwing off the heavy cloak of official colonialism and by the emergence of Rastafari—itself a statement of independence from European-imposed icons for worship and ideals of beauty. In their place, Rastafari embraced an African-inspired aesthetic that reformed music, dress, worship, and diet. Perhaps because of this, reggae never gained wide appeal for local audiences until it traveled and returned with international approbation, or, to put it another way, until it had passed through the cynosure of Western eyes and been pronounced "fit" for intramural admission. For the local watchdogs of culture and the national image, the terms by which products of the yard could be granted egress outside the containing wall still lay outside the country and the region, and so reggae comes to signify the "nervous condition" of the post-colony as opposed to the powers of the free state.

In the use of the term "Reggae Revival" is the awareness of the political currency *reggae* carries. Reggae signifies a particular brand of sound—for the attuned ear. It signifies, as well, a response to oppression and societal dis-ease that had to remain marginal to sustain a fierce critique of the center. It is the sound of a newly independent nation, and it is perhaps the sound that put Jamaica on the (musical) map. In the Jamaican context, revival also signifies indigeneity. What I mean by this is that in the Jamaican context it is difficult to see the word *revival* as it pertains to culture without thinking about another indigenous religion (the first being Rastafarianism), which is Revivalism. Martin and Pamela Mordecai, in their study *Culture and Customs of Jamaica*, argue, "Revival endures as more than a theological oddity or colorful footnote. It is the well-spring of a peculiarly Jamaican spirituality, presenting a unique view of man's place in the cosmos and his relationship with eternity. The influence of Revival on Jamaican culture also is significant: in the music, rhythms, and most of all style of singing that can be found in churches of the fully Christian denominations; also in popular music, in the growing religious music sector, in reggae, and even in dancehall" (Mordecai and Mordecai, 2000, 45). It is certainly significant that many Rastafarian symbols emerged from Revivalism. Barry Chevannes, in "New Approach to Rastafari" from his edited collection *Rastafari and Other African-Caribbean Worldviews*, traces a number of Revivalist elements that persist in Rastafari, mostly in "ritual structure" and in "ritual instruments" (Chevannes, 1995, 20–42).[2] As well, in common parlance there is a fascinating language slippage whereby people would leave off the "reggae" and simply refer to the revival or refer to the artists as "revivalists." This linguistic slippage signified many possibilities for the Reggae Revival's future unfolding: Would the revival have a similar leavening effect as Revivalism on Jamaican culture? How did this linguistic slippage and the possibilities bound up in the slippage suggest the uncertainty and unchartedness about the future of the revival of which I have previously spoken?

It is compelling to think about this Reggae Revival moment as another cultural rendition that harkens back to a genealogy of indigenous religious sound. What this suggests about the genealogy of the Reggae Revival is not that there is an Afro-Christian worldview as there was in Revivalism, nor is there an Afro-centric worldview as there was in Rastafari reggae of the 1960s, but rather there are elements of both positions as well as a uniquely twenty-first-century indigenous religious aesthetic. In other words, then, the revivalists found power and agency in constructing their own relationship to religious practice, creating an idiom that was outside of previous forms, because these were confining and not quite enough. Whether reggae revivalists are aware of this genealogy in their choice of nomenclature is irrelevant, because it is difficult not to see that it is there.

If reggae emerged in an anti-colonial-into-postcolonial moment, we could say that dancehall emerged as the soundtrack for the influence and the response to the impact of globalization and free trade on Jamaica as well as the insistent realities of a quickly globalizing world. As I have previously outlined, the sound and culture of reggae are what Pam O'Gorman calls "essentially non-European" (O'Gorman, 1972, 50), and while dancehall arguably is a genre and aesthetic unconcerned with mainstream societal expectations and respectability—what Carolyn Cooper terms "slackness"—it is not as purposefully concerned with marginal and traditional aesthetics such as Afro-centricity or the brand of cultural wholeness that reggae performs. Rory "Stone Love" Gilligan, renowned producer and DJ, recounts the shift from reggae "rub a dub" to dancehall as the move from one turntable to two turntables and from a live DJ to "juggling," that is, absent the live DJ (Rory Gilligan, producer, in conversation with the author, July 10, 2014). Mikie Bennett argues that the advent of the drum machine had a startling and rapid impact on the tempo of the music, hurtling reggae into dancehall (Mikie Bennett, producer, in conversation with the author, July 10, 2014). The grittier, faster beats of dancehall found lyrics that were unapologetic about performing blatant materialism, sexual and verbal violence, violence in the community, and "video light" beauty that did not hide Jamaica's conflation of light brown skin and long, straight hair with beauty and social mobility.

118 • Inside Tenement Time

One could say that dancehall exposed the contradictions and paradoxes of Jamaican social structure and the wide fluidities of the power dynamic by going to extremes to *acquire* the status quo. The practice of skin whitening, or bleaching, is an example of this, since many bleachers see lighter skin as a more effective social tool than education or a good job. Sonjah Stanley Niaah argues in *Dancehall* that dancehall, the grittier, younger sibling of reggae, "occupies a tenuous place, a 'war zone,' in Jamaican society: there are relations of tension between [a] mostly lower-class performance practice and the middle-and-upper-class status quo" (Niaah, 2010, 3). The relations of tension that Niaah highlights are not so easily distinguished in the dancehall of the moment. While many of the artists may have their roots in the inner city or in poverty, their audiences are equalized and indistinguishable across class lines. Dancehall, and reggae before it, created a new class, an entertainment class if you will. As part of the performance and evidence of their success, this entertainment class straddled inner-city/poor and middle class; they were people with flexible feet. It is in this open, complex, and flexible positioning of dancehall that we find a bridge to the Reggae Revival.

As twenty-first-century observers, we note that class boundaries are often positioned, or are desired to be positioned, as porous and permeable. That value becomes materialized when these different genres occupy shifting positions on the class ladder. Indeed, as Cooper in *Sound Clash* cautions, "Misreading both reggae and dancehall, shortsighted historians of Jamaican popular music often fail to recognize continuities across seemingly fixed generic boundaries" (Cooper, 2004, 80). So I speak in generalizations here, then, when I say that if reggae was working class in the 1960s and 1970s, it has since the emergence of dancehall climbed the social ladder with agility. This is not to say that reggae has sought the cool hills of upper St. Andrew,[3] but rather that dancehall replaced reggae as the sound that took to the rest of the populace the working-class imaginary, *which has always revolutionized the national consciousness*. The Reggae Revival emerges not only as a counterculture response to dancehall but as an active contestation of the revolutionary space, that is to say, a direct attempt to wrest the revolutionary space that dancehall occupies. I do not wish to suggest that reggae, dancehall, and the Reggae Revival are separate and discrete, but that they are genealogically related. Indeed, the emergence of the revival demands a return look at the cultural and religious landscape.

Community

For certain, the aesthetic born in the 1960s has had a significant impact on the contemporary music that some now call the Reggae Revival, though, unlike the 1960s moment that almost exclusively casts itself as musical, the revival moment, perhaps consistent with the age, is unchained from any specific singular form. What I mean by this is that within the movement itself, there are practitioners of dub and theater, visual artists, videographers, producers, and, of course, writers, bands, and vocalists; as well, a great many "stragglers" and adherents who would call themselves simply "thinkers" are included in the revival's composition. While no one in the movement would suggest that there is a creed from which the revivalists operate, there is easy agreement that the revival has sought a revisionary aesthetic of Jamaican music culture and the arts more generally. One shift embedded in the ideology of the revival is the centrality of community. This has not simply meant the rewriting of the sound-clash/border-clash culture, which found potency as a marketing strategy and as creative cussing, otherwise known as "lyrics," in dancehall. It has also signified in the myriad ways community is invoked and evoked in the revival. The fact that the Reggae Revival includes different art forms is the first sense in which it is community.

There are important resonances between the artistic community of the Reggae Revival and the Caribbean Artists Movement (CAM), which was founded in London in 1966. The founders of CAM were Caribbean writers (and their partners). Key members included the poets Edward Kamau Brathwaite, John La Rose, their partners Doris Brathwaite and Sarah White, and Andrew Salkey. Other members of the collective included poets, writers, textile artists, sculptors, painters, actors, and later musicians. While the Reggae Revival had its roots in Jamaica partly in response to the neoliberal showdown in Tivoli Gardens where politics, surveillance, and heavy-handed U.S.-backed power epitomized a Jamaica where even the artists were in the pockets of politicians and other "bad men," CAM was an artistic statement in support of the spirit of federation; in its genesis, it was pan-Caribbean—but its vision was for the collective to be a larger Third World project united across the globe as an anti-colonial movement. In contrast, while the revival thrives in Jamaica with enough musicians and artists to draw international attention and to spark conversation as well as to change the vibe of the music in the international arena, the revival's vision was fundamentally locally centered in and toward Jamaica. The difference between the two anti-colonial movements is largely the product of their times: the community that CAM envisioned emerged out of a moment of regional and to some extent global hope; the one envisioned by the revival emerged out of a moment when global encounters had once again compromised Jamaica's/the Caribbean's press for sovereignty. While CAM and the revival—like movements generally—no longer exist as movement or revival, they can be assessed as legacy and genealogy. As communities, they have inspired powerful currents and futures in the larger story of Caribbean art and life and the groundations of an anti-colonial archive.

I return to Dutty Bookman's story here to expand the discussion of community, especially because in the Jamaican context any such discussion must acknowledge the problematics of class. Bookman's journey to naming the Reggae Revival is parallel to his coming to a kind of consciousness in

Rastafari. Bookman's perceived and perhaps implied uptown status as a "browning" educated at Campion College (which has become the most elite high school in Jamaica) and in Miami is compromised once he finds Rastafari. In fact, Bookman's transformation from Gavin Hutchinson to Dutty Bookman is a narrative very similar to other so-called enlightenment narratives, in which spiritual gain parallels diminishing social status—at least at first. Perhaps the more accurate term is "social shift," as Bookman finds himself aligned with a different social cohort of culturally conscious youth. It is this cohort of young Jamaicans and others who are similarly ideologically aligned and artistically minded that Bookman calls the Reggae Revival. Ultimately, he was not fully aware at this point of the impact this naming would have, nor was he fully aware of the extent of the spiritual and artistic resurgence of reggae and the culture surrounding it, but his close interactions with Oje Ollivierre, known as Protoje; with Janine Cunningham, known as Jah9; and with the Uprising Roots Band and the Bebble Rock Team suggest that Bookman and his contemporaries were already gathering around Rasta and music at an ideological base away from the mainstream.

In the chapter of his book titled "Spot Check," Bookman describes an encounter he and Protoje had with the police. His account suggests that this encounter facilitated an important spiritual and creative connection:

> On another occasion, this time in Kingston, we were at a gathering and he was going on the road to get something that we determine necessary for the enhancement of the meditation. I went along with him and, in the car, our mutual respect for each other became apparent. I sensed the potential for cooperation. . . . Not until I dreamed about Haile Selassie I did it begin to dawn on me that Oje and I potentially had the combined capacity to effect significant and positive change in society through our different modes of self expression. I still did not know what we would create together or how we would do it, but I felt very sure we had to cooperate on a mission. (Bookman, 2011, 97, 83, 101)

The story of what they create together and of their shared mission is manifest in the narrative of Dutty and Oje being pulled over for a spot check on Mountain View Avenue in Kingston. The officers find Dutty's chalice and his recently purchased herb, and he is arrested for a short period. For the hour or so that he is behind bars, Dutty uses a treasured notebook to record the scene. He admits that he assails the officers with sarcastic comments and the bitter contempt he feels for the law, and perhaps this manifestation of the law that he deems to be ignorant, incapable, and ultimately unfair.

It is very difficult not to see Jamaican class politics being played out here—Dutty and Protoje (Gavin and Oje) read as "brown," "uptown" youngsters making a foray into a world that is not quite their own, likely by way of music or some other artistic interest. Dutty notes that the officers find them to be "comedians at heart" (Bookman, 2011, 83). And Dutty, more than Oje, for many more reasons than he mentions—perhaps the register in which the officers speak, where they are stationed, and all the other social marker readings that such an encounter would encourage—feels great "upset" that these "squaddies" (low-ranking officers) and the arrogant inspector never return the chalice nor the herb to him. Perhaps one thing Dutty does not consider is that just as he reads the squaddies and the inspector as working class and ignorant, they read and treat him as privileged and thus exercise as much of their power as they can, even if to symbolically articulate their positions. Their seeming incompetence and dedication to the letter of the law is, rather, a statement of police resistance in a place where there are no laws for the wealthy and well-connected. In the Mountain View Avenue police station, the officers have the power only to inconvenience and humiliate. In a very real and potent sense, policing as the surveillance machinery of the state breaks down in the face of class. The class politics at play here may not be true for everyone in the revival, but the encounter does point to the ways the inclusiveness of the revival remains fraught and tenuous by class. Most of the practitioners are associated not with a rigid middle class but certainly with an educated class, which even as it embraces a twenty-first-century egalitarian class consciousness is connected, inadvertently or otherwise, with societal hierarchies.

It is the teaching of His Majesty's[4] principles, and indeed Rasta as a central ideological gathering ground, that the revivalists agree connect them. In Chronixx's "Here Comes Trouble," Protoje's "Who Dem a Program," Jah9's "New Name," and Kabaka Pyramid's "Lead the Way," the call of Rasta is a call to a renewed spiritual investment, in a renewed form, and in a renewed message. A total embrace and support of other revivalists and their artistic endeavors as well as a philosophy of economic inclusion is an important tenet of the movement. As a business model, these practices eliminate the need for a "big man" producer/promoter/investor/overseer and instead encourage reliance on the range of artistic and socioeconomic resources available among those in the movement. In live shows as well as in music videos and collaborations, the community-centeredness of the revival is striking.[5]

The lyrics of Protoje's "A Who Dem a Program" and the official music video are in many ways a textual exposé of the Reggae Revival. The video has a very different beginning from Papa San's 1993 version of the song, which included Stan Ryck (when "who dem a program" meant who are they staring at, fassing with, maco-ing). Protoje's "programming" has little or nothing to do with Papa San's bad boy–pretty girl standoff, where materialism and sex are the territorial cornerstones, yet it uses some of the words from the Papa San version. In Protoje's video, the first images besides the artist himself, who is dressed to immediately signal Rasta, are flashes of the symbols of Babylon: the Inland Revenue Department, the Jamaica Stock Exchange, Jamaica Public Service, the Bank of

Jamaica, and various government ministries, including the Ministry of Education. The (Big Brother) "programming" here is done by Babylon, and the resistance to that programming comes in a revived artistic product. While the general rhythm is the same, the texture and pace of the song are not led by digitized sounds but by the live music of the Indiggnation Band, who are also foregrounded. Always close behind Protoje, in a kind of march-chant-trod, is the revivalist photographer and videographer Puru, reading a holy text. Other revivalists in the video include the NoMadzz, Jah9, Yaadcore, and Karece—a virtual village of support.

The final image in the video is of visual artist Matthew McCarthy finishing the painting of the Lion of Judah as part of a mural on the wall of Grafton Studios in Kingston.[6] Protoje in this song and video reprograms the Jamaican music scene. He rejects the usual oppressive overseeing forces of Babylon and the materialism and mechanization internalized and born out of its gilded cities. The "brand new prince on the scene" (Protoje) does not stand alone; he has beside him, behind him, and before him others like himself, reading, standing, painting, meditating, playing their support. In "A Who Dem a Program," then, there is plenty of evidence of reggae speaking with a new vocabulary, not only in its response to dancehall culture but in the sense of a collective artistic project. Perhaps more than that, Protoje's resistance to programming challenges the label of the revival at the very moment that it celebrates its possibilities. This is just one example of the complicated and flexible dynamics that interpolated the bongo futures that the revival reached after.

Roots of the Revival

Matthew McCarthy, whose paintbrush and mural are signal visuals in the final frame of the Protoje video, has been described as a visual artist of the Reggae Revival.[7] McCarthy, a graduate of the Edna Manley College of the Visual and Performing Arts, is an illustrator and mural painter. Petrona Morrisson, in her introduction to the exhibit New Roots at the National Gallery from July to September 2013, of which McCarthy was a part, describes McCarthy's work: "The site-specific work of Matthew McCarthy and the New Jamaica Collective is defiant in its emphasis on collective engagement, and forces the audience to reevaluate their ideas about 'art' in the museum space" (Morrison, 2013). McCarthy's discomfort with defining spatial categories is evidenced in his outsized and odd-sized pieces not made for museums or for the walls of collectors but rather for the outside and for the elements; it is also evidenced in his resistance to labels and categories.

McCarthy, who grew up on Red Hills Road in Kingston, a very long street that is residential and commercial, with working-class through middle-class communities, says he has always been a student of the flamboyancy of Jamaican street art and typography. He was fascinated by signboards and shop signage and spent much of his time doodling replications. He also cites the paintings of mainstream artist Barrington Watson as an influence on his work because he sees in Watson elements of a cartoonist. As well, McCarthy has been inspired and influenced by artists who "portray their society in the way they actually see it," and for McCarthy, the Japanese are very effective here. He notes the work of Shigeru Miyamoto, Takashi Murakami, and Akira Toriyama—Japanese animators and game artists whose work includes Mario Brothers games, *Dragon Ball Z*, and the movie *Akira* (Matthew McCarthy, artist, in conversation with the author, November 13, 2013). His work with Protoje and other revivalists began on sets for music videos, and he found among the young musicians an unflinching attention to the ills in Jamaican society. He also sees chimera in Rastafari and Japanese anime, in their preoccupation with apocalypse and futures unchained by the realities of social norms and cultures soon to implode. McCarthy's vision here is of a place for futures in the revival and, more than that, a place for iconoclastic cultural meetings. Certainly, a question that arises from this is, how does the revival suggest a new genealogy of reggae? One could say, then, that by naming these influences and using the term *reggae*, revivalists are suggesting that reggae is not so much a phenomenon situated in a particular historical moment but rather a principle that they are resurrecting.

I return to McCarthy's mural *Rise Up* on the Deanery Road walls of Grafton Studios to begin an analysis of the connections between the revival and visual art, but also as a way to consider how the making/painting of the mural, a crucial visual in the video, extends the possibilities of interpretation and also gives further insight into the roots of the revival. The mural painted on the burnt orange wall depicts in the foreground a Black Rastaman covering the camera lens of a man with a gray crew cut. The man holding the camera could easily be from the police or the military. The angularity of the man's side profile obscures his race but almost certainly confirms him as official and powerful. The severity of

FIGURE 4. *Rise Up*: Mural by Matthew McCarthy on the wall of Grafton Studios, a recording studio and popular meeting place for musicians. Grafton Studios is on the corner of Grafton Road and Deanery Road, Kingston 3.

his features is compounded by his camera, which could also be read as a weapon—a gun, perhaps, so that the Rastaman's hand covering the lens seems to be in danger. The man with the camera is not the only gray figure, however; hovering above his head is a gray bird with a camera for a face. The steely grayness of both the man holding the camera and the camera-headed surveillance bird are in marked opposition to the local merino-clad torso and muscular arms of the Rastaman. There is no airborne support above the Rastaman's head, only the thought presumably responsible for the Rastaman's covering of the camera: "Who dem a program?" In the background of the mural is a bright yellow Lion of Judah, looking regal and conquering, presumably overseeing the standoff in the foreground. The lion carries a scepter with a swath of red, green, and gold flying from its end. Like the lion's tail, which seems to be alive and in motion, the red, green, and gold flying from the scepter has the same impact. The flying tricolored "flag/tail" suggests victory. The mural very clearly depicts the song's concern with and resistance to local Jamaican "programming" mentioned earlier. There are various symbolizations of power at multiple levels: the supremacy of Rasta against Babylon, iterating the foundational principle of Rasta against Babylon; in the context of the Tivoli incursion and the blatant use of intimidatory force by the United States, an assertion of transcendent spirituality as an effective antidote to hegemonic neoliberalism and its instruments of surveillance; and the standoff that positions Rasta as a political force within the nation, the only one effectively standing against the incursions of the West.

But perhaps without the mural, we would pay much less attention to the global programming presented in the video as well. For instance, the angular man in official gray, his camera, and the camera-headed bird cause me to see and pay closer attention to the passing shot in the video of a gray surveillance airplane in gray skies, just as Protoje sings the word *spy*. The U.S. military-style drone above Jamaica's skies is a very weighty and effective reminder of the Tivoli Gardens incursion, in which it is now widely believed that Jamaican and U.S. forces joined to capture and extradite Tivoli don and Shower Posse leader/drug lord Christopher "Dudus" Coke. When, in response to Prime Minister Bruce Golding's initial refusal to extradite Dudus, the United States began revoking visas of politicians, top entertainers, and businessmen, this "programming" evoked fear and silence among many powerful people and groups in Jamaica. Perhaps the most booming silence sounded when, after the incursion and massacre, a usually quickly prolific local music industry produced no songs about the incursion.

The only song directly recounting the incursion is "Kingston Town" by a Trinidadian artist recording in Jamaica named Ataklan:

I was working on my album
voicing some wicked sounds

police started looking for the biggest don
chaos all around.
Man, so many dead bodies
so few recovered guns
and I feel it for those mothers
who still weeping for their sons. (Ataklan, 2013)

But perhaps what was a perceived silence in terms of songs and lyrics had a grander efficacy for the provenance of a movement. McCarthy locates his work and his art as part of a revival, though it is not necessarily conceived in reggae. Rather, he sees Jamaican art and music responding to critical sociocultural and political "tipping points" that have affected the island and the globe. McCarthy locates the Reggae Revival and a more general cultural revival of a certain brand of consciousness as a response to a tipping point, in this case, the Tivoli Gardens incursion. For him, it is an occasion when visual art speaks with music and for music. We could say the mural speaks where the music is silenced; we could say that the mural amplifies the complaint in the song—globalizing the programmers and threatening their power.

Tivoli

The broader sociopolitical and economic moment to which the "Dudus-Golding fiasco" and the incursion belong, what McCarthy terms a "tipping point" in Jamaican culture, is that of a worldwide embrace of neoliberalism and local responses to top-heavy, self-serving powers.[8] In *A Brief History of Neoliberalism*, David Harvey defines the concept: "Neoliberalism is in the first instance, a theory of political economic practice that proposes that human well-being can best be advanced by liberating individual entrepreneurial freedoms and skills within and an institutional framework characterized by strong private property rights, free markets and free trade." Harvey goes on to explain that "the process of neoliberalization has ... entailed much 'creative destruction,' not only of prior institutional frameworks and powers ... but also of divisions of labour, social relations, welfare provisions, technological mixes, ways of life and thought, reproductive activities, attachments to the land and habits of the heart" (Harvey, 2007, 2, 3). Free trade agreements and the "reorganization of international capitalism" have had a marked effect on the Jamaican economy. In the decades following the destruction of key local industries, sans government protections, private enterprises have exploited natural and human resources and then banked their profits abroad.

The resulting inequalities have plagued the social and cultural fabric of Jamaica. In her book *Exceptional Violence*, Deborah Thomas establishes, "Within Latin American and Caribbean contexts ... the scholarly emphasis has been on the structural violence that has become part of the fabric of everyday life. Of crucial importance here has been a sense that the state, which should be protecting people from violence and providing social order and justice, has shattered." She goes on to argue, "Neoliberalism is the culprit here—shaping civil wars, legitimizing U.S. interventions, and generating gross social inequalities" (Thomas, 2011, 10). In the Dudus-Golding fiasco, the general acceptance and silence of underreported corporate bad-manism and the very carefully reported gang corruption could no longer remain hidden, not with an international audience looking on. What was also revealed was the alternative social structure under which residents of Tivoli Gardens lived. In the absence of state protection and welfare, "residents went to Coke for tuition, legal aid, business loans, food, and medicine" (Schwartz, 2011, 65). Under Dudus's rule, crime was under (his) control. The state had so failed the residents of Tivoli, and Dudus had so saved them, that despite the evidence of international courts and in the face of the Jamaica police force and the army, residents marched, fought, and died for President Dudus.

The contours of neoliberal logic still couched in well-entrenched colonial hegemonies are manifest in the Dudus-Golding fiasco. Jamaicans knew for certain that Golding's uptown brown supporters would not have died like Dudus's downtown Black ones. They also knew that the same power that forced Golding to agree to Dudus's extradition had silenced the bards. Perhaps it is in this moment of silence and cultural drought that the sounds of the revival begin to be heard. The lyrics of Chronixx's "Capture Land" and Kabaka Pyramid's "We No Want No Capitalist" are in good company with the corpus of music that comes out of the revival: "Watch dem pon top a di hill / a look inna dem plate how it proper and it fill," Chronixx sings. "Because downtown people have shotta fi kill / Dem tell the tourist fi stop a Negril" (Chronixx, 2014). Kabaka sings, "We nuh want no capitalist / I man suss dem out wid I man chalice / and we nuh want no big business plan / we nuh want no promise from the UN" (Kabaka Pyramid, 2013). Chronixx uncovers the insidious nature of class in Jamaica, overturning the widely held notion that poor people steal land or capture land by becoming squatters on it. Chronixx suggests instead that the original squatters were Columbus and his crew and that the powerful (locally and internationally) are bold and pernicious thieves. Kabaka's refrain is largely concerned with global thievery; not only does he openly condemn capitalism and the United Nations, but he also lights his chalice as open symbolic opposition. The rejection of neoliberalism as an alternative way of negotiating the Jamaican experience in the world is evidenced on at least two levels here. The first is that the music speaks in clear tones about these themes. The second is that the Reggae Revival community sees their shared stage as their anti-capitalist plan—a way forward, a new future—and this not only implies dissatisfaction with Jamaican politics but implicates the direction of the Jamaican cultural scene.

Neoliberalism and Futures

The collocation of forms and influences that I have discussed so far as central to the revival are not only evidenced in the work of Protoje and McCarthy. Protoje's reggaefying dancehall and McCarthy's fascination with Japanese anime only become more interesting in company with the jazziness of Jah9, who considers Nina Simone her musical forebear, and with Kabaka Pyramid, who names Wu Tang Clan as his main influence. Perhaps one group that embodies the breadth and the possibilities in the Reggae Revival is the No-Maddz, a four-member band consisting of Sheldon "Sheppie" Shepherd, Everaldo Creary, Chris Gordon, and Oniel Peart. The No-Maddz, who began their artistic endeavors in the drama club at Kingston College, see dub poetry as the root of their art. According to Sheppie, the four entered a number of Independence Festival competitions, winning both gold and confidence in their talent as performance poets.[9] That they came to their music through dub and theater has significantly marked their style and expanded the possibilities in their politics. Michael Bucknor begins his essay "Dub Poetry as Postmodern Art Form" with, "Dub poetry is Jamaica's gift of a new art-form to the literary world," a significant claim in light of the No-Maddz, a reggae band whose music is inspired by and emerges from their work in theater and dub poetry. Bucknor outlines the debates among dub poets and critics about how to name this poetry, "characterized by its reliance on musical support and sound techniques, its use of demotic language—creole speech, dread talk, 'nation language'—its exploitation of speech rituals and resources of the oral tradition—warning, prophecy, name-calling, cursing, call and response—and by allusiveness, proverbial wisdom and verbal wit" (Bucknor, 2011, 255).

The presence of the No-Maddz's music in the moment of revival invites us to talk about music that begins in dub poetry, thus complicating the genealogy of their art. What, then, is dub, a poetic form that comes out of a particular musical tradition, when it doubles back to its origin as music but with a new and different musical sound? Where the dub poet has written to the rhythm and sound of a particular musical form, the dub musician makes music an equal accompaniment to the poetry as well as a translation of it. Translation can come in several forms—for example, through the tonality of the music interpreting the poem or through the remaking of song or story into a music-accompanied poem. Certainly, it would seem that in its place in the history of the No-Maddz's evolution, dub poetry becomes part of the revival's genealogy, making a significant impact on reggae and the musical culture as a whole. "Bongo music" is the term the No-Maddz use to describe their art. We could say that bongo music makes music the accompaniment to the essential poetry, stretching the limits of poetry.

Another possibility is in the consideration of the No-Maddz's art as reggae theater. In the song written to celebrate Jamaica's fiftieth anniversary of independence—"Sort Out Yuh Life, Jamaica!" or "It is time to get the nation in order, Jamaicans"—they begin with an ode to creativity. The lyrics "performance, integrity, teamwork, respect, and communication" are sung on a ledge of the dilapidated Ward Theatre, now closed to the public (No-Maddz, "Sort Out Yuh Life, Jamaica!" *Sort Out Yuh Life*, 2011). The theater, which opened officially on December 16, 1912, was a gift from the "Honorable Charles James Ward, Lieutenant Colonel, Custos of Kingston." From its inception, the Ward Theatre was seen as a performance space for the support of local groups. In *Jamaican Theatre*, Wycliffe and Hazel Bennett explain, "Despite the fact that the theatrical scene continued to be dominated by touring companies from overseas, local enthusiasts ensured that a show produced locally would mark the opening of the Ward Theatre" (Bennett and Bennett, 2011, 25). That the site of disrepair itself is a stage for the No-Maddz and the theater the stage for their bongo music is instructive. The No-Maddz see their music as firmly rooted in the Jamaican theater and perhaps even as redemption from its current reality. If the disrepair of the Ward signifies faltering official and unofficial support of local creative enterprise, then the No-Maddz's call for Jamaica and Jamaicans to "sort out" their lives is a call for renewed support of artistic and cultural institutions. Indeed, the theme of the local is explored throughout the song.

The music video underscores the No-Maddz's support of local industry and the indigenous cultural spaces from which they emerged. While the narrative frame begins with the broken windows and the peeling paint of the Ward Theatre, the performance on the ledge and the terrace below breathes new life into the space. The revival of the Ward begins a more general celebration of the local. The No-Maddz's journey around the island—by bus, taxi, police escort, and bike back—takes us to banana plantations, dancehall sessions, a Rastafarian drumming session, vistas of the roiling seas, roadside stalls, and beaches unspoiled by tourists. The video for "Sort Out Yuh Life, Jamaica!" signals the group's commitment to Jamaican theater, as do many of their live shows. Their reggae theater production *Breadfruit Is the New Bread, Baby* offered as its central aim a kind of rededication to local Jamaican food and culture to sustain the nation. Breadfruit, brought to Jamaica by Captain William Bligh in the 1790s, was one of many alternative food staples sought as a cheaper way to feed the slaves. *Breadfruit Is the New Bread, Baby* recounts Jamaica's dependence on food and products that it cannot afford and suggests through a return to more sustainable physical sustenance a renewed commitment to more carefully chosen cultural sustenance.

The No-Maddz interrogate neoliberal hegemonies in many of the same ways that others in the revival do, primarily through Rastafari. Engrained in this religious philosophy is *fiya bun* (indignation and rejection) for systems of inequality and injustice. In the Jamaican context, these have included the imposition of British colonial cultural values and the subsequent embodiment of those values by the colonized. In *Breadfruit* the No-Maddz propose a New Bread Order, with critiques of corporate Jamaica and of the Christian church and its role in cultural underdevelopment and with an exposé of local music and sound. The line that ends the second verse of "Sort Out Yuh Life, Jamaica!" is a striking rewriting of local importance and desirability: "Everybody want a piece of the Jamaican dream." That there is a Jamaican dream, a play on the American dream, is itself a novel concept. It is an inward-looking vision looking outward, a recasting of the meaning of success, a statement of values that is concerned with the well-being of more of the nation, not less. The emphasis on including the concept of the nation is in concert with other revivalists such as Protoje and Chronixx, whose music reveals this as part of a revival of spiritual and political consciousness.

Conclusion

This bongo futures aesthetic remakes the boundaries of reggae by extending it to a principle that not only undergirds but also, significantly, brings together artists of various genres—performance, spoken and written word, visualization, and installation—to create an umbrella genre that is at once local and indigenous and is linked conceptually and phenomenologically, and certainly in terms of explicitly espoused influences, to contemporary postmodernist movements in the global arena. By their shared ideologies of community and their performance collaborations, the artists extended the meaning and contours of performance space and call for the construction of new physical spaces in which to house such productions, since clearly the old, separated demarcations of dance/music hall, outdoor open stages for music bands, indoor theater for dramatic productions, and closed museum spaces for visual art and installations are no longer adequate. More than that, they renamed Babylon by rallying around a common outrage that marks a particular moment of crisis in Jamaica's postcolonial history—the Dudus moment becomes as defining and as apocalyptic as the 2010 earthquake in Haiti or 9/11 in the United States; it replaces C.E. as much as C.E. replaced A.D. In this way, the movement marked off its insistently Jamaican genealogy from its global associations. This is only one of its many complexities of doubleness, if you like—for as we have seen, the anomalies and contradictions of its class-inclusive ideology as well as the disparate ideological orientations of its practitioners and their refusal of labels while marking themselves off as a signal (re)defining moment in Jamaican art history and culture are among the features that showed the Reggae Revival as the child of a future that is past and is imagined in its present.

Doubleness in the life of this Caribbean modern moment appears from another angle as I shift to contemplate the revival's present. It may be argued that the greatest challenge to the spirit of the revival has been its outsized success: that while visibility and community were crucial to the movement in its beginning, international attention and all it entails have obliterated the need for the particular kind of community that the revival espoused. Moreover, international success may well have compromised the movement's aim to dissociate from Babylon in the form of big (Brother) state/small state, big business, and the unhumananizing rat race of competition. The shapes of ambiguities that I have discussed in this book, however, offer an alternative view. Thinking through the lens of flexible hegemonies allows us to see that power and influence are not a one-way street but a space that is shared, kinetic, and contested. The revivalists' ethos and message and their sound are part of the global flow, alongside losses they have undoubtedly sustained in consequence of their success in the global marketplace and soundscape. More crucial is the fact that the revival remains an integral part of Jamaica's recuperative self-imaginary post 2010.

Much of the residue of the Tivoli affair was a vast national shame, a sense that the country had been exposed to a dirty-laundry washing under the international gaze. The Reggae Revival emerged as a corrective vision of what the country wanted to be and a mirror on its imagined past. Though the moment of the revival's beginning is different from its present phase—partly because of the passing of time and partly because of the immense success that the movement has attained—one cardinal principle has remained unchanged: the Reggae Revival's grounding in Rastafari. (This remains true though, as I have discussed, this is not Africa-centric or vintage Rasta, but Rasta as a twenty-first-century consciousness that echoes various strands of indigenous religious sound and political action.) Perhaps it is Rastafari—and the larger realm of the spirit— that is the link between the revival and yards, slums, and other *downpressed*, high-surveillance spaces. Rasta bredren of the Dungle continue to face the often brutal, always surveilling eye of the state. Less directly subject to the brutalities of the state, twenty-first-century Rastas of the ilk of the revivalists have used their music to speak out against injustice, capitalism, corruption, environmental degradation, treatment of the poor, political schemes and scams, money-loving, gunman and shotta, and to speak up for those who have no public forum to speak up for themselves. They position themselves as seers and redemption chanters for the common good. Yet there is a way in which the theme of Babylon's surveillance of Rastafari is overarching. In the lyrics of most revivalists, legal prohibitions against the sacraments of Rasta are consistently condemned as an intrusion of the law into sacred space and practice.[10]

The insistence on the sacrality of the human is the long thread and the break in official time that we perceive in the strategies of resistance and self-making from Carnival to suss to Revival to Rastafari to revival, and others.

Coda

• • • • • • • • • • • • • • • • • • • •

> On this island things fidget.
> Even history.
> The landscape does not sit
> willingly
> as if behind an easel
> holding pose
> —Kei Miller, "What the Mapmaker
> Ought to Know"

In a state of emergency, or in this nineteenth-century version—the declaration of martial law by Governor John Eyre—troops were mobilized to quell peasant-led foment in St. Thomas in the east at its capital, Morant Bay. It was 1865, just twenty-seven years after full freedom. When the troops completed their mission, 465 black Jamaicans had died and many more were brutally flogged. One thousand houses were burned to the ground.

In a state of emergency, the longest in Jamaica's history—from June 19, 1976, to June 6, 1977—the Smile Jamaica concert headlining reggae superstar Bob Marley was held at the National Heroes Park. Over 40,000 people attended.

In a state of emergency during the Tivoli incursion of 2010, seventy-three people were killed. Seventy were civilians and three were members of the security forces. Thousands of men were arrested.

In a state of emergency, eight of Jamaica's fourteen parishes—St. Ann, Clarendon, St. Catherine, Kingston, St. Andrew, St. James, Westmoreland, and Hanover—rang in the new year, 2023. In red block letters, the caption "SOE's Dilemma" was the front-page story of the January 1, 2023, edition of the

Sunday Gleaner. The caption was placed under a photograph of fireworks and wishes for a Happy New Year.

In a state of emergency, citizens' rights are restricted. Limited mobility is imposed through curfews, and citizens are exposed to the full surveilling force of the state. But "the landscape does not sit/willing." In opposition to the hegemonic narrative which *marks off* space and time with formal brushstrokes of law and social geography, another perspective emerges here, which is that "[o]n this island things fidget. / Even history." That is to say that in states of emergency, sometimes parties are held and concerts attended. And even when the state's will is silence and fear, demonstrations are held, bold stories are told and retold, and inquiries are launched. The reiterative history of states of emergency in Jamaica is also the story of the people's resilience and the irrepressible sounds of another narrative of history via the vernacular arts and *higher sciences*. This is history that the cartographer cannot read. These are maps the cartographer cannot draw.

The State of Public Emergency Act of 1938 explains the legal process and the circumstances under which the governor general of Jamaica could declare a fourteen-day period of public emergency. The period can be extended to three months after its expiration if both houses of Parliament agree. Implicit in the Act but not explicitly stated is the delicate relationship between a targeted space and a specific period of time, fourteen or thirty days. The entire island may experience a period of public emergency, or the state of emergency may be specific to hot spots. Even more, while the entire island is under a state of emergency, different people experience the public emergency differently.

At various times since the 1960s, the concept of the state of emergency has escalated to even more extreme forms of surveillance and control. One permutation that has become important to controlling crime in Jamaica is the use of zones of special operation, or ZOSOs. These zones, staffed by soldiers and police, are placed strategically in communities with high crime rates in times of heightened criminal activity (gang war, turf war, flare-ups of violence, etc.). The Law Reforms (Zones of Special Operations) Act of 2017, which invokes the use of ZOSOs, is "an act to provide for special measures for upholding and preserving the Rule of Law, public order, citizen security, and public safety within certain geographically defined areas of Jamaica; and for connected matters" (https://docs.google.com/document/d/1Nw2H0EU8sxkn98Ft6j7IveWOtqCj YfjgtWxm4AxRwpA/edit). The law's concern with "certain geographically defined areas" makes it different from the usual declaration of a state of public emergency, because these are always targeted areas and not ever (even potentially) the entire country. Unlike a public emergency that begins as a fourteen-day period, ZOSOs are declared for sixty days with the possibility of extension. ZOSOs have become a fixture on the Jamaican social landscape. They work as a kind of fixed but movable surveillance technology. Driving through one of these checkpoints by Flankers, St. James; Spanish Town; or

August Town—all urban spaces with primarily either working-class/poor populations or high concentrations of such—means vehicular traffic slowing significantly as it passes through a wall of police officers or soldiers carrying semiautomatic weapons. Drivers and passengers are expected to be fully visible to the combined forces, and it is routine for select vehicles to be pulled over for a more careful search. ZOSOs and the question of their efficacy have continued to be a prominent issue in a present and ongoing national debate about state power, surveillance, and the measures used for curbing crime in Jamaica. While debates about their effectiveness as crime-fighting mechanisms are numerous and topical, questions about the politics of space or the issue of "geographically defined areas" have garnered much less attention.

States of emergency not only restrict movement and heighten state surveillance—they also *mark off places and people*. Often these marks are long historical scars still tender to the touch. And often too, the state of emergency may not be de jure—that is, not officially declared—but the machinery including surveillance deployed in a specific place is a de facto execution of emergency. Morant Bay and the quelling of the 1865 uprising, Coral Gardens where Rastafari were tortured and shot amid an upswing in anti-Rasta sentiment across the island (1963), Green Bay and the ambush and massacre of Jamaica Labour Party supporters by members of the Jamaica Defence Force (1978), and Tivoli Gardens (2010) have been sites of formalized, state-designated surveillance in Jamaica. Indeed, the employment of ZOSOs may be regarded as a formalization of the kinds of practices that were already long in use, as in Coral Gardens and Green Bay. Names of places become seared into national memory as sites of contestation between the poor and the surveillance state (the state becomes a surveillance state mainly only in contestation with the poor); names of places that assert alternative histories emerge in aphorisms, proverbial sayings, the established ways of marking history.

The urbanscape of Jamaica has been of cardinal importance to this project. Repeatedly I and the writers and scholars I engage in this project are exercised by lists of the names of communities in Jamaica used to indicate space-specific information. I am struck by this practice. What does it mean to mark space like this? Is a litany of names cartography too? "Tivoli, Denham Town, Stadium Gardens" (introduction). "Rae Town, Brown's Town, Lindo's Town, Hannah Town and Smith Village to which were added Fletcher's Town, Kingston Gardens, Allman Town, Franklin Town and Passmore Town" (Clarke, 2006c, 34). "Hannah's Town, Smith's Village, Jones' Pen, New Town, out into the Spanish Town Road" (Moore and Johnson, 2000, 109). In other narrations, the geography and landscape of Jamaica have been critical as spaces that are traversed and described in surveillance contexts: in newspaper reports, the path of the demonstration that the women in white from Tivoli take; in Patterson's fictive-sociological geography, Dinah's circular movement from the Dungle to the tenements back to the Dungle; in de Lisser's sussveiling perambulations,

Jane's walks through the city of Kingston, but perhaps most memorably when she leaves Mrs. Mason's house for the tenements, "the innumerable yards in . . . the numerous lanes of Kingston" (de Lisser, 1972, 95).

This book is also concerned with defined spaces that signify beyond their geographic boundaries: the spirit pull of the Dungle, 56 Hope Road as an uptown yard, the Smile Jamaica concert at the National Heroes Circle as a signifier of the tense, frowning time in 1976 Kingston, and Tivoli Gardens in the aftermath of the incursion are examples. The island fidgets, the landscape does not sit willingly, and the cartographer's lines surrender to *other* ways of thinking about space. The metaphysics of suss and the spirit undermine the cartographer's grid of the city.

The issues discussed in this book invite reflection not only about space but also about how time is marked under surveillance. On the one hand, this is what David Scott describes in *Omens of Adversity* as the "apprehension of temporal insecurity and uncertainty" (Scott, 2014a, 12) that arises from the definition of time conceived as a linear phenomenon and history conceived as a narrative of progress along time's linear continuum. Obviously, for the tenement dweller, living in the constant shadow of progress unrealized, such definitions constitute an existential anomaly. For the tenement dweller—and here we go back to the Caribbean quotidian—the crisis of temporal insecurity and uncertainty is the fabric of everyday life *at home*. To live every day in a moment of crisis is to live in a double relation to time (and space). And this produces the other side: a great facility in re-creating—that is to say, making over—the future *in the moment*, even in situations of heightened crisis. Tenement time in the narratives of those who experience it is flexible, nimble, insistent against the teleology of temporal uncertainty.

In this light, I am struck by how Deborah Thomas witnesses the incursion from the perspective of Tivoli residents who survived the incursion. Thomas invites her readers into the residents' experience of space and time: "If you were a male youth in Tivoli Gardens the week of 24 May 2010, you likely experienced something like what Shawn Bowen went through" (Thomas, 2019, 24).

"If you were a woman with children in Tivoli Gardens during the incursion, you might have had an experience like Claudette Morgan's on that Monday morning of 24 May" (Thomas, 2019, 26). Tivoli is the space, May 24, 2010, is the marked time. Already we know that this couldn't happen in Cherry Gardens, Hope Gardens, Mona, or Beverly Hills. Their chilling testimony is a marker of time and place. Shawn, Claudette, and Annette Irving's stories show them thinking in tenement time. They appear to remain acutely aware and observant, cerebrally documenting events in minute detail even in the most heightened moments of terror.

"Shawn noticed soldiers on top of the buildings with masks covering their faces—looking up at them earned him several smacks across his back with a piece of wood—and he saw men lined up 'neat in a row' on their knees. After about six or seven hours at that location, another truck came, and they were told to get in. . . . He was kept there for several days 'for processing,' during which time he was unable to sleep or bathe" (Thomas, 2019, 25).

"During those long four days, thirteen people occupied their kitchen." Claudette prepared food every day, but no one could eat—"we just barely take like a mouthful and that was it because shots fired nonstop, nonstop. . . . [I]t was like we're in Vietnam" (Thomas, 2019, 26).

"[Annette's] sister Pet was on the way to church because she didn't feel comfortable staying at her house; Annette argued with Pet and told her to stay put at home. Some moments later, she received a call from a friend telling her that Pet had been shot on the corner of North Street and Chestnut Lane. Annette's sister's body stayed in the road for three days" (Thomas, 2019, 27).

Thomas's form of narration highlights two layers of the history from inside: first, the perspective of the citizens pressing to be seen and heard. Second, the vast *compression of time* in which a long historical arc of terror is lived in a handful of days or a moment: "six or seven hours," "several days," "long four days," "shots fired nonstop, nonstop," "some moments later," "three days." Tracking the experience in this way, between time markers of the invasion and everyday activities by which residents kept their feet balanced on the shifting ground (the simple act of cooking, walking to church), we visualize time and history not as abstract concepts but as the pulse of how life and death are experienced within the tenement under pressure. Time is calibrated in heartbeats; the space between one breath and another; the gap between a sudden death and the waiting for a burial. The litany of time markers reoutlines the geography of the space that is Tivoli, not by its location as the once-upon-a-time Back O' Wall or by its present identity as a garrison community in the inner city of downtown, but by its division between the inner and the outer scapes: the kitchen, crowded closely with thirteen refugees; the church not reached; the roofs of buildings taken over by police and military; the familiar streets now sites of choreographed humiliations and disappearances; the interior lanes as contingent morgues. The sense of a familiar alienation is conveyed by Claudette's "it was like we're in Vietnam" (Thomas, 2019, 26).

Shawn recalls himself thinking at the moment when he was sure he was going to be killed, "Mama a go miss a son now" (Thomas, 2019, 25). In the *compression* of the moment, he restructures the expectation of his own death with a calm message to himself that yet functions as a matter-of-fact "psychic telegram" to his mother, who is his first thought. Shawn's statement is arresting in the familiarity of its subject (the annual statistics of young men dying by violence are high; the idea that it is women who lose their sons is endemic)[1] and in the concentrated quietude with which he appears to contemplate his expected death, beyond the moment of terror. In this apparent garnering of thought and relation in a heartbeat of time, there is a way in which terror is not allowed to have the last word.

Another version of Jamaica erupts out of Shawn's, Annette's, and Claudette's stories and other stories of the Caribbean's long history of oppression. This version is a narrative of resistance, of claiming the right to speak and to be heard. It emerges in the alternative geographies by which the people remapped the island in names of warning (Me-No-Sen-Yu-Nuh-Come, Shotover, Gimme Mi Bit, Nannyville, Angola, Gaza); in names that established family land and free villages as statements of prophecy (Mount Peace, Mount Horeb, Pinnacle, Mt. Salem); and in aftermaths like the Reggae Revival. It signifies in the irresistible trace of Africa manifested in markings at Afro-syncretic church doorways, the sound of Nyabinghi drums, and the figure of the flying African—examples of a panoply of spiritual arts that adhere stubbornly to ideas of metaphysical time.

Inside tenement time is also that infinitesimal space or hesitation when the inmate of the yard stops for a moment of self-care (a sip of water, a straightened shirt, a word with Jah) and walks with purpose in the direction of the curfew.

Acknowledgments

I hope this book will look its age, because Jah know, it's taken a long time to get to what you are reading. Over the years and the miles, I have many to thank for their kindness, generosity, colleagueship, and presence. Give thanks, thank you.

The seed idea for this book didn't come from a dream or a voice from the heavens. I have a memory of sitting in a café in Liguanea (down the road from Mona, Jamaica) with Deborah Thomas talking about our work on the Tivoli incursion—hers big and mine quite small. And Deborah asking me, who is working on surveillance in Caribbean literature? Give thanks, Deborah, for asking such a generative question.

My own work on Tivoli began with an interest in the Reggae Revival and its emergence after Tivoli 2010. Give thanks for Mikie Bennett (Grafton Mikie), who was instrumental to my research on the artists and the culture of the revival. Mikie B put me in touch with all kinds of people. Sheldon Shepherd of the No-Maddz, Jah9, Kabaka Pyramid, T'Jean Bennett, Jesse Royal, I-Nation (bookseller), Matthew McCarthy (visual artist), Puru (videographer), Rory "Stone Love" Gilligan (producer), and a host of good-up others. Obviously, my library life woke up for these blessings.

Mikie also gave me a start in the conversations that helped frame chapter 3 on the Smile Jamaica concert. He connected me with Cat Coore and Colin Leslie—who put me in touch with Elaine Wint-Leslie. He organized a link up with I-Nancy, a St. Andrew High School girl, no less. Thanks also for connecting me with Sir Pooh, the original Stevie G(olding). Give thanks for the links, Mikie B; I am ever grateful.

Give thanks for the conversation from Devon House to Deanery Road and back with veteran policeman Bigger Ford, who suggested I talk with Alan Skill Cole. And thank you for your time, Arnold Bertram.

138 • Acknowledgments

I am grateful to my friends and colleagues at Colgate University. Some of my steadiest support has come from my colleagues in the English Department. Nimanthi Rajasingham read a very early version of the revival chapter, Lynn Staley talked with me about the medieval roots of the word barrack. Linck Johnson suggested I focus chapter 3 on the concert, Michael Coyle seriously engages me on reggae music all the time. I spend a lot of time with Margaret Maurer, who has taught me that no detail is too small. Ben Child is a bruva from another muva who always takes my questions seriously. And because Ben is so brilliant, he always has an answer.

Thank you, Maura Tumulty, for all your wisdom and for sending me home that summer morning to contact an editor and start the process of getting this longtime book out. Brenda Sanya, thanks for the walks and talks about Agamben and others. Michelle Stephens made the Rutgers connection easier. Thanks for looking out for me for a long time now.

Give thanks for all librarians. Special big ups to Chantelle Richardson at the National Library of Jamaica. I am grateful for the kindness and willingness of others whose names I do not remember in the West Indies Collection at UWI, Mona, and the British Library. Thanks to the librarians at Colgate, who have been so helpful. Peter Tagtmeyer for helping me find the 1770 laws of Jamaica and securing full access to the *Jamaica Gleaner* archives as well as Josh Finnell for his help and patience with the minutiae of citations.

I had a most enjoyable day with Miss Erna (Brodber) at the National Archives in Spanish Town, Jamaica. I did the driving and got the learning.

All of my visits to libraries and archives were generously supported by the Colgate Research Council. Give thanks.

The King of ITS, Ahmad Khazaee, has helped me with everything tech, big and small. My gratitude for you is saved on all the clouds.

Give thanks for Michael Bucknor and Faith Smith for the bellyful laughter, conversations, and especially for your thoughts on the introduction. Special thanks to my COVID reading group: Val Carnegie, Matthew Chin, and Donette Francis. Thanks for your generous comments on an early version of chapter 2 and, of course, for bringing Zoom solace in those locked-in days.

Thank you, Alison Donnell, for the invitation to share from this project at the University of East Anglia, for the ginger tea, and the generous offer to read for me.

Many friends and colleagues have given insight on the project over the years. Many others have through their kindness and love offered sustaining friendship. Katie and Ben Child, Brian Moore and Yvonne Senior Moore, Hazel Jack, Rachel and Jeb Beagles, Kim Kaiser, Sally Isbell, Konrad Kirlew, Michelle Stephens, Donette Francis, Connie Harsh, Dana Cypress, Ariel Martino, Tess Jones, Dominique Hill, Danny B, Paul Humphrey, Maura Tumulty, Joy Daniel, Rhonda Frederick, Carol Bailey, Antonia McDonald-Smythe, Simone James-Alexander, Nicky Dawson, Simone Banhan. Give thanks to Saru Matambanadzo, Sonya

Stephens, Ella Tour, my faculty success (FSP) sisters. Thanks to my students, especially the ones who allowed me to show them Jamaica.

Thanks also to the folks at Rutgers University Press, especially Kim Guinta, who has been patient and generous from the start.

Extra special, deep and wide, boononoonus thanks to Curdella Forbes for the countless conversations, the gracious editing, the insights and outsights. Missssss! Biggest respect.

Give thanks and love to Andrew Fagon for balancing the books and the parenting. Matthias and Jude, apologies for missing all those movie nights and thanks for your encouragement. Thanks to rest of my family for the prayers and support: my parents and sister, my parents-in-law and siblings in law, my aunts and cousins, and all my other family dem. Big love for Nelia Watten for understanding so well. And for John Page, who taught me to love my country and region deeply.

Notes

Introduction

1 I have chosen the word incursion and not some of the other terms that have been used (massacre, siege, invasion) because it seems to balance the tensions of political power that I describe as flexible hegemonies in this chapter.

2 A *shotta* in Jamaican slang is an outlaw or gangster who depends on guns and violence to maintain power. The *Urban Dictionary* tracks the etymology of shotta to the term "shot caller"—that is, someone who makes his/her own decisions, someone at the top of the food chain.

3 Jim Brown, whose given name was Lester Lloyd Coke, was the founder and leader of the Shower Posse, a transnational organization with its headquarters in Jamaica that was said to deal in drugs and weapons. Brown grew very powerful as the head of the Shower Posse and became the de facto leader/community leader or don of the Tivoli Gardens community in West Kingston. Brown was the father of Christopher "Dudus" Coke. He died mysteriously in a prison cell at the General Penitentiary in Kingston while awaiting extradition to the United States.

4 *Politricks* in Jamaican parlance is politics with corruption and tricks, especially to the detriment of the socially and economically vulnerable.

5 Curdella Forbes discusses the connection between "masculinist messianism and performative representation" in *From Nation to Diaspora: Samuel Selvon, George Lamming and the Cultural Performance of Gender* (2005, 42). Forbes quotes at length from a speech by Norman Manley describing the performances of power by recently arrived governors: "We . . . can remember, that Governor when they arrived here proceeded on a grand tour of the island wearing the fantastic colonial uniform designed for no other purpose than to impress the natives with the magnificence of the rulers from abroad. From one end of the country to the other they used to take themselves around with high ceremony, and give promises of what, as representatives of the king, they were supposed to do for this unfortunate island" (Manley, 1983, 114). Sometime after Governor John Eyre's inaugural procession, he performed his power by brutally murdering those who questioned the efficacy of his rule. He hanged Paul Bogle and other rebels like broken ornaments from the Morant Bay

142 • Notes to Pages 3–5

courthouse. Indeed, as Orlando Patterson proves in *Slavery and Social Death*, "[n]aked might—violence . . . is essential for the creation of all such systems" (Patterson, 1982, 3).

6 I am using the word *indigenous* not to refer to first peoples, but to describe Africa-based, Jamaican-grown cultural practice. This usage is akin to the sense in which it was used by the thinkers of the Haitian indigenous movement as exemplified in the work of Jean Price-Mars, *So Spoke the Uncle*, and more precisely as explicated by Sylvia Wynter. Wynter says, "[h]istory has mainly been about the European superstructure of civilization. Yet in the interstices of history we see in glimpses, evidences of a powerful and pervasive cultural process which has largely determined that unconscious springs of our beings: a process which we shall identify and explore as the process of 'indigenization'—a process whose agent and product was Jamaican folklore, folksongs, folk-tales, folk dance" (Wynter, 1970, 35).

7 I appreciate Simone Browne's unpacking of the term surveillance and the usefulness of the root word *veillance* to her discussion and here now to mine. "Surveillance is understood here as meaning 'oversight,' with the French prefix sur-meaning 'from above' and the root word *-veillance* deriving from the French verb veiller and taken to mean observing or watching. The root word -veillance is differently applied and invoked, for example, with the terms 'überveillance' (often defined as electronic surveillance by way of radio-frequency identification or other devices embedded in the living body)" (Browne, 2015, 18).

8 Naipaul's linked short stories, though they are set in a street, capture the ethos of the barrack yard.

9 Roger Mais was surveilled by postal censors and imprisoned for sedition in 1944. Martin Carter was surveilled and imprisoned during the British anti-Marxist military occupation in 1953 and 1954.

10 The question of how evidence was gained to confirm Dudus Coke's criminal and illegal activities and whether the methods by which that evidence was obtained made it admissible in Jamaican courts to support a U.S. extradition request for Coke was of great importance to the unfolding Tivoli drama. So murky was this issue that a U.S. law firm, Manatt, Phelps and Phillips, was retained by the JLP to help. The report of the Commission of Enquiry into the Extradition Request for Christopher Coke is the most useful document on this. The report is accessible at https://jis.gov.jm/media/Manatt-Final-Report-1.pdf.

11 In section 2 of the West Kingston Commission of Enquiry report, Deputy Commissioner of Police Glenmore Hinds says of Coke, "He operated a surrogate government. He operated his own court and persons who breached his code were brought to him, tried and sentenced" (2016, 2.13). As well, former Commissioner of Police Owen Ellington described Tivoli as a "state within a state." The report explains further, "Evidence before the Commission revealed that utility companies such as those providing electricity, water and telephones were unable to go into Tivoli Gardens to collect outstanding monies due to them. In fact, for very many years residents of Tivoli Gardens received the services of utility companies but paid no money for them. According to DCP Hinds, Coke himself collected payment for these services" (2016, 2.14, 18–19).

12 Sheri-Marie Harrison argues that the events leading up to May 2010 and the extradition of Coke "produced a multifaceted experience of confusion and dissonance that illuminated the lingering problems of sovereignty in the Caribbean's postcolonial present and the limitations of our critical ability to fully interpret and understand these problems" (2014, 1).

13 See, for example, images on page A4 of the May 21, 2010, issue of the *Daily Gleaner*. In the six small frames of photographs, the women photographed do not simply capture the working classes. There is a woman with bleaching cream on her face, another two in "skin out" positions, another two women posing with a cell phone, and another with her mouth open in a shout. The caption: "The supporters were angry that their benefactor was in trouble with the law and made the world know, in no uncertain terms, that they were not hostages in their own communities and had not had their phones confiscated as reported by the police" ("Diehards Defend Dudus," 2010, A4).

14 This refers to prime minister and leader of the Jamaica Labour Party Bruce Golding, who was as well the member of Parliament for West Kingston. Bruce Golding served as prime minister and leader of the Jamaica Labour Party from 2007 to 2011.

15 The Monroe Doctrine is U.S. foreign policy, first articulated by President James Monroe in 1823, stating that European powers were to see the Western Hemisphere as the extended domain of the United States. As time went on, countries in the Western Hemisphere began to see how their political, social, and environmental affairs are also considered the business of the U.S.

16 Rupert Lewis's article "Party Politics in Jamaica and the Extradition of Christopher 'Dudus' Coke" argues that "the extradiction of Coke and the subordination of Tivoli Gardens to the rule of law are the first major assaults on garrison politics and the power of dons whose financial and gun power give them influence, putting them in a position to significantly determine the outcome of both local and national politics" (2012, 41–42). Lewis also argues that the Dudus affair caused Jamaicans to look outward: There has been an unprecedented national discussion of sovereignty and "constitutional" freedom in politics, formal versus informal political processes, and the role of the political party machinery. This is taking place in and out of parliament, in the Jamaican Diaspora (especially in North America), as well as in the Caribbean and international media during 2010 and 201l" (2012, 40–41).

17 See Adrian Green, "Get Real: The Drug Lord Dilemma," *Nationnews Barbados*, 2015; also Kito Johnson, "Coke War Pushes Jamaica to the Brink," 2010, and "The Legend of Dudus: And Its Lessons for T&T," 2010, both in the *Trinidad and Tobago Guardian*.

18 Historian William Green notes that "The Morant Bay uprising, its brutal repression, and the reaction to those events in England and the colonies brought into focus the great divisions, animosities, and anxieties which permeated West Indian society and affected British attitudes toward the Caribbean colonies during the thirty years following emancipation. Though the rebellion was confined to one district of Jamaica, its ramifications were deeply felt throughout the Caribbean" (1991, 381). Roy Augier also discusses this in "Before and After 1865" (n.d.).

19 The first Maroon War between the British government and maroons began in Jamaica in 1728.

20 I am thinking here of Deborah Thomas's book *Political Life in the Wake of the Plantation*, where she documents stories by citizens who lived through the incursion. These moving testimonies are very revealing of the complex story from inside Tivoli Gardens.

21 This argument is made by Paul Gilroy (1993), Frederick Douglass (1893), and Wynter (1990).

22 See Michel Foucault's work on believing oneself to be watched as being just as effective as being watched.

144 • Notes to Pages 19-34

23 Carolyn Cooper refers to a (female) slave song, "Mi nuh know no law/mi nuh know no sin," in her book *Noises in the Blood* (1995).

24 I use this term to indicate the fundamental shift in human interaction and in the Western narrative of *Homo sapiens sapiens* that was initiated by the idea that a category of people were in fact not human but household chattel or movable goods (in some narratives, at best, livestock). See Sylvia Wynter's discussion in "Beyond Miranda's Meanings" (1990), especially pages 357 and 362. Wynter uses the term "epochal shift." "Break" seems to me to represent more fully the radical nature of this turn in the linear shape of the "history" of the human.

25 I refer here to Giorgio Agamben's *Homo Sacer* (1998), where *Homo sacer* is in this Kingston context the embodiment or incarnation of Dungle life—destitute, exposed, barely human.

26 Kamau Brathwaite engineers this term to capture the rooted possibilities in the word *alternative*. See Brathwaite (1974b, 30) and (1974a, 209).

27 An onomatopoeic way to represent the sound of reggae music.

Chapter 1   In the Shadow of the Wall

1 In Harry Franck's *Roaming through the West Indies*, Kingston is described as "the most disappointing town of the West Indies. With the exception of a few bright yellow public buildings and a scattered block or two of new business houses, it is a negro slum spreading for miles over a dusty plain" (Franck, 1920, 404).

2 Deborah Thomas includes a brief history of how Back O' Wall became Tivoli Gardens in *Political Life in the Wake of the Plantation* (2019, 43).

3 The arts of subterfuge in the Caribbean are often referred to as science and higher science, the latter indicating that these ways of knowing and doing outsmart Western science, and by extension, the epistemologies of the West.

4 Browne examines the arrangement of enslaved Africans on the slave ship *Rogers*. She argues that even in representations of the ship based on the ship's journals, the bodies of the enslaved were organized in such a way as to keep them with the constant sense that they were being surveilled. Brown's work does not extend to a close reading of the plantations or to a discussion of yards, but the idea of the "white eye" obtains in these settings as well.

5 *Suss* is not to be confused with *Sus* as in Sus laws, a term used to refer to the British laws by which, during the 1970s, a Black person could be arrested on suspicion that they may be about to commit a crime.

6 "Siddung pon di Wall" appears in Mutabaruka's collection, *The First Poems/The Next Poems*. The collection was published in 2005 but, as in Mutabaruka's work generally, the vernacular idioms of protest and satire characteristic of the Reggae Revolution that emerged in the 1970s resonate in the lyrics and the sound. The millennial publication underscores the longevity of the issues. of surveillance.

7 "Tenement Yard" was written by Roger Lewis and Jacob Miller. It was produced by Inner Circle, courtesy of SoundBwoy Entertainment Inc.

8 The yard already impacts how Caribbean scholars read early twentieth-century Jamaica: its emerging (urban) interclass relationships, and even the politics of intimacy. Scholars who have grappled with these themes include Kenneth Ramchand in his seminal identification of C.L.R. James's *Minty Alley* as a yard novel (2004) and Leah Rosenberg (2016) in her analysis of Trinidad's *Beacon* Group.

9 After emancipation and into the first decades of the twentieth century, the trajectory of social mobility as traced by residence in Kingston followed this

pattern: from West Kingston to East Kingston and then toward the suburbs of St. Andrew. Of course, this was not always the case for all residents, but it obtained for many. According to Colin Clarke, "In 1900 three times as many whites were living in Kingston as in St. Andrew. . . . By 1943 four times as many whites were living in St Andrew as in Kingston, and out-migration has transformed Kingston Gardens. . . . By 1935 the black population of St Andrew exceeded that of Kingston. Their association with areas of low status and high population density was offset spatially, if not socially, by their employment as servants in the most exclusive suburban areas" (Clarke, 2016, 20).

10 According to the *Dictionary of Jamaican English*, "carry go bring come" is "tale bearing" or "the tale bearer." In the *Dictionary of Caribbean English Usage*, the Jamaican "carry go bring come," "bring and carry" in St. Vincent, and "lick-mouth" in Barbados mean to "carry news" or to be a "tittle-tattle."

11 The warrant for Bedward's arrest, published in the January 22, 1895, issue of the *Jamaica Gleaner*, gives some insight into the nature of suss at the national level. Bedward's words had been regularly published and the *Gleaner*'s conservative colonial bias used to shape their presentation. Ironically, the legalese of the warrant echoes the *Gleaner*'s disparaging tone. "Whereas information has this day been laid before the undersigned Resident Magistrate that Alex. Bedward being a wicked, malicious, seditious and evil disposed person, and wickedly, maliciously and seditiously contriving and intending the peace of Our Lady the Queen, to incite and move to hatred and dislike of the person Our Lady the Queen and of the Government established by law, in this island to incite and move and persuade great numbers of the liege subjects of our said Lady the Queen to insurrections, riots, tumults and breach of the Peace, and to prevent by force and arms the execution of the Laws of this island the preservation of the public peace on the 16th January 1895, at Mona, in the Parish of St Andrew" ("Bedward Arrested on a Charge of Sedition," 1895, 3).

12 Rhonda Frederick, Leah Rosenberg, and Belinda Edmondson have called attention to this work as journalism. The use of the term "ethnography" here highlights de Lisser's commitment to observing cultural detail in the minutest degree.

13 Interestingly, Kenneth Ramchand in his seminal treatise *The West Indian Novel and Its Background* opines that de Lisser had no interest in arguing for "a Jamaican literature" (Ramchand, 2004, 55). Yet, at the same time, Ramchand assigns de Lisser a major place in Caribbean literary history. In a chapter significantly titled "New Bearings," he argues that "de Lisser's attitude to his raw material and to his characters comes closest to being like that of later West Indian writers" (Ramchand, 2004, 37). Both *Jane's Career*, carefully subtitled *A Story of Jamaica*, and *Susan Proudleigh* treat the close domestic space of the yard within the frame of large national issues: the advancing and class-troubling education of the poor; the issue of labor unrest in the opening decades of the century; the advent of Panama (the Canal Zone) into Jamaica and wider Caribbean socioeconomics. From this close interweaving of the inner-city yard and the public sphere, the novels convey an irresistible sense of an emerging nation whose contours are being battled out in domestic arenas. Paired with de Lisser's careful signaling of his self-authorization as an authentic Jamaican voice in the journalistic writings (his outlining of his ethnographic procedure, his credentials as a participant-observer), these narrative and thematic choices give credence to the contention that de Lisser was invested in a literary Jamaica to which he sought to help give shape.

14 Both de Lisser and Claude McKay had a white British patron. McKay's *Banana Bottom* reveals more expressly the influence of Oliver, perhaps because it was

published many years after McKay left Jamaica (1933). McKay's *Constab Ballads*, however, and even more so *Songs of Jamaica*, his first poetry collection, is clearly influenced by another white English patron, Walter Jekyll.

15 In this way, de Lisser's work can be read as a precursor to V. S. Naipaul's. Both de Lisser and Naipaul offer stark critiques of the class to which they belong, even though Naipaul's is starker and more sustained in *A House for Mr. Biswas* than is de Lisser's in this novel.

16 *Badmind* (noun and adjective) is a way to describe people who are jealous of another's success.

17 According to the *Dictionary of Caribbean English Usage*, "mampa(r)la-man is "A worthless, effeminate or impotent man; [by extension] a homosexual male playing the female role" (Allsopp, 2003, 366).

18 Donette Francis has drawn my attention to a piece by Neville Dawes titled "Preliminary Sketch for an Autobiography" in *Fugue and Other Writings*. "When I was sixteen I walked the same route every night—up Elleston Road, along Banana Street, on Cumberland Avenue, up St. James's Road, then after an uncertain zig-zag through Vineyard Town, I walked down Merrion Road into South Camp Road: then I turned seawards at Kingston College and made my first halt at the back of the Palace Cinema" (Dawes and Dawes, 2012, 127). Dawes's Kingston is an intimate maze, the street names a sacred text, and his recitation of them like a rosary or invocation. He says, "he walked alone at night for the restless days were friendless, but the nightly familiar streets were dark enough for me to flaunt my loneliness before them" (127), signaling his positioning as a young Black man who finds some respite in the nighttime streets of his city, respite that he does not find in the day. David Scott's article "Stuart Hall's Vernacular Modernism" (2021) traces Dawes's walks through the city. Scott suggests that James Joyce's Stephen Dedalus, though "not explicitly evoked," haunts Dawes's wanderings. Scott argues that Dawes and Stuart Hall in *Familiar Stranger* experiment with this "modernist memoir-form." Jane is not an artist, and she is not educated like Dawes and Hall, but this walk begins the work to create herself.

19 The other was Thomas MacDermot (Tom Redcam).

Chapter 2   "The Dungle Is an Obeah Man"

1 Sylvia Wynter's work on what she terms "After Man" is succinctly explained by Anthony Bogues: "In this paradigm those who are poor and jobless become in Wynter's thought a certain category of man. They are not just materially poor or exploited but are fixed within a normative order of the human that allows for their constant reproduction as poor. In the end therefore the transformation of the capitalist order requires not only economic and political changes but normative epistemic breaks about the nature of man" (Bogues, 2005, 327). Zakiyyah Jackson's *Becoming Human* advances "After Man" in this way: "Thus in order to become human without qualification, you must already be Man in its idealized form, yet Man, understood simultaneously as an achievement and bio-ontology, implies whiteness and specifically nonblackness" (Jackson, 2020, 33).

2 Johannes Fabian, Chinua Achebe, and others have written on this image of Africa, imagined by the European, passed on and proliferated like truth. In "An Image of Africa: Racism in Conrad's *Heart of Darkness*," Achebe comments on this image: "Africa as setting and backdrop which eliminates the African as human factor. Africa as metaphysical battlefield devoid of all recognizable humanity, into which

the wondering European enters at his peril. Of course there is a preposterous and perverse arrogance in thus reducing Africa to the role of props for the breakup of one petty European mind" (Achebe, 1978, 9).

3 These voices, especially as they concerned slum clearance, were not postindependence phenomena, nor one-time events. The Slum Clearance and Housing Law was passed in 1939, and it was under this law that squatter communities were cleared, ostensibly for the purpose of revitalizing poor and dangerous communities. (See *Jamaica Gleaner*, July 27, 1939; November 3, 1954.)

4 Browne and Bigo's iterations of exclusion also differ from Giorgio Agamben's history of *Homo sacer* (1998)—abject man, the sacrifice/excluded, who must be kept outside the city's walls for the city to be conceptualized or brought into being. Agamben's history charts the Jewish Holocaust as the outer limit of exclusion. Bigo and Browne bring other particularities that highlight the work of context in surveillance. Wynter's and Jackson's histories allow us to see the foundational shift in the discourse and practice of exclusion and surveillance produced by the invention of race—that is to say, the invention of Blackness as the means to justify chattel slavery. See also Paul Gilroy on the relation between blackness and modernity (1993). In Jamaica of the 1930s, ultra-poor and Black intersect to produce the slum, otherwise, as in *Children of Sisyphus*, called the Dungle, or trash heap.

5 Operation Friendship was an interdenominational group formed as a response to the dastardly conditions faced by poor people in West Kingston, specifically the Ackee Walk and Back O' Wall communities. First led by Reverend William Blake, the group carried out its work of "practical salvation" with grants from the government and with donations from local and international donors (*Sunday Gleaner*, May 26, 1963, 8–10).

6 Kingston Pen was known colloquially as "Back-a-Wall." Here and elsewhere, I spell it Back O' Wall as in Back of Wall, but in Jamaican speech the shortened, creolized "of" sounds like an "A." In *The Star* newspaper the community is called Back O Wall, but in other publications it is called Back-a-Wall, which is more consistent with Jamaican speech patterns but less accessible to the non-creole ear.

7 The folk song, with many verses, bemoans substandard but expensive housing that many poor people were forced to inhabit. In the version by the Jolly Boys, the second couplet includes a hilarious testimony of the experience of living in a rented or "dry weather house": "Early one morning the landlord went / To one of his tenants to collect some rent / The tenant sey 'Massa, mi nuh fool' / 'Mi nah pay nuh rent fi nuh swimming pool.' / Dry-weather house . . . dem nuh worth a cent. / Man! A shouldn't pay so much fi mi rent." Though I have not found any commentary on this song, written by Louise Bennett Coverley, it seems to me that the song is about urban housing experiences.

8 The color contradiction here has to do with the fact that there were light-skinned people in the slums, and while the hue of their skin would have served them well in that context, it would not assure them the full range of privilege that is brownness accompanied by wealth and/or high social position.

9 According to the CIA factbook, 92.1 percent of Jamaicans are Black and 6.1 percent are mixed with Black. This Black majority and the conclusions one might assume about a Black nation are perhaps one of the reasons the Jamaica census does not collect data on race. (They collect data on age and sex, people's movements in Jamaica, marriage and divorce, employment and earnings, education, and justice and crime.) This fact of Blackness has ironically struggled for prominence in the

148 • Notes to Pages 66–80

nation's concept of itself. The Jamaican motto, "Out of Many, One People," for instance, "reflects the ethos of the independence moment when nationalizing elites focused considerable energy on fostering a nation-based kinship ideology in an attempt to unify Jamaicans" (Kelly and Bailey, 2018, 693). Rachel Mordecai (2014) argues that scarcely a decade later, in the 1970s, the national struggle was to establish the parameters of a Black nation, first and foremost, not the parameters of democratic socialism articulated in the People's National Party manifesto. In *Modern Blackness*, Deborah Thomas explains that "by the late 1990s, a significant shift had occurred within Jamaica's public sphere whereby the creole vision of Jamaicanness, consolidated by political and intellectual elites at the time of independence became publicly superseded by a racialized vision of citizenship that [she calls] modern blackness" (Thomas, 2004, 11).

10 Here I am glossing George Lamming's famous declaration in *The Pleasures of Exile* that the West Indian novelist was the first to elevate the peasant to his true and original status of personality (Lamming, 1992, 39).

11 I make reference here to the song by Stanley and the Turbines, "Come Sing with Me," which won the Jamaica Independence Festival competition in 1980. The song begins, "I am dreaming of a new Jamaica / a land of peace and love / some say they cannot see no hope / that's why they keep us down." The song, written for the festival song competition, joined a tradition begun in 1962 of songs written about Jamaica. Many of these songs became extremely popular across the island way beyond the independence season in August.

12 "Yardie" can refer to someone who is from Jamaica, and it can refer to a gunman from Jamaica—particularly in Britain in the 1980s and 1990s. I use the term in the first sense.

13 In the *Dictionary of Caribbean English Usage*, to *read* is "to interpret the future of and forewarn; to interpret signs, dreams, etc." (Allsopp, 2003, 469).

14 Edward Seaga quotes Hartley Neita's essay "A Slum Is a Smell," which Neita wrote after he toured Back O' Wall with Norman Manley, who was chief minister of Jamaica at the time. Seaga's description of "the social predicament" of newly independent Jamaica is part of the first volume of his autobiography, *My Life and Leadership*. Neita writes, "We walked from early morning until mid-afternoon through some four acres of squalor. . . . The smell from the combination of the rotting wood, mud, sour water and faeces and scraps of cooked food waste, was a nauseous, stomach-turning smell" (quoted in Seaga, 2010, vol 1, 153).

15 Oil of fallback, an obeah-inspired potion or oil intended to return someone to the place or thing they attempt to escape.

16 Miss Mollypols appears in *The Children of Sisyphus* near the end of the novel (174–176). She is emblematic of a brown/white uptown perspective that is fascinated with the Rastafari brethren and the Dungle, yet at the same time fearful of them.

17 Anancy is not only the cunning trickster of Caribbean folklore but also, according to the *Dictionary of Caribbean English Usage*, "a person whose cunning or untrustworthiness is detected or revealed" (29). The *Dictionary* also gives the following definitions: ginnal: "A trickster; a person who is so cunning as to be dangerous" (255); samfie: "A confidence trickster; a swindler" (486).

18 I am thinking here of David Scott's argument in "The Tragic Vision in Postcolonial Time," where he uses Patterson's *The Children of Sisyphus* as example of a text in which the postindependence vision is not about "redemptive compensation and the radiant prospect of repair and justice" (803), but is rather a vision of tragedy and catastrophe (Scott, 2014b).

Notes to Pages 82–94 • 149

19 I'm riffing here on Frantz Fanon in *Black Skin, White Masks*, where the white child pointing at him exclaims, "Look, a Negro!"

Chapter 3 Smile Jamaica, for the Camera

1 See earlier reference to Rachel Mordecai's discussion of the shift toward Blackness as the face of the nation in the 1970s (2014, 42).
2 Garrison communities are politically aligned inner-city communities, often riddled with crime because of burdensome political affiliations. See Rupert Lewis (2012) and Kevin Edmonds (2016).
3 Criticism includes Rachel L. Mordecai's *Citizenship under Pressure*, already cited. Fiction includes Michelle Cliff's *No Telephone to Heaven* (1996), Margaret Cezair-Thompson's *The True History of Paradise* (2009), and Marlon James's *A Brief History of Seven Killings*.
4 The tourist's gaze" refers to the then practice by the Jamaica Tourist Board of staging smiley welcomes for tourists arriving at the island's airports, tourism being considered a major source of national income. While conceivably the government might have been worried about how negative press was impacting tourist arrivals, the point here is that the concert moved the concept of Smile Jamaica beyond that audience.
5 Chronixx's "Smile Jamaica" is framed in terms of a heteronormative romance, which is not a huge surprise considering the artiste's commitment to Rastafari.
6 On Monday, December 6, 1976, the morning after the Smile Jamaica concert, *The Star* reported that "a crowd estimated at 40,000" had gathered and waited for the reggae superstar ("The Show Goes On," 1976, 1). Chris Salewicz in *Bob Marley: The Untold Story* posits higher numbers: "Although Bob had not been expected to perform, by 5 P.M. there were fifty thousand people at the venue: three hours later, there were eighty thousand in the audience" (Salewicz, 2014, 304).
7 Higman and Hudson give a summary of the name changes: "National Heroes Park was formerly called George VI Park, which was in turn an imperial relabelling of Kingston Racecourse" (Higman and Hudson, 2009). The area was commonly called Racecourse because it was originally a horse-racing venue.
8 As the venue for the concert, National Heroes Circle emblematized the contradictions of the recently achieved postcolonial status, but it also emblematized the ideal of a nation that chose Black people, rebels who fought and won against the British, as its heroes. The park's connections with meetings across class lines and the imagination of a new nation are amplified by Marley's and reggae's own origins in the urban yard of Trench Town. But National Heroes Circle is only one of the many crossroad geographies involved in the concert's signifiers and scenes of action. The chapter addresses the complex of surveillance and countersurveillance writ large as it plays out in the greater Kingston area (in common reference, "Kingston" designates both Kingston and urban sections of St. Andrew. Together they are referred to as the Corporate Area).
9 See Roger Steffens's conversation with Carl Colby Jr. (Steffens, 2002).
10 While the theoretical and research work is vast and varied, I think in particular here of Sylvia Wynter's thought and research on folk culture in the early essays "Jonkonnu in Jamaica" (1970) and "Novel and History" (1971), and Carolyn Cooper's *Noises in the Blood* (1995), all of which emphasize the work of carnivalesque play and folk music as arts of resistance, self-making, and transformation; Rex Nettleford's similar thoughts on national dance in *Inward Stretch, Outward Reach* (1995); Wilson Harris's essay on limbo and Voudun in the seminal essay "History, Fable and Myth

150 • Notes to Pages 95–114

in the Caribbean and Guianas" (1970); Gordon Rohlehr on calypso in *Calypso and Society in Pre-Independence Trinidad* (1990); and the work of recent scholars such as Jason Allen-Paisant, "Towards a National Theatre" (2021).

11 Of course, this is modulated by different types of stage. For example a theater stage like the Ward Theatre, located in what would have been upper-class Kingston when it was first built, replicated much of the distancing design of the traditional English stage, with its upper galleries perched high above the stage, whereas a small dinner theater such as the Barn Theatre or an intimate circle such as the theater in the round of the Philip Sherlock Centre for the Creative Arts at the University of the West Indies, Mona, shrinks that space and allows for audience–actor interaction.

12 *The Dictionary of Caribbean English Usage* confirms that "Babylon" entered into Jamaican English via the beliefs and positions of Rastafari. Babylon is "any Western-style society or government and its supporters, particularly in the Caribbean, the Caribbean Establishment." Babylon also refers to the police or "any agent employed in the established protective services of any (Caribbean) society." Chanting down Babylon, then, is using the voice through speech, chants, and song to defuse and destroy the power and impact of Babylon (Allsopp, 2003, 55).

13 *So Jah seh*—meaning "so Jah says. This is what Jah says. Jah's will be done."

14 Njelle Hamilton's work also prompts us to ask what kinds of collective memories are sourced (and exploited) in this music (Hamilton, 2019).

15 In 2010, dancehall artistes including Beenie Man, Mavado, Aidonia, Bounty Killer, and Ricky Trooper all had their U.S. visas revoked by the U.S. embassy in Jamaica, which gave directives to all U.S.-bound airlines "stating that the aforementioned artists were barred from boarding any U.S. bound aircraft." While the embassy never commented on why the artistes' visas were revoked, it was widely speculated that they had had close ties with Christopher "Dudus" Coke prior to his extradition to the U.S. See also "US Bars Dudus Pal: Embassy Revokes Justin O'Gilvie Visa," *Gleaner*, July 13, 2011, and a similar report in the Guyana *Staebroek News* of the same date (https://www.stabroeknews.com/2011/07/13/news/guyana/us-revokes-visa-of -dudus%E2%80%99-associate/).

16 I-Nancy was a close friend of Cindy Breakespeare, who was lover and mother of Bob Marley. I-Nancy was Breakespeare's chaperone at the 1976 Miss World competition. She was a regular visitor and friend at 56 Hope Road.

17 Bam Bam's name is striking. First perhaps recalling the child-talk word for buttocks and, according to Cassidy and Le Page, "echoic" of beating the bottom. Bam Bam's contracted childhood is alluded to in another meaning of his name, which is trouble, as in Sister Nancy's song "Bam Bam," which has widely popularized the Jamaicanism "what a bam bam!" (here's trouble now!).

18 Anglophone writers who have pursued this cultural trope include Kei Miller (2012), Derek Walcott (1971), Michelle Cliff (1996), and several poets (Mervyn Morris, Lorna Goodison, Anthony McNeill, Kwame Dawes) writing on the legendary Jamaican musician, "folk hero," and "mad genius" Don Drummond. From the Hispanophone diaspora, Cristina Garcia's *Dreaming in Cuban* (1993) fits into this trope. See also scholars on the image of the madman/woman in Caribbean literature, for example, Kelly Baker Josephs (2013) and Evelyn O'Callaghan (1993).

Chapter 4 Bongo Futures after Tivoli

1 Afifa Nzinga Badiliko Aza, in "Who Is the Reggae Revival For?" (paper presented at the International Reggae Studies Conference, University of the West Indies,

Mona, February 12–13, 2015), registers her discomfort with the wholesale acceptance and celebration of the Reggae Revival in the local Jamaican and international press. She questions why the artists are "reggae" artists, what exactly is the nature of their consciousness given the pressing sociocultural needs of Jamaica, and the absence of critical work on what she views as their closely kept class privilege.

2 Barry Chevannes explains that Revival meetings are divided into two parts—"an initial period of drumming, singing, dancing and spirit possession, followed by the specific rituals which define the purpose of the meeting" (Chevannes, 1997, 33). He suggests that Rastafari meetings retain these same elements: "At one ceremony . . . in Westmoreland the Table from which the Elder spoke hosted a glass of water—another Revival trace" (34). He also finds that the drums used in Rastafari Nyabinghi sessions are continuities from Revival ceremonies, as are many of the songs.

3 There is some irony in this statement. One of the prime locations for hearing reggae music is the Kingston Dub Club on Skyline Drive. Skyline Drive, also called "Reggae Mountain," is accessible both from Jacks Hill, a mostly middle- and upper-class community with pockets of working-class settlement, and from Papine, a lower-middle-class community. This meeting place, a middle ground of sorts, challenges many of the easy binaries that are used to mark uptown and downtown spaces as one or the other. One can see how imaginative and expressive spaces are at once materialized and dematerialized: the hillside location, the heavy bass line of loud, disruptive music, and copious amounts of ganja smoke are not easily one or the other.

4 *His Majesty* is the moniker that Rastafari use to refer to Emperor Haile Selassie of Ethiopia.

5 Among the arts in the Caribbean, Jamaica featuring dominantly, there is a move toward collaborative projects. The New Caribbean Cinema movement is another example of this. Young filmmakers have worked together to produce Ring di Alarm, described as seven stories, six directors, and one island. The seven short, no-budget films were written, directed, and produced by the collective.

6 Grafton has been a central space in the becoming and production of the Reggae Revival. It has close links with the Edna Manley College of the Visual and Performing Arts, where many of these artists were trained/educated, and has given discounted studio time to emerging artists.

7 Tanya Batson-Savage writes about McCarthy's role in the creating the visuals of the revival and also in what she calls "visualizing" the revival (Batson-Savage, 2013).

8 By using "Dudus-Golding fiasco," I intend to signify two men, two communities, and two brands of power in Jamaica, and I mean to suggest that they were and are closely, though unofficially, connected. When the U.S. government sought the extradition of Dudus Coke on drug charges, Golding refused at first and then complied under pressure, setting in motion the Tivoli Gardens incursion.

9 An Independence Festival is a celebration of Jamaican culture and independence from Britain through an exposé of music and the arts, recognizing talent in the service of patriotism.

10 Many songs by reggae revivalists hit out against the law that criminalizes marijuana, which is used as part of Rasta ritual and is seen by Rastas as an herb of enlightenment. Songs also celebrate the recent legalization of marijuana in small amounts. In the overall body of their works, songs that address this subject far outnumber songs that address love or political issues.

Coda

1 Police statistics reported in the *Sunday Gleaner* of December 26, 2010, show 1,376 men being murdered in 2009, the year before the incursion. The number decreased to 1,168 in 2010, and the *Gleaner* credits the Tivoli incursion for the decrease. Most of the men killed were young men between the ages of eighteen and twenty-five. According to the commissioner of police, Major General Antony Anderson, as reported in the *Gleaner* of December 21, 2021, "young males have become endangered species in the country."

References

Achebe, Chinua. 1978. "An Image of Africa." *Research in African Literatures* 9, no. 1: 1–15.

Agamben, Giorgio. 1998. *Homo Sacer: Sovereign Power and Bare Life*. Stanford, CA: Stanford University Press.

Agee, Philip. 1975. *Inside the Company: CIA Diary*. New York: Farrar, Straus & Giroux.

Alexander, Gail. 2010. "The Legend of Dudus and Its Lessons for T&T." *Trinidad and Tobago Guardian*, July 9. https://www.guardian.co.tt/article-6.2.338241.630284fd2e.

Allen-Paissant, Jason. 2021. "Towards a National Theatre." In *Caribbean Literature in Transition, 1920–1970*, vol. 2, edited by Raphael Dalleo and Curdello Forbes. Cambridge: Cambridge University Press.

Allsopp, Richard, ed. 2003. *Dictionary of Caribbean English Usage*. Kingston: University of the West Indies Press.

Altink, Henrice. 2022. *Public Secrets: Race and Colour in Colonial and Independent Jamaica*. Liverpool: Liverpool University Press.

Ataklan. 2013. *One Morvant Night*. TAJ Records.

Augier, Roy. n.d. "Before and After 1865." *New World Journal*. Accessed June 26, 2023. https://newworldjournal.org/jamaica/before-and-after-1865/.

Bailey, Wilma R. 1974. "Kingston, 1692–1843: A Colonial City." Doctoral dissertation, University of the West Indies, Kingston, Jamaica.

———. 1976. "What the Yard Is Said to Be." *Social and Economic Studies* 25, no. 2: 168–175.

Batson-Savage, Tanya. 2013. "Matthew McCarthy: Visualizing the Reggae Revival." *Susumba*, December.

"Bedward Arrested on a Charge of Sedition." 1895. *Jamaica Gleaner*, January 22.

Beenie Man. 2011. "I'm OK." https://www.discogs.com/release/3423723-Beenie-Man-Khago-Im-Ok-Nah-Sell-Out.

Bennett, Alvin. 1973 (1964). *God the Stonebreaker*. London: Heinemann.

Bennett, Wycliffe, and Hazel Bennett. 2011. *The Jamaican Theatre: Highlights of the Performing Arts in the Twentieth Century*. Kingston: University of the West Indies Press.

154 • References

Bigo, Didier. 2007. "Detention of Foreigners, States of Exception, and the Social Practices of Control of the Banopticon." In *Borderscapes: Hidden Geographies and Politics at Territory's Edge*, edited by Prem Kumar Rajaram and Carl Grundy-Warr, 3–33. Minneapolis: University of Minnesota Press.

———. 2008. "Globalized (In)Security: The Field and the Ban-Opticon." In *Terror, Insecurity and Liberty: Illiberal Practices of Liberal Regimes after 9/11*, edited by Didier Bigo and Anastassia Tsoukala. London: Routledge.

Bob Marley and the Wailers. 1975. "No Woman, No Cry (Live at the Lyceum, London)." https://www.discogs.com/master/101428-Bob-Marley-And-The-Wailers-No-Woman -No-Cry-Live-At-The-Lyceum-London.

———. 1976. "Smile Jamaica." https://www.discogs.com/master/311119-Bob-Marley-The -Wailers-Smile-Jamaica.

Bogard, William. 2006. "Surveillance Assemblages and Lines of Flight." In *Theorizing Surveillance: The Panopticon and Beyond*, edited by David Lyon. Abingdon, UK: Willan.

Bogues, Anthony. 2005. *Caribbean Reasonings: After Man, towards the Human: Critical Essays on Sylvia Wynter*. Kingston: Ian Randle.

"A Book You Will Like." 1914. *Jamaica Gleaner*, January 8.

Bookman, Dutty. 2011. *Tried and True: Revelations of a Rebellious Youth*. Washington, DC: Bookman Express.

Bradley, Lloyd, and Dennis Morris. 2002. *Reggae: The Story of Jamaican Music*. London: BBC Books.

Brathwaite, Edward Kamau. 1974a. "The African Presence in Caribbean Literature." *Daedalus* 103, no. 2: 73–109.

———. 1974b. *Contradictory Omens: Cultural Diversity and Integration in the Caribbean*. Mona, Jamaica: Savacou Publications.

———. 1988. *The Arrivants: A New World Trilogy*. Oxford: Oxford University Press.

Brodber, Erna. 1975. *A Study of Yards in the City of Kingston*. Kingston: Institute of Social and Economic Research, University of the West Indies.

Browne, Simone. 2015. *Dark Matters: On the Surveillance of Blackness*. Durham, NC: Duke University Press.

Bucknor, Michael A. 2009. "Sounding Off: Performing Ritual Revolt in Olive Senior's 'Meditation on Yellow.'" *Mosaic: An Interdisciplinary Critical Journal* 42, no. 2: 55–71.

———. 2011. "Dub Poetry as Postmodern Art Form." In *The Routledge Companion to Anglophone Caribbean Literature*, edited by Michael A. Bucknor and Alison Donnell. London: Routledge.

Caluya, Gilbert. 2010. "The Post-Panoptic Society? Reassessing Foucault in Surveillance Studies." *Social Identities* 16, no. 5: 621–633. https://doi.org/10.1080/13504630.2010 .509565.

Carter, Martin Wylde. 1954. *Poems of Resistance from British Guiana*. London: Lawrence and Wishart.

Cassidy, Frederic G., and Robert Brock Le Page. 2002. *Dictionary of Jamaican English*. Kingston: University of the West Indies Press.

Césaire, Aimé. 1969. *Return to My Native Land*. Baltimore: Penguin Books.

Cezair-Thompson, Margaret. 2009. *The True History of Paradise*. New York: Random House.

Chang, Kevin O'Brien, and Wayne Chen. 2012. *Reggae Routes: The Story of Jamaican Music*. Kingston: Ian Randle.

Chevannes, Barry, ed. 1997. *Rastafari and Other African-Caribbean Worldviews*. New Brunswick, NJ: Rutgers University Press.

Chronixx. 2013a. "Here Comes Trouble." https://www.discogs.com/release/4818825 -Chronixx-Here-Comes-Trouble.

———. 2013b. "Smile Jamaica." https://www.discogs.com/release/4591868-Chronixx -Jah-9-Smile-Jamaica-Brothers.

———. 2014. *Dread and Terrible.* https://www.discogs.com/master/705934-Chronixx -Dread-Terrible.

———. 2017. *Chronology.* https://www.discogs.com/master/1225384-Chronixx -Chronology.

C.I.A. Briefing: Jamaica Destabilised: British Guiana Repeated? 1976. London: Agee-Hosenball Defence Committee. https://www.abebooks.com/first-edition/C.I .A-BRIEFING-JAMAICA-DESTABILISED-author-stated/30909747742/bd.

"CIA on Trial: Jamaica Gives Evidence." 1978. *Struggle,* September 14.

Clarke, Colin. 2006a. *Decolonizing the Colonial City: Urbanization and Stratification in Kingston, Jamaica.* Oxford: Oxford University Press.

———. 2006b. "From Slum to Ghetto: Social Deprivation in Kingston, Jamaica." *International Development Planning Review* 28, no. 1: 1–34. https://doi.org/10.3828 /idpr.28.1.1.

———. 2006c. *Kingston Jamaica Urban Development and Social Change 1692–2002.* Kingston: Ian Randle.

———. 2016. *Race, Class, and the Politics of Decolonization: Jamaica Journals, 1961 and 1968.* Basingstoke, UK: Palgrave Macmillan.

Cliff, Michelle. 1996 (1987). *No Telephone to Heaven.* New York: Plume.

Cobham-Sander, C. Rhonda. 1987. "The Creative Writer and West Indian Society: Jamaica 1900–1950." Doctoral dissertation, University of St. Andrews, Scotland.

Cooper, Carolyn. 1995. *Noises in the Blood: Orality, Gender, and the "Vulgar" Body of Jamaican Popular Culture.* Durham, NC: Duke University Press.

———. 2004. *Sound Clash: Jamaican Dancehall Culture at Large.* New York: Palgrave Macmillan.

Curtin, Philip D. 1955. *Two Jamaicas: The Role of Ideas in a Tropical Colony, 1830–1865.* Cambridge, MA: Harvard University Press.

"Dancehall Acts Hit by U.S. Visa Cancelations." 2010. *Billboard,* April 27. https://www .billboard.com/music/music-news/dancehall-acts-hit-by-us-visa-cancelations-1207820/.

Davies, Carole Boyce, and Elaine Savory, eds. 1990. *Out of the Kumbla: Caribbean Women and Literature.* Trenton, NJ: Africa World Press.

Dawes, Kwame. 1999. *Natural Mysticism: Towards a New Reggae Aesthetic.* Leeds, UK: Peepal Tree Press.

Dawes, Neville, and Kwame Dawes. 2012. *Fugue and Other Writings.* Leeds, UK: Peepal Tree Press.

De Lisser, Herbert George. 1913. *Twentieth Century Jamaica.* Kingston: Jamaica Times.

———. 1915. *Susan Proudleigh.* London: Methuen & Co.

———. 1972 (1913). *Jane's Career: A Story of Jamaica.* London: Heinemann.

"Diehards Defend Dudus." 2010. *Jamaica Gleaner,* May 21, section A.

Douglass, Frederick. 1893. "Lecture on Haiti: The Haitian Pavilion Dedication Ceremonies Delivered at the World's Fair, in Jackson Park, Chicago, Jan. 2d, 1893." Accessed June 26, 2023. https://www.loc.gov/item/02012340/.

"Dudus Caught in Police Spotcheck in Jamaica." 2010. *Jamaica Gleaner,* June 22.

Edelman, Lee. 2004. *No Future: Queer Theory and the Death Drive.* Durham, NC: Duke University Press.

Edmonds, Kevin. 2016. "Guns, Gangs and Garrison Communities in the Politics of Jamaica." *Race & Class* 57, no. 4: 54–74.

156 • References

Edmondson, Belinda. 1998. *Making Men: Gender, Literary Authority, and Women's Writing in Caribbean Narrative*. Durham, NC: Duke University Press.

———. 2009. *Caribbean Middlebrow: Leisure Culture and the Middle Class*. Ithaca, NY: Cornell University Press.

Ericson, Richard V., and Kevin D. Haggerty. 2006. *The New Politics of Surveillance and Visibility*. Toronto: University of Toronto Press.

Forbes, Curdella. 2005. *From Nation to Diaspora: Samuel Selvon, George Lamming and the Cultural Performance of Gender*. Kingston: University of the West Indies Press.

Foucault, Michel. 1995. *Discipline and Punish: The Birth of the Prison*. Translated by Alan Sheridan. New York: Vintage Books.

Franck, Harry Alverson. 1920. *Roaming through the West Indies*. New York: Century.

Frederick, Rhonda D. 2005. *"Colón Man a Come": Mythographies of Panamá Canal Migration*. Lanham, MD: Lexington Books.

García, Cristina. 1993. *Dreaming in Cuban*. New York: Ballantine Books.

Gilroy, Paul. 1993. *The Black Atlantic: Modernity and Double Consciousness*. London: Verso.

Glissant, Edouard. 1999. *Caribbean Discourse: Selected Essays*. Translated by J. Michael Dash. Charlottesville: University of Virginia Press.

Gray, Obika. 1991. *Radicalism and Social Change in Jamaica, 1960–1972*. Knoxville: University of Tennessee Press.

———. 2004. *Demeaned but Empowered: The Social Power of the Urban Poor in Jamaica*. Kingston: University of the West Indies Press.

Green, Adrian. 2015. "Get Real: The Drug Lord Dilemma." *Nationnews*, May 17. https://www.nationnews.com/2015/05/17/get-real-the-drug-lord-dilemma/.

Green, William A. 1991. *British Slave Emancipation: The Sugar Colonies and the Great Experiment, 1830–1865*. Oxford: Clarendon Press.

Haggerty, Kevin D., and Richard V. Ericson. 2006. "The New Politics of Surveillance and Visibility." In *The New Politics of Surveillance and Visibility*, edited by Kevin D. Haggerty and Richard V. Ericson, 3–26. Toronto: University of Toronto Press. https://www.jstor.org/stable/10.3138/9781442681880.4.

Hamilton, Njelle W. 2019. *Phonographic Memories: Popular Music and the Contemporary Caribbean Novel*. New Brunswick, NJ: Rutgers University Press.

Harriott, Anthony. 1997. "Reforming the Jamaica Constabulary Force: From Political to Professional Policing?" *Caribbean Quarterly* 43, no. 3: 1–12.

Harriott, Anthony D., and Marlyn Jones. 2016. *Crime and Violence in Jamaica*. Washington, DC: Inter-American Development Bank. https://doi.org/10.18235/0000333.

Harris, Wilson. 1970. "History, Fable and Myth in the Caribbean and Guianas." *Caribbean Quarterly* 16, no. 2: 1–32. https://doi.org/10.1080/00086495.1970.11829042.

Harrison, Sheri-Marie. 2014. *Jamaica's Difficult Subjects: Negotiating Sovereignty in Anglophone Caribbean Literature and Criticism*. Columbus: The Ohio State University Press.

Hartman, Saidiya V. 1997. *Scenes of Subjection: Terror, Slavery, and Self-Making in Nineteenth-Century America*. New York: Oxford University Press.

Harvey, David. 2007. *A Brief History of Neoliberalism*. Oxford: Oxford University Press.

Hearne, John. 1972. "The Novel as Sociology as Bore." *Caribbean Quarterly* 18, no. 4: 78–85.

Henzell, Perry, dir. 2000 (1972). *The Harder They Come*. Criterion.

Higman, B. W., and Brian J. Hudson. 2009. *Jamaican Place Names*. Kingston: University of the West Indies Press.

Hope, Donna. 2013. "New Name? Conceptualizing the Second Wave of Post-Millennial 'Rastafari Renaissance'/Reggae Revival in Jamaican Popular Music." Rastafari Studies Conference and General Assembly, University of the West Indies, Mona Campus, Jamaica, August 13–16.

"Housing Rehabilitation Programme." 1960. *Public Opinion*, December 3.

Jackson, Zakiyyah Iman. 2020. *Becoming Human: Matter and Meaning in an Antiblack World*. New York: NYU Press.

Jah9. 2013. *New Name*. https://www.discogs.com/release/4855577-Jah9-New-Name.

Jamaica. 1786. *Acts of Assembly: Passed in the Island of Jamaica; from 1770, to 1783, Inclusive*. Kingston: Lewis and Eberall. https://link.gale.com/apps/doc/CB0130434518/ECCO?sid=bookmark-ECCO&xid=5c659585.

Jamaica Constabulary Force. 2019. "About Us." https://jcf.gov.jm/about-us/history/, https://jcf.gov.jm/about-us/history/.

Jamaica Journal. n.d. Digital Library of the Caribbean. Accessed June 27, 2023. https://www.dloc.com/UF00090030/00010.

James, C.L.R. 1997 (1936). *Minty Alley*. Jackson: University Press of Mississippi.

James, Marlon. 2014. *A Brief History of Seven Killings*. New York: Riverhead Books.

Jefferson, Tony. 2012. "Policing the Riots: From Bristol and Brixton to Tottenham, via Toxteth, Handsworth, Etc." *Criminal Justice Matters* 87, no. 1: 8–9. https://doi.org/10.1080/09627251.2012.670995.

Johnson, Kito. 2010. "Coke War Pushes Jamaica to the Brink." *Trinidad and Tobago Guardian*, May 28. https://www.guardian.co.tt/article-6.2.335246.co1dad266b.

Josephs, Kelly Baker. 2013. *Disturbers of the Peace: Representations of Madness in Anglophone Caribbean Literature*. Charlottesville: University of Virginia Press.

Kabaka Pyramid. 2013. *Lead the Way EP*. https://www.discogs.com/release/8906183-Kabaka-Pyramid-Lead-The-Way-EP.

Kabaka Pyramid/Iba Mahr. 2014. "The Revival"/"Step Away." https://www.discogs.com/release/5524474-Kabaka-Pyramid-Iba-Mahr-The-Revival-Step-Away.

Kelly, Monique D. A., and Stanley R. Bailey. 2018. "Racial Inequality and the Recognition of Racial Discrimination in Jamaica." *Social Identities* 24, no. 6: 688–706.

Lamming, George. 1992. *The Pleasures of Exile*, 2nd ed. Ann Arbor: University of Michigan Press.

———. 1999 (1960). *Season of Adventure*. Ann Arbor: University of Michigan Press.

———. 2011 (1958). *Of Age and Innocence*. Leeds, UK: Peepal Tree Press.

"The Laws of Jamaica." Acts of assembly. Passed in the island of Jamaica; from 1770, to 1783, inclusive. Kingston: Lewis and Eberall, 1786.

Lewis, Rupert. 2012. "Party Politics in Jamaica and the Extradition of Christopher 'Dudus' Coke." *Global South* 6, no. 1: 38–54.

Lyon, David. 2006. "9/11, Synopticon, and Scopophilia: Watching and Being Watched." In *The New Politics of Surveillance and Visibility*, edited by Kevin D. Haggerty and Richard V. Ericson, 35–54. Toronto: University of Toronto Press. https://doi.org/10.3138/9781442681880-003.

———. 2010. "Liquid Surveillance: The Contribution of Zygmunt Bauman to Surveillance Studies 1: Liquid Surveillance." *International Political Sociology* 4, no. 4: 325–338. https://doi.org/10.1111/j.1749-5687.2010.00109.x.

Mais, Roger. 2004 (1954). *Brother Man*. Kingston: Macmillan Caribbean.

Manley, Michael. 1983. *Jamaica: Struggle in the Periphery*. London: Third World Media.

Mann, Samuel. 1994. "Wearable Computing as a Means for Personal Empowerment." Paper delivered at the First International Conference on Wearable Computing, Cambridge, MA.

Mann, Steve, and Joseph Ferenbok. 2013. "New Media and the Power Politics of Sousveillance in a Surveillance-Dominated World." *Surveillance & Society* 11, nos. 1/2: 18–34. https://doi.org/10.24908/ss.v11i1/2.4456.

Mann, Steve, Jason Nolan, and Barry Wellman. 2002. "Sousveillance: Inventing and Using Wearable Computing Devices for Data Collection in Surveillance Environments." *Surveillance & Society* 1, no. 3: 331–355. https://doi.org/10.24908 /ss.v1i3.3344.

Maoz, Eilat. 2023. "Black Police Power: The Political Moment of the Jamaica Constabulary." *Comparative Studies in Society and History* 65, no. 1: 115–140. https://doi.org/10 .1017/S0010417522000421.

Marley, Rita, and Hettie Jones. 2005. *No Woman No Cry: My Life with Bob Marley.* New York: Hachette Books.

McCaulay, Diana. 2018. "The Sacrifice Zone: The Riverton City Dump." *Addastories .org,* December 11. https://www.addastories.org/the-sacrifice-zone/.

McKay, Claude. 1974 (1933). *Banana Bottom.* New York: Ecco.

———. 2022 (1912). *Constab Ballads: Including the Poem "If We Must Die."* Redditch, UK: Read Books.

Mendes, Alfred, and Rhonda Cobham. 1984 (1935). *Black Fauns.* London: New Beacon Books.

Miller, Jacob. 1975. "Tenement Yard." https://www.discogs.com/master/490474-Jacob -Miller-Tenement-Yard.

Miller, Kei. 2012. *The Last Warner Woman.* Minneapolis: Coffee House Press.

_____. 2014. *The Cartographer Tries to Map a Way to Zion.* Manchester, UK: Carcanet Press.

Ministry of National Security. 1977. "Review of the State of Emergency." Ministry Paper no. 22. http://www.nlj.gov.jm/MinistryPapers/1977/22.pdf.

Moore, Brian, and Michele A. Johnson, eds. 2000. *"Squalid Kingston" 1890–1920: How the Poor Lived, Moved and Had Their Being.* Mona, Jamaica: Social History Project.

Mordecai, Martin, and Pamela Mordecai. 2000. *Culture and Customs of Jamaica.* Westport, CT: Greenwood Press.

Mordecai, Rachel L. 2014. *Citizenship under Pressure: The 1970s in Jamaican Literature and Culture.* Kingston: University of the West Indies Press.

Morrison, Petrona. 2013. Opening remarks, "New Roots: 10 Emerging Artists, National Gallery of Jamaica Exhibit," July 28.

Moten, Fred. 2003. *In the Break: The Aesthetics of the Black Radical Tradition.* Minneapolis: University of Minnesota Press.

Murrell, Nathaniel Samuel. 2010. *Afro-Caribbean Religions: An Introduction to Their Historical, Cultural, and Sacred Traditions.* Philadelphia: Temple University Press.

Mutabaruka. 2005. *Mutabaruka: The First Poems/The Next Poems.* Kingston: Paul Issa Publications.

Naipaul, V. S. 1976 (1958). *The Suffrage of Elvira.* London: Penguin Group.

———. 2002 (1959). *Miguel Street.* New York: Vintage.

Nettleford, Rex M. 1970. *Mirror Mirror: Identity, Race and Prejudice in Jamaica.* Kingston: LMH Publishing.

———. 1995. *Inward Stretch, Outward Reach: A Voice from the Caribbean.* Brooklyn, NY: Caribbean Diaspora Press, Caribbean Research Center, Medgar Evers College, CUNY.

Newell, Bryce Clayton. 2020. "Introduction: The State of Sousveillance." *Surveillance & Society* 18, no. 2: 257–261.

Niaah, Sonjah Stanley. 2010. *DanceHall: From Slave Ship to Ghetto*. Ottawa: University of Ottawa Press.

O'Callaghan, Evelyn. 1993. *Woman Version: Theoretical Approaches to West Indian Fiction by Women*. London: Macmillan Caribbean.

O'Gorman, Pamela. 1972. "An Approach to the Study of Jamaican Popular Music." *Jamaica Journal* 6, no. 4: 50.

"Operation Friendship: Will Need Police Aid to Succeed in Back-O-Wall." 1962. *The Star*, February 14.

Papa San, Featuring Stan Ryck. 1993. "The Program." https://www.discogs.com/release/2923060-Papa-San-Featuring-Stan-Ryck-The-Program.

"Parliamentary Report on Survey of Squatters in Jamaica." n.d.

Parsard, Kaneesha Cherelle. 2018. "Barrack Yard Politics: From C.L.R. James's The Case for West-Indian Self Government to Minty Alley." *Small Axe: A Caribbean Journal of Criticism* 22, no. 3: 13–27. https://doi.org/10.1215/07990537-7249089.

Paton, Diana. 2015. *The Cultural Politics of Obeah: Religion, Colonialism and Modernity in the Caribbean World*. Cambridge: Cambridge University Press.

Patterson, Chris. 2022. "States of Public Emergency Declared in Eight Parishes." *Jamaica Information Service*, December 28. https://jis.gov.jm/states-of-public-emergency-declared-in-eight-parishes/.

Patterson, Orlando. 1964. *The Children of Sisyphus*. Kingston: Bolivar Press.

———. 1982. *Slavery and Social Death*. Cambridge, MA: Harvard University Press.

———. 1986. *The Children of Sisyphus*. Harlow, UK: Longman Group. https://www.abebooks.com/9780582785717/Children-Sisyphus-Longman-Caribbean-Writers-0582785715/plp.

———. 2011. *The Children of Sisyphus*. Leeds, UK: Peepal Tree Press.

Poupeye, Veerle. 2022. *Caribbean Art*, 2nd ed. London: Thames & Hudson.

Price-Mars, Jean. 1983. *So Spoke the Uncle*. Washington, DC: Passeggiata Press.

"Protestors Cause Panic at Parliament." 2010. *Jamaica Gleaner*, May 21, section A.

Protoje. 2013. *The 8 Year Affair*. https://www.discogs.com/release/4554008-Protoje-The-8-Year-Affair.

Rajaram, Prem Kumar, and Carl Grundy-Warr, eds. 2007. *Borderscapes: Hidden Geographies and Politics at Territory's Edge*. Minneapolis: University of Minnesota Press. http://ebookcentral.proquest.com/lib/colgate/detail.action?docID=340771.

Ramchand, Kenneth. 2004. *The West Indian Novel and Its Background*. Kingston: Ian Randle.

"Reggae Revival Discussion in the United States Today." 2013. *Jamaica Gleaner*, June 12.

Reid, Victor Stafford. 1980. *Sixty-Five*. Jamaica: SOS Free Stock.

———. 2016. *New Day*, rev. ed. Leeds, UK: Peepal Tree Press.

Rohlehr, Gordon. 1990. *Calypso and Society in Pre-Independence Trinidad*. Port of Spain: Gordon Rohlehr.

Rosenberg, Leah Reade. 2016. *Nationalism and the Formation of Caribbean Literature*. New York: Palgrave Macmillan.

Russell, Stephen C. 2022a. "Skin for Skin: Biblical Language in Jamaica's Morant Bay Rebellion." *Journal of the American Academy of Religion* 90, no. 3: 636–653. https://doi.org/10.1093/jaarel/lfac071.

———. 2022b. "'Slavery Dies Hard': A Radical Perspective on the Morant Bay Rebellion in Jamaica." *Slavery & Abolition* 43, no. 1: 185–204. https://doi.org/10.1080/0144039X.2021.1993736.

Salewicz, Chris. 2014 (2009). *Bob Marley: The Untold Story*. New York: Farrar, Straus and Giroux.

Satchell, Veront M. 2004. "Early Stirrings of Black Nationalism in Colonial Jamaica: Alexander Bedward of the Jamaica Native Baptist Free Church 1889–1921." *Journal of Caribbean History* 38, no. 1: 75–106.

Schwartz, Mattathias. 2011. "A Massacre in Jamaica." *New Yorker*, December 2. https://www.newyorker.com/magazine/2011/12/12/a-massacre-in-jamaica.

Scott, David. 1999. *Refashioning Futures: Criticism after Postcoloniality*. Princeton, NJ: Princeton University Press.

———. 2004. *Conscripts of Modernity: The Tragedy of Colonial Enlightenment*. Durham, NC: Duke University Press.

———. 2013. "The Paradox of Freedom: An Interview with Orlando Patterson." *Small Axe: A Caribbean Journal of Criticism* 17, no. 1: 96–242.

———. 2014a. *Omens of Adversity: Tragedy, Time, Memory, Justice*. Durham, NC: Duke University Press.

———. 2014b. "The Tragic Vision in Postcolonial Time." *PMLA* 129, no. 4: 799–808.

———. 2021. "Stuart Hall's Vernacular Modernism." In *Life between Islands: Caribbean-British Art, 1950s–Now*, edited by Alex Farquharson and David A. Bailey. London: Tate.

Seaga, Edward. 1980. "Central American and the Caribbean: The Continuing Crisis." *World Affairs* 143, no. 2: 135–144.

———. 2010. *Edward Seaga: My Life and Leadership*. Oxford: Macmillan Education.

"Security Watch on Rastafarians, Reds." 1961. *The Tribune*, January 8.

Sheller, Mimi. 2019. "Complicating Jamaica's Morant Bay Rebellion: Jewish Radicalism, Asian Indenture, and Multi-Ethnic Histories of 1865." *Cultural Dynamics* 31, no. 3: 200–223. https://doi.org/10.1177/0921374019847585.

"The Show Goes On." 1976. *The Star*, December 6.

"Significant Plunge in Murders." 2010. *Jamaica Gleaner*, December 26.

"Sisyphus." n.d. *Britannica Academic*. Accessed April 23, 2024. https://academic-eb-com.exlibris.colgate.edu/levels/collegiate/article/Sisyphus/68010.

Sives, Amanda. 2012. "A Calculated Assault on the Authority of the State? Crime, Politics and Extradition in 21st Century Jamaica." *Crime, Law and Social Change* 58, no. 4: 415–435. https://doi.org/10.1007/s10611-012-9391-0.

Smith, Matthew J. 2010. "H. G. and Haiti: An Analysis of Herbert G. De Lisser's 'Land of Revolutions.'" *Journal of Caribbean History* 44, no. 2: 183–200.

———. 2014a. "Footprints on the Sea: Finding Haiti in Caribbean Historiography." *Small Axe: A Caribbean Journal of Criticism* 18, no. 1: 55–71. https://doi.org/10.1215/07990537-2642755.

———. 2014b. *Liberty, Fraternity, Exile: Haiti and Jamaica after Emancipation*. Chapel Hill: University of North Carolina Press.

Smith, Michael, and Mervyn Morris. 1989. *It a Come*. San Francisco: City Lights Publishers.

"Squatters Clash with Police." 1963. *The Star*, October 14.

Steffens, Roger. 2002. "We Shot Bob Marley! Behind the Scenes with the Film Crew at the 1976 Smile Jamaica Concert." *The Beat*. https://www.proquest.com/magazines/we-shot-bob-marley-behind-scenes-with-film-crew/docview/217549427/se-2?accountid=10207.

———. 2017. *So Much Things to Say: The Oral History of Bob Marley*. New York: W. W. Norton & Company.

Stone, Carl. 1981. "Party Voting Trends in Jamaica (1959–1976)." In *Perspectives on Jamaica in the Seventies*, edited by Carl Stone and Aggrey Brown. Kingston: Jamaica Publishing House.

Stone, Carl, and Aggrey Brown. 1981. *Perspectives on Jamaica in the Seventies*. Kingston: Jamaica Publishing House.

Taylor, Don. 1995. *Marley and Me: The Real Bob Marley Story*. New York: Barricade Books.

Thelwell, Michael. 1980. *The Harder They Come*. New York: Grove Press.

Thomas, Deborah A. 2004. *Modern Blackness: Nationalism, Globalization, and the Politics of Culture in Jamaica*. Durham, NC: Duke University Press.

———. 2011. *Exceptional Violence: Embodied Citizenship in Transnational Jamaica*. Durham, NC: Duke University Press.

———. 2019. *Political Life in the Wake of the Plantation: Sovereignty, Witnessing, Repair*. Durham, NC: Duke University Press.

Thomson, Ian. 2011. *The Dead Yard: A Story of Modern Jamaica*. New York: Nation Books.

"Under Siege." 2010. *Jamaica Gleaner*, May 20, section A.

Walcott, Derek. 1971. *Dream on Monkey Mountain and Other Plays*. New York: Farrar, Straus and Giroux.

Waters, Anita M. 1985. *Race, Class, and Political Symbols: Rastafari and Reggae in Jamaican Politics*. Abingdon, UK: Routledge.

"The West Kingston Commission of Enquiry Report (Tivoli Report)." 2016. http://go-jamaica.com/TivoliReport/files/assets/basic-html/page-1.html.

White, Timothy. 2006 (1983). *Catch a Fire: The Life of Bob Marley*, rev. ed. New York: Holt Paperbacks.

Wynter, Sylvia. 1970. "Jonkonnu in Jamaica: Towards the Interpretation of Folk Dance as Cultural Process." *Jamaica Journal* 4, no. 2: 34–48.

———. 1971. "Novel and History, Plot and Plantation." *Savacou* 5 (June): 95–102.

———. 1977. "We Know Where We Are From: The Politics of Black Culture from Myal to Marley." Paper presented at the joint meeting of the African Studies Association and the Latin American Studies Association, Houston, TX, November.

———. 1990. "Beyond Miranda's Meanings: Un/Silencing the 'Demonic Ground' of Caliban's Woman." In *Out of the Kumbla: Caribbean Women and Literature*, edited by Carole Boyce Davies and Elaine Savory Fido, 355–370. Trenton, NJ: Africa World Press

———. 2003. "Unsettling the Coloniality of Being/Power/Truth/Freedom: Towards the Human, after Man, Its Overrepresentation—An Argument." *CR: The New Centennial Review* 3, no. 3: 257–337. https://doi.org/10.1353/ncr.2004.0015.

"Young Men Endangered Species." 2021. *Jamaica Gleaner*, December 21.

Index

Page numbers in *italics* indicate figures.

Achebe, Chinua, 146n2

Adams, Reneto, 12

Africa, 27, 34, 73, 136; religions popular in Jamaica that originated in, 18, 22, 31, 32, 57, 69, 76–79, 115; perceived threat posed by, to the new nation of Jamaica, 56, 61, 146n2. *See also* Ethiopia; obeah; Rastafari; Revivalism; "white eye"

Agamben, Giorgio, *Homo Sacer*, 144n25, 147n4

Agee, Philip, 86

Aidonia, 150n15

Altink, Henrice, 66

Anancy, 79, 148n17

Asian Jamaicans, 13, 34, 59, 60

Ataklan, "Kingston Town," 124–125

Aza, Afifa Nzinga Badiliko, 150n1

Back O' Wall, 57, 135, 147n5, 148n14; in *The Children of Sisyphus*, 69, 71; history of (how it became Tivoli Gardens), 27–28, 60, 144n2; name of, 147n6; surveillance of and treatment of as shameful spectacle, 61, 63–64. *See also* Kingston Pen

Bailey, Wilma, 32, 33, 34–35

Bandwagon campaign (PNP, 1972), 99–100

banopticon, 16, 61–62, 68, 70, 71

Barbados, 4, 20, 145n10

Batson-Savage, Tanya, 151n7

Bauman, Zygmunt, 16, 17

Bebble Rock Team, 120

Bedward, Alexander, 30, 35–36, 145n11; Bedwardism, 31, 72

Beenie Man, 150n15; "I'm OK," 111–112

Bennett, Alvin, *God the Stone Breaker*, 3, 53

Bennett, Hazel, 128

Bennett, Louise, "Jamaica 'Oman," 73

Bennett, Mikie, 117

Bennett, Wycliffe, 128

Bentham, Jeremy, 16, 29. *See also* panopticon

Bertram, Arnold, 99, 100, 101

Bigo, Didier, 16, 61, 62, 68, 70, 147n4

Blackness/the Black body, 13–14; association of with poverty and slum dwelling, 44, 45, 60, 61, 66, 146n1; and bongo futures, 115; invention of, as the means to justify chattel slavery, 147n4; and the Jamaican concept of self, 147n9; lynching of, and colonial power, 15; and the march of women in Tivoli Gardens, 7; power of, seen as a threat, 27; readings of, in the Caribbean, 17; shift toward, as the face of the nation (1970s), 53–54, 149n1

Bligh, William, 128

Bogle, Paul, 12, 13, 15, 141n5

Bogues, Anthony, 146n1

Bois Caïman ceremony, 18, 113

163

164 • Index

bongo futures, defined, 115, bongo futures aesthetic, 112, 122, 129

Bookman, Dutty: and the Reggae Revival, 113–114, 119–121; *Tried and True*,113–114, 120–121

Boukman, Dutty, 18, 113

Bounty Killer, 150n15

Bowen, Shawn, 134–136

Bradley, Lloyd, 116

Brathwaite, Doris, 119

Brathwaite, Edward Kamau, 17–18, 119, 144n26

Breakespeare, Cindy, 150n16

Brief History of Seven Killings, A (James, 2014), 20, 87, 89, 95, 97, 104–109

Britain, 142n9, 148n12, 149n8, 151n9; attitudes of, toward the Caribbean colonies following emancipation, 143n18; and colonial cultural values, 128–129; and the design of Kingston, 58; Jamaica's independence from, 21, 149n8; Labour Party of, 86; and the Maroon Wars, 78, 143n19; and the model "English gentleman's" influence on West Indian literature, 66; and the Morant Bay Rebellion, 12–13; and Sus laws, 144n5. *See also* colonialism

Brodber, Erna, 32, 33–34

Brown, Jim, 1, 10, 141n3

Browne, Simone, 61, 142n7, 144n4, 147n4; *Dark Matters*, 16–17, 77–78

Bucknor, Michael, 51, 127

Burke, I-Nancy, 103, 150n16

Byles, Junior, 99

CAM. *See* Caribbean Artists Movement

Canal Zone, 20, 52, 53, 145n13

Caribbean: art and literature of, 40, 48, 51, 56, 108, 109, 119; Black power and revolutionary movements in, 102, 113; demography of, 17–18; gangs in, 8; performance in, 90, 92–95, 111; size of, 17–18; spirituality in, 17, 18; structural violence of, 126; surveillance and countersurveillance across, 3–5, 16–20, 24, 29–30, 33; and the Tivoli incursion response, 10–11, 16. *See also specific countries and topics*

Caribbean Artists Movement (CAM), 24, 119. *See also* nationalism, in Jamaican art and literature

Carnival, 95; and language games, 111; and the staging of countersurveillance and resistance, 2, 19, 90, 92–93, 94, 130, 149n10

Carter, Martin, 142n9; *Poems of Resistance from British Guiana*, 4

Cassidy, Frederic G., 30, 150n17

Castro, Fidel, 22

Central Intelligence Agency. *See* CIA

Chevannes, Barry, 116–117, 151n2

Children of Sisyphus, The (Patterson, 1964), 3–4, 20, 21–22, 53, 60, 63, 147n4, 148n16, 148n18; editions of, 72–73; spiritveillance in, 80–83; surveillance in, 66–71; women in, 72–80

Christianity: critiques of, 128–129; norms of, 77, 105; and Revival, 116, 117

Chronixx, 113, 115, 129; "Capture Land," 126; "Here Comes Trouble," 121; "Smile Jamaica," 91, 149n5

CIA (Central Intelligence Agency), 86, 90, 91, 92, 93, 102

city planning. *See* Jamaica: city planning in

Clarke, Colin, 58–59, 144n9

Cliff, Michelle, 82, 150n18

Cobham-Sander, Rhonda, 40

Coke, Christopher "Dudus": and artistic production in response to Tivoli affair, 23, 102, 110, 124, 129; father of, 1, 10, 141n3; rule of, 4–5, 126; and the Tivoli incursion, 1, 4–11, 14, 102, 124–126, 142nn10–12, 143n16, 150n15, 151n8

Coke, Lloyd Lester. *See* Brown, Jim

Cold War, 10

Cole, Alan Skill, 97, 98, 101

colonialism/postcolonialism/neocolonialism: codes of, and respectability, 7, 19, 57; and crisis, trauma, and global visibilities of shame, 20, 108, 112; spaces of, and policing/monitoring of, 2, 3,12, 14, 15, 18–19, 27–28, 31, 32, 33, 35, 36, 42, 53, 54, 56, 62, 87, 89. *See also* Britain; neoliberalism; Reggae Revival; slavery/the enslaved

Columbus, Christopher, 19–20, 126

Cooper, Carolyn, 73, 117, 118, 144n23, 149n10

Coverley, Louise Bennett, 147n7

Creary, Everaldo, 127

creole speech/speech patterns, 48, 50–51, 111, 127, 147n6

crime, 61, 149n2; and the attempt on Bob Marley's life, 104, 105; and Dudus's narrative about Tivoli Gardens, 4–5, 126; and gun violence, 89; and the JCF, 12; and the

state of emergency during the Jamaica
Smile concert, 88, 94, 105; and Sus laws,
144n5; and the targeting of the slums by
police, 61–63; and ZOSOs, 132–133. *See also*
drugs: trafficking of; Jamaica Constabulary Force; police
Cuba, 10, 102; agents from, 86
Cunningham, Janine. *See* Jah9
Curtin, Philip, 62–63
cybersurveillance, 3

dancehall, 113–119, 122, 128; artists/
performers of, 111, 114, 127, 150n15
Dawes, Kwame, 116
de Lisser, H. G., 20, 21, 22, 26–32, 33, 37–40;
journalistic work of, 37, 38–39, 145n12;
patron of, 40, 145n14; place of, in Jamaican
literary history, 145n13; as a precursor to
V. S. Naipaul, 146n15; *Twentieth Century
Jamaica*, 38–39, 40, 51. See also *Jane's
Career*; *Susan Proudleigh*
democratic socialism, 54; PNP's experiment
with, 86, 87, 101, 102, 147n9
drugs: and Rastafari, 76, 84, 151n3, 151n10;
trafficking of, 1, 4, 11, 141n3, 151n8
dub poetry, 31, 119, 127
Dudus. *See* Coke, Christopher "Dudus"
Dungle (slums of West Kingston), 23, 108,
130, 133; demographics of, 60; description
of, 59; explanation of term, 55, 61; life in,
63; as "obeah man," 68–71, 76, 78–83;
setting of, as central to critique of postcolonial Jamaica, 22, 57–58, 67, 134; women
in, 72–75

East Kingston, 24, 26, 45, 144n9
Eccles, Clancy, 99
Echo Squad, 93, 94, 102, 103
Edelman, Lee, 115
Edmondson, Belinda, 44, 66, 145n12
Edna Manley College of the Visual and
Performing Arts, 122, 151n6
Ellington, Owen, 5, 142n11
England. *See* Britain
Ericson, Richard V., 16
Ethiopia, 25, 80, 151n4
Europe: musicians touring, 98, 110; rejection
of cultural norms of, 77, 115, 116, 117, 142n6;
relationship of to the U.S., 143n15; view of
Africa in, 146n2
Eyre, John, 12–13, 131, 141n5

Fabian, Johannes, 146n2
Fanon, Frantz, 149n19
Fantan Mojah, 114
Ferenbok, Joseph, 30
Forbes, Curdella, 141n5
Ford, Bigger, 103
Foucault, Michel,143n22. *See also* panopticon
Francis, Donette, 146n18
Franck, Harry, 144n1
Frederick, Rhonda, 51, 145n12

ganja. *See* drugs: and Rastafari
gaze: male, 73, 75, 76; tourist's, 76, 91, 149n4;
the turning away of, from the slums,
61–62. *See also* "white eye"
gender: and the march of women in Tivoli
Gardens, 5–8, 10, 133; and mobility, 41, 51;
oppression, and patriarchy, 72–75, 76;
and Rastafari, 74; and spiritveillance, 68;
and surveillance, 44, 54
ghetto school of thought, 100, 101–102,
103–104
Gilligan, Rory "Stone Love," 117
Gilroy, Paul, 147n4
Glasspole, Sir Florizel, 88
Glissant, Edouard, 81
globalization/free trade, 106, 113, 115, 117, 125
Golding, Bruce, 143n14; and the Tivoli
incursion, 4, 8, 9, 124, 125, 126, 151n8
Gordon, Chris, 127
Gordon, George William, 12, 13, 15
Grafton Studios, 122, 123, *123*, 151n6
Grammys, 113
Gray, Obika, 27
Great Britain. *See* Britain
Green, William, 143n18
Grenada, 10
Guianas, 18. *See also* Guyana
Guyana, 4

Haggerty, Kevin D., 16
Haiti, 10, 40, 56, 129, 142n6; Haitian
Revolution, 18, 113. *See also* Voudun
Hamilton, Njelle, 150n14
Harriot, Anthony, 8, 12
Harrison, Sheri-Marie, 142n12
Hartman, Saidiya, 64, 66
Harvey, David, 125
Henzell, Perry, 33
Higman, B. W., 149n7
Hinds, Glenmore, 142n11

166 • Index

His Majesty. *See* Selassie, Haile
Hope, Donna, 114
Hudson, Brian J., 149n7

Independence Festival, 127, 148n11, 151n9
independence in Jamaica. *See* Jamaica: independence of
indigeneity, 21, 32, 100, 128, 129; author's use of term, 3, 142n6; and feminist ideology, 73; and spiritualism/religion, 18, 57, 76, 117, 130. *See also* Reggae Revival; Revivalism
Indiggnation Band, 122
intelligence agencies. *See* CIA; KGB; surveillance: by the U.S. government
International Monetary Fund, 101
I-Wayne, 114

Jack, Deborah, 18
Jackson, Zakiyyah, 146n1, 147n4
Jah9, 120, 121, 122, 127
Jamaica: city planning in, 57–66; independence of, 3–4, 21, 28, 33, 55, 56, 58, 60, 66–67, 70, 73, 77, 78, 90, 128, 147n3, 147n9, 148n18; the 1970s in, 22, 31, 54, 82, 84, 86, 87, 89–92, 97, 99, 100, 104, 108. *See also specific cities/neighborhoods and historical events*
Jamaica Constabulary Force, 5, 12, 14. *See also* police
Jamaica Defence Force, 5, 14, 133
Jamaica Gleaner (daily newspaper), 6, 37, 59, 76, 103, 132, 145n11; ads in, 38, *39, 85*; conservatism of, 76, 86; on the Tivoli incursion, 7, 9, 152n1
Jamaica Labour Party: massacre of supporters of, 133; as a pro-imperialist party, 102; songs critical of, and banning of political lyrics by, 99, 100; surveillance by, 100, 101; and the Tivoli incursion, 4, 6, 142n10. *See also* Golding, Bruce; Seaga, Edward
Jamaican Diaspora, 143n16
Jamaica Times, 37, 48, 50
James, C. L. R., *Minty Alley*, 3, 66, 144n8
James, Marlon. See *Brief History of Seven Killings, A*
Jane's Career (de Lisser, 1913), 3, 26, 53, 145n13; source of, 38–40, 50; suss and surveillance in, 28, 41–48, 133–134
Japanese artists, 123, 127
JCF. *See* Jamaica Constabulary Force

JDF. *See* Jamaica Defence Force
Jekyll, Walter, 50, 145n14
Jesse Royal, 113
Jewish Jamaicans, 12, 13
JLP. *See* Jamaica Labour Party
Johnson, Michele A., 37, 59
Johnson, Robert A., 11, 13
Jolly Boys, 147n7
Jones Town, 58, 68, 71, 74, 80, 81, 97
Jonkunnu, 94
Joyce, James, 146n18

Kabaka Pyramid, 113, 115, 121, 126, 127
Kalonji, Sizzla, 114
Karece, 122
KGB, 87
Kingston, 29, 112, 120, 122; city planning in, 58–66; de Lisser on, 37, 41–43, 45, 50, 51, 53, 134; as the emblem of national identity, 21; history of, 32–36; Patterson on, 56, 67, 68–71, 80; and the Smile Jamaica concert, 91–93. *See also* Dungle; East Kingston; Grafton Studios; National Heroes Park; Riverton City; Tivoli Gardens; West Kingston; yards, urban
Kingston College, 58, 127, 146n18
Kingston Pen, 59, 60, 61, 63–64, *65*, 147n6. *See also* Back O' Wall
Kumina, 31

Lamming, George: *In the Castle of My Skin*, 20; *Of Age and Innocence*, 4; *The Pleasures of Exile*, 148n10; *Season of Adventure*, 4
La Rose, John, 119
law enforcement. *See* police
Le Page, Robert Brock, 30, 150n17
Leslie, Colin, 97, 98
Levien, Sidney Lindo, 12, 13
Lewis, Roger, 144n7
Lewis, Rupert, 143n16
"liberation politics," 99–100
Lyon, David, 16

MacDermot, Thomas. *See* Redcam, Tom
Mais, Roger, 33, 142n9; *Brother Man*, 3, 53, 66, 79
Manley, Edna, 15, 73
Manley, Michael, 22, 86, 87, 88, 92, 97–100, 102
Manley, Norman, 63, 141n5, 148n14
Mann, Stephen, 16–17, 30

Maoz, Eilat, 12

marijuana. *See* drugs: and Rastafari

Marley, Bob: attempt on life of, 22–23, 87, 89, 92, 93–94, 96, 104, 108; death of, 116; empire of, 113; Jamaican people's shared identity with, 95–96; mother of, 150n16; "No Woman No Cry," 31–32, 91; and politics, 87–88, 92; "Smile Jamaica" (song), 90–91; works on life of, 97–104 (see also *Brief History of Seven Killings, A*). *See also* One Love Peace concert; Smile Jamaica concert

Marley, Rita, *No Woman No Cry: My Life with Bob Marley*, 97, 101

maroons, 9, 13, 14, 78, 109, 113, 143n19

Maroon Wars, 78, 143n19

Marshall, Bucky, 87

masquerade, 94, 95, 96

Massop, Claudie, 87

Mathieson, Thomas, 16

Mavado, 150n15

McCarthy, Matthew, 122–125; *Rise Up*, 123–124, *123*

McCaulay, Diana, 82–83

McKay, Claude, 21; *Banana Bottom*, 51, 66–67, 79, 145n14; *Constab Ballads*, 50, 145n14; *Songs of Jamaica*, 145n14

Mendes, Alfred, *Black Fauns*, 3

middle class, 7, 62, 66, 95; communities in Jamaica, 112, 122, 151n3; de Lisser on, 21–22, 28, 29, 32, 40, 42, 43, 44, 45, 47, 48, 50, 53, 104; Patterson on, 56, 57, 58, 68, 104; and the Reggae Revival, 24, 118, 121

Miller, Jacob, "Tenement Yard," 31, 53, 84–86, 96, 144n7

Miller, Kei, 131, 150n18

Miller, the Reverend Al, 9–10

misogyny. *See* gender

Monroe, James, 143n15

Monroe Doctrine, 11, 143n15

Moore, Brian, 37, 59

Morant Bay Rebellion of 1865, 11–15, 35, 131, 133, 141n5, 143n18

Mordecai, Martin, 116

Mordecai, Pamela, 116

Mordecai, Rachel, 53–54, 147n9, 149n1

Morgan, Claudette, 134–136

Morris, Dennis, 116

Morrisson, Petrona, 122

Moten, Fred, 111

Murrell, Nathaniel, 77

music: bongo, 115, 127–128; calypso and soca in Trinidad, 19; works that address the yard, 53. *See also* dancehall; reggae; Reggae Revival; Smile Jamaica concert; *and specific artists and texts*

music industry in Jamaica, 24; response of, to the Tivoli incursion, 124–125; U.S. retaliation against, for failure to extradite Dudus, 110–111

Mutabaruka, 31, 107, 144n6

Naipaul, V. S., 3, 4, 142n8, 146n15

National Heroes Park, 23, 88, 92, 97, 131, 134, 149nn7–8

nationalism, in Jamaican art and literature, 21, 24, 31, 37–38, 54, 66–67, 82

Neita, Hartley, 148n14

neoliberalism, 114; Rastafari/Reggae Revial as an antidote to, 112, 115, 119, 124; and the Tivoli incursion, 125–127, 128

Nettleford, Rex, 66, 149n10

New Caribbean Cinema movement, 151n5

Niaah, Sonjah Stanley, 118

Nolan, Jason, 95

No-Maddz, The, 122, 127–129; *Breadfruit Is the New Bread, Baby*, 128–129; "Sort Out Yuh Life, Jamaica," 128

obeah, 148n15; and the Dungle's spiritual power (as exemplified in *The Children of Sisyphus*), 22, 57, 63, 66, 68, 70–80; as a religious practice, 57, 76–79

Obeah Act, 78

O'Gorman, Pam, 117

Oliver, Sydney, 40, 145n14

Ollivierre, Oje. *See* Protoje

One Love Peace Concert (Bob Marley), 87, 88

Operation Friendship, 63–64, 147n5

Orange Street fire, 97

pan-Africanism, 11

Panama, 20, 25, 51–52, 145n13

pan-Caribbeanism, 119

panopticon, 2, 16, 29, 33, 54, 61, 62

Papa San, 121

Parliament of Jamaica: and states of emergency, 132; and the Tivoli incursion, 6, 7–8. *See also* Golding, Bruce

Parsard, Kaneesha, 34

Paton, Diana, 76, 78

patriarchy. *See* gender

168 • Index

Patterson, Orlando, 33, 104, 133, 141n5.
  See also *Children of Sisyphus, The*
Peart, Oniel, 127
People's National Party (PNP), 6; and
  democratic socialism, 86, 147n86, 87,
  101, 102, 147n99; and the Smile Jamaica
  concert, 87, 92, 98–101, 103
performance: backdrop and afterlives of
  Marley's, 97–104; in the Caribbean, 92,
  94, 95; Marley's, at the Smile Jamaica
  concert, 93–96; as a response to/pushback
  against surveillance, 2, 5, 9, 10, 15, 22–23,
  24, 87, 89–90, 94–95; street, 94. *See also*
  Carnival; masquerade
Phillips, Peter, 7–8
PNP. *See* People's National Party
police, 52; as the Beast, 84, 86; Bookman
  and Protoje's encounter with, 120; and
  clashes with Rastafari, 76; and class, 121;
  de Lisser on, 50–51; inability of to intervene in Tivoli Gardens, and the Tivoli
  incursion, 4–10, 14, 126; Patterson on,
  68–70, 74; and the rebellion in Morant
  Bay, 12–14; and the Smile Jamaica concert, 92, 93, 103; surveillance by, 63, 68,
  90, 121; and the targeting of the slums,
  61–64, 65, 102. *See also* Echo Squad;
  Jamaica Constabulary Force; zones of
  special operations
"politricks," 1, 141n4
Pollack, Andrew, 86
Presidential Click (gang), 1, 4–5, 8, 23
Price-Mars, Jean, 142n6
Protoje, 113, 115, 120–122, 123, 124, 127, 129;
  "Who Dem a Program," 121
Puru, 122

race, in the Caribbean, 18
Ramchand, Kenneth, 144n8, 145n13
Rastafari, 68, 99, 133, 149n5, 150n12, 151n4;
  in *The Children of Sisyphus*, 72, 73–74,
  148n16; and the gendered power of men,
  72, 73–74; Marley and, 96, 103; meetings,
  151n2; and the Reggae Revival, 112, 113,
  114–117, 119–120, 121, 128, 130, 151n10;
  in the *Rise Up* mural, 123–124; and the
  slums, 22, 31, 57, 70, 72, 82, 113; targeting
  and surveillance of, 75–76, 84–86
Ray, Ellen, 86
Redcam, Tom, 21, 146n19

Rees, Merlyn, 86
reggae, 144n27, 144n6; artists, 91, 113; lyrics
  of, on the slums, 31; origins of, 23, 32,
  149n8; and politics, 100–102; venue for,
  151n3. *See also* Marley, Bob; Reggae Revival;
  Smile Jamaica concert
Reggae Revival: artists/community of, 20,
  118–125, 127–129; contrasted with reggae,
  116–118; origins of, 23–24, 111, 113–115; and
  Rastafari, 130; as a response to surveillance,
  3, 24, 112; success of, 113; and the Tivoli
  incursion, 125–127
Reid, V. S., 15
religion. *See* Christianity; obeah; Rastafari;
  Revivalism; spiritveillance
Revivalism: African origins of, 22, 31, 57; in
  The Children of Sisyphus, 68, 72, 74–75,
  76; influence of, on Jamaican culture,
  116–117; and the march of women in
  Tivoli Gardens, 6–7; meetings, 151n2; and
  the slums, 22, 36, 68, 72
Rhone, Trevor, 33
Rhys, Jean, *Wide Sargasso Sea*, 79
Riverton City, 82–83
Romeo, Max, 99
Rosenberg, Leah, 40, 144n8, 145n12
Russell, Stephen, 13
Ryck, Stan, 121

Salewicz, Chris, *Bob Marley: The Untold
  Story*, 97, 98, 99, 101, 149n6
Salkey, Andrew, 119
Saulter, Storm, 33
Scott, David, 2, 73, 112, 115, 134, 146n18,
  148n18
Seaga, Edward, 86–87, 88, 148n14
security forces. *See* police; Tivoli incursion
Selassie, Haile, 120, 151n4
Sheller, Mimi, 13
Shepherd, Sheldon "Sheppie," 127
shottas, 1, 5, 8–9, 130; in *A Brief History of
  Seven Killings*, 104–109; defined, 141n2
Shower Posse, 1, 8, 124, 141n3
Simone, Nina, 127
Sister Nancy, 150n17
Sisyphus, 78–79
slavery/the enslaved, 12, 21, 27, 42, 128, 147n4;
  and the history of surveillance, 11, 15–19,
  29, 61, 101, 144n4; and the inception of
  the tenement yard, 32–35, 60, 62; and

obeah, 77; and the staging of countersurveillance, 2

slums. *See* Back O' Wall; Dungle

Smile Jamaica concert (Bob Marley), 20, *85*, 131, 134; backdrop of, 97–104; geographies and description of, 90–93; and performance and surveillance, 3, 22–23, 87–90, 93–96. *See also Brief History of Seven Killings, A*

Smith, M. G., 66

Smith, Matthew, 40

Smith, Mikey, 31, 33

sousveillance, 16–17, 30, 95

Spanish Town, 6, 50, 58, 59, 132

spiritveillance, 93; in *The Children of Sisyphus*, 66, 68, 69, 71, 75–83; definition of, 56–57, 68; relation of, to surveillance, 2, 19, 22, 68

squatters, 55, 58, 60, 64–66, *65*, 69, 76, 126; and the Slum Clearance and Housing Law,147n3

St. Andrew (Jamaican parish), 112, 118, 144n9, 149n8

Stanley and the Turbines, 148n11

Star, The (Jamaican newspaper), 63–64, *65*, 76, 86, 149n6

states of emergency: and the Smile Jamaica concert, 88, 97; surveillance and repression during, 14, 93, 102, 131–133

surveillance studies, 16

Susan Proudleigh (de Lisser, 1915), 3, 145n13; suss, surveillance, and female agency in, 28, 38, 41, 48–54

sussveillance, 2, 19, 56; contextualizing, 32–36; definition of, 29–31; in de Lisser's fiction, 21, 28–32, 37, 41–54, 133

synopticism, 16

Tacky's Rebellion, 78

Taylor, Don, 91, 97, 98; *Marley and Me: The Bob Marley Story*, 97–98, 101, 102

tenements. *See* Back O' Wall; Dungle; yards, urban

Thelwell, Michael, 33; *The Harder They Come*, 53

Thomas, Deborah: *Exceptional Violence*, 125; *Modern Blackness*, 147n9; *Political Life in the Wake of the Plantation*, 134, 143n20, 144n2

Thomson, Ian, 58

Tivoli Gardens, 58, 105; Back O' Wall reinvented as, 28, 60, 135, 144n2; Jim Brown

as head of, 10, 141n3; Dudus as head of, 4–5, 10, 126, 142n11. *See also* Back O' Wall; Tivoli incursion

Tivoli incursion, 1–12, 14–15, 20, 23, 56, 60, 131, 133; and de Lisser's fiction, 27–28; and the march of women, 5–8, 10, 133; the Reggae Revival's roots in, 24, 110–111, 115, 119, 124–127, 130; witnesses to, 134

Trench Town, 23, 31, 60, 97, 103, 149n8

Trinidad: and the Black Power uprising of 1970; literature on, 3; and masquerade, 95; music of, 19, 125

Trooper, Ricky, 150n15

Turbulence, 114

United Kingdom. *See* Britain

United States: embassy of, 10; and entry privileges for Jamaican artists, 110, 111, 150n15; impact of, on Jamaican domestic relations and culture, 23, 25; and the Monroe Doctrine, 143n15; 9/11 in, 129; race in, 18, 52; surveillance by, and intervention in Jamaican politics, 22, 56, 88–90, 93, 101–102, 110–112, 115. *See also* CIA; neoliberalism; Tivoli incursion

Uprising Roots Band, 120

urban yard. *See* yards, urban

Voudun, 18, 81, 113, 149n10

Wailers. *See* Marley, Bob

Ward Theatre, 128, 150n11

Waters, Anita, *Race, Class, and Political Symbols: Rastafari and Reggae in Jamaican Politics*, 97, 99–100

Watson, Barrington, 15, 123

Wellman, Barry, 95

West Kingston, 143n14; poverty and slums of, 24, 56, 58–60, 64, 66, 83, 143n14, 144n9, 147n5. *See also* Back O' Wall; Dungle; Morant Bay Rebellion of 1865; Tivoli Gardens

West Kingston Commission of Enquiry, 5, 14, 142nn10–1

White, Sarah, 119

White, Timothy, *Catch a Fire*, 97, 98, 99, 101, 103

"white eye," 16, 29–30, 144n4

Wilson, Delroy, 99

Wint-Leslie, Elaine, 92, 97
women. *See* gender
World Bank, 101
Wu Tang Clan, 127
Wynter, Sylvia, 21, 100, 142n6, 144n24, 146n1, 147n4, 149n10

Yaadcore, 122
yard fiction, 2, 3–4, 30, 54, 66, 144n8. *See also specific writers and works*

yards, urban, 55–56, 112, 144n4, 145n13; as creative hotbeds, 31; history of, 32–36; Marley's residence as uptown version of, 103–104, 134; Reggae Revival's idealization of, 113, 130; surveillance of, 18–23, 84–86, 105, 130. *See also* Trench Town; yard fiction

zones of special operations (ZOSOs), 132–133

About the Author

KEZIA PAGE is associate professor of English and Africana and Latin American studies at Colgate University. Her first book, *Transnational Negotiations in Caribbean Diasporic Literature: Remitting the Text*, was published in 2010. She was born and raised in Kingston, Jamaica. She lives with her family in Hamilton, New York.

Available titles in the Critical Caribbean Studies series

Giselle Anatol, *The Things That Fly in the Night: Female Vampires in Literature of the Circum-Caribbean and African Diaspora*

Alaí Reyes-Santos, *Our Caribbean Kin: Race and Nation in the Neoliberal Antilles*

Milagros Ricourt, *The Dominican Racial Imaginary: Surveying the Landscape of Race and Nation in Hispaniola*

Katherine A. Zien, *Sovereign Acts: Performing Race, Space, and Belonging in Panama and the Canal Zone*

Frances R. Botkin, *Thieving Three-Fingered Jack: Transatlantic Tales of a Jamaican Outlaw, 1780–2015*

Melissa A. Johnson, *Becoming Creole: Nature and Race in Belize*

Carlos Garrido Castellano, *Beyond Representation in Contemporary Caribbean Art: Space, Politics, and the Public Sphere*

Njelle W. Hamilton, *Phonographic Memories: Popular Music and the Contemporary Caribbean Novel*

Lia T. Bascomb, *In Plenty and in Time of Need: Popular Culture and the Remapping of Barbadian Identity*

Aliyah Khan, *Far from Mecca: Globalizing the Muslim Caribbean*

Rafael Ocasio, *Race and Nation in Puerto Rican Folklore: Franz Boas and John Alden Mason in Porto Rico*

Ana-Maurine Lara, *Streetwalking: LGBTQ Lives and Protest in the Dominican Republic*

Anke Birkenmaier, ed., *Caribbean Migrations: The Legacies of Colonialism*

Sherina Feliciano-Santos, *A Contested Caribbean Indigeneity: Language, Social Practice, and Identity within Puerto Rican Taíno Activism*

H. Adlai Murdoch, ed., *The Struggle of Non-Sovereign Caribbean Territories: Neoliberalism since the French Antillean Uprisings of 2009*

Robert Fatton Jr., *The Guise of Exceptionalism: Unmasking the National Narratives of Haiti and the United States*

Rafael Ocasio, *Folk Stories from the Hills of Puerto Rico/Cuentos folklóricos de las montañas de Puerto Rico*

Yveline Alexis, *Haiti Fights Back: The Life and Legacy of Charlemagne Péralte*

Katerina Gonzalez Seligmann, *Writing the Caribbean in Magazine Time*

Jocelyn Fenton Stitt, *Dreams of Archives Unfolded: Absence and Caribbean Life Writing*

Alison Donnell, *Creolized Sexualities: Undoing Heteronormativity in the Literary Imagination of the Anglo-Caribbean*

Vincent Joos, *Urban Dwellings, Haitian Citizenships: Housing, Memory, and Daily Life in Haiti*

Krystal Nandini Ghisyawan, *Erotic Cartographies: Decolonization and the Queer Caribbean Imagination*

Yvon van der Pijl and Francio Guadeloupe, eds., *Equaliberty in the Dutch Caribbean: Ways of Being Non/Sovereign*

Patricia Joan Saunders, *Buyers Beware: Insurgency and Consumption in Caribbean Popular Culture*

Atreyee Phukan, *Contradictory Indianness: Indenture, Creolization, and Literary Imaginary*

Nikoli A. Attai, *Defiant Bodies: Making Queer Community in the Anglophone Caribbean*

Samuel Ginsburg, *The Cyborg Caribbean: Techno-Dominance in Twenty-First-Century Cuban, Dominican, and Puerto Rican Science Fiction*

Linden F. Lewis, *Forbes Burnham: The Life and Times of the Comrade Leader*

Keja L. Valens, *Culinary Colonialism, Caribbean Cookbooks, and Recipes for National Independence*

Kim Williams-Pulfer, *Get Involved! Stories of Bahamian Civil Society*

Preity R. Kumar, *An Ordinary Landscape of Violence: Women Loving Women in Guyana*

Kezia Page, *Inside Tenement Time: Suss, Spirit, and Surveillance*